# Content

# QUEEN ELIZABETH I

## Life and Legacy of the Virgin Queen

Paul Kendall

FRONTLINE
BOOKS

**Queen Elizabeth I: Life and Legacy of the Virgin Queen**

This edition published in 2022 by Frontline Books,
An imprint of Pen & Sword Books Ltd,
Yorkshire - Philadelphia

ISBN 978 1 39901 835 7

CIP data records for this title are available from the British Library

Pen & Sword Books Limited incorporates the imprints of Atlas, Archaeology, Aviation, Discovery, Family History, Fiction, History, Maritime, Military, Military Classics, Politics, Select, Transport, True Crime, Air World, Frontline Publishing, Leo Cooper, Remember When, Seaforth Publishing, The Praetorian Press, Wharncliffe Local History, Wharncliffe Transport, Wharncliffe True Crime and White Owl.

PEN & SWORD BOOKS LTD
47 Church Street, Barnsley, South Yorkshire, S70 2AS, England
E-mail: enquiries@pen-and-sword.co.uk
Website: www.pen-and-sword.co.uk

Or
PEN AND SWORD BOOKS
1950 Lawrence Rd, Havertown, PA 19083, USA
E-mail: Uspen-and-sword@casematepublishers.com

For more information on our books, please visit
www.frontline-books.com, email info@frontline-books.com
or write to us at the above address.

Printed and bound in the UK by CPI Group (UK) Ltd.

Typeset in 10/14pt Adobe Caslon by SJmagic DESIGN SERVICES, India.

# QUEEN ELIZABETH I

*Life and Legacy of the Virgin Queen*

# Introduction

This book is about the life and legacy of one of the most iconic of English sovereigns. Queen Elizabeth was the daughter of Henry VIII and Anne Boleyn. She was the last monarch of the Tudor dynasty and reigned for forty-four years and four months. When she died in 1603, she became the longest serving English sovereign up to that time. Given that she was the second child of Henry VIII and that her step-siblings, Edward and Mary, were ahead of her in the line of succession, her chances of becoming sovereign seemed remote when she was a child. Being raised and educated within the royal household, Elizabeth learned from a young age that the court was a dangerous place to be, where she had to be cautious in her actions, careful about what she said and who she could trust. Her life was in perpetual danger throughout her life, as princess, when falsely implicated in a plot against her sister, Queen Mary, and later as Queen of England, when she was the focus of numerous attempts to usurp her throne.

Elizabeth was 25 when she became queen. In the view of her father and her peers, being a female sovereign was a distinct disadvantage, a weakness that could be taken advantage of within her realm and by foreign nations. Elizabeth was resolute, resilient, intelligent and possessed the strength of character to defy misogynistic opinion to succeed as a strong sovereign. She inherited a litany of problems, both national and international. The country had been mismanaged during the reigns of Edward VI and Mary. The reformation instigated by Henry VIII still caused problems. Religion had divided Protestants and Catholics within the nation, although the majority of the populace wanted a national church independent of the authority of the Pope, the Bishop of Rome in the Vatican, with simple services that could be understood. Corruption was prevalent and there was a sense of distrust in those that led the country. The army had been weakened since the days of Henry VIII. Catholic countries such as Spain and France wanted to impose their Catholic faith upon Protestant England, which was sanctioned by the Pope, and the prospect of invasion from those countries was a real threat. England was already at war with France, with the French besieging Calais and its army present in Scotland when Elizabeth ascended the throne. Elizabeth was also regarded as Queen of Ireland and during the course of her reign she had to confront several revolts in Ireland.

Elizabeth was renowned as the 'Virgin Queen' for she never married or conceived children. Instead, Elizabeth believed that she was married to the kingdom. These circumstances would pose a perpetual problem throughout her reign, because of the uncertainty of who would succeed her if she died without producing an heir. Instability had caused violent struggles in the past such as the Wars of the Roses, between the Houses of York and Lancaster during the fifteenth century, and there was great reluctance to return to that situation. In the absence of a successor, the next direct heir to succeed Elizabeth was her Catholic cousin, Mary, Queen of Scots. The Catholics in England saw Mary as a figurehead, as an alternative Queen of England and the person to champion their faith, which meant that she remained a dangerous threat to Elizabeth's position.

The Privy Council tried to resolve the problem of succession by encouraging Elizabeth to marry, but she resisted. Potential suitors were willing to marry the Queen of England, including Philip II of Spain, who was married to her step-sister, Queen Mary. He was enthusiastic about maintaining an alliance between the two countries, and being a Catholic, keen to promote the faith in England during Elizabeth's reign. Francis, Duke of Anjou and Alençon, the brother of the French king, was also put forward as a husband when Elizabeth was 46. He too was Catholic, but given the fact that Elizabeth was likely beyond child-bearing age a childless marriage to Francis would mean England would be controlled by France after her death.

It was her relationship with Robert Dudley, Earl of Leicester that probably brought her closest to a loving, intimate union. He had been a friend since childhood and they had both been imprisoned in the Tower of London at the same time and lived under the threat of death. Dudley became a prominent figure in Elizabeth's court and many courtiers believed that they were lovers. However, any prospect of marriage with Elizabeth was improbable because he was already married. When his wife died in mysterious circumstances, there was speculation that Dudley was involved so that he could be free to marry the queen. Elizabeth would never marry him because of this scandal, however she did keep him close to her in her court by appointing him Master of the Horse and frequently visited his country home at Kenilworth during royal progresses.

Elizabeth did not like change and maintained an inner circle of ladies-in-waiting, courtiers and privy councillors. When Robert Dudley died in 1588, she replaced him with his step-son, the Earl of Essex, as Master of the Horse, although this would prove to be an ill-judged decision, given that he would lead a rebellion against her. When William Cecil, Lord Burghley became ill, she appointed his son, Robert Cecil, as a privy councillor to maintain continuity.

Elizabeth was the most important legacy of Henry VIII, becoming a highly respected queen whose reign would see great national achievements and have a lasting impact on England as a nation in the following centuries. Elizabeth would build upon Henry's English navy, which brought triumphs that Henry aspired to but failed to achieve. The Elizabethan era is remembered for being an age of discovery and exploration. Her patronage of seafaring privateers such as John Hawkins, Francis Drake, Martin Frobisher and Walter Raleigh to discover new lands and support attacks upon Spanish shipping to plunder their wealth and exert British dominance of established trade routes saw the beginning of the formation of the British Empire, which would expand during the following three centuries. Exploration enabled England to acquire wealth, power and territory. The colonisation of Virginia in America was named after Elizabeth, 'The Virgin Queen'. The English navy defeated the Spanish Armada and emboldened England as a powerful nation and evolved into the Royal Navy, cementing Elizabeth's place in history and her iconic persona of Gloriana.

Literature and entertainment flourished during the Elizabethan period, in particular the work of writers such as Edmund Spenser, Christopher Marlowe and William Shakespeare. The plays of Marlowe and Shakespeare are still performed 400 years later and retain their relevance in the twenty-first century.

Although her reign has been regarded a 'golden age', this could be open to challenge. The fact that Elizabeth sanctioned piracy and shared the profits plundered from foreign vessels is morally questionable. The formative years of the British Empire were tainted by the involvement of Elizabeth's mariners such as Hawkins and Drake in the establishment of the slave-trade routes. It marked one of the darkest episodes from which Elizabeth and England as a nation profited and prospered to the detriment of other communities. The colonisation of other lands, the oppression of its people and the theft of resources from those lands is indefensible. Elizabeth demonstrated throughout her reign that she was as ruthless as her father, allowing the torture of traitors, the burning of Catholics and the executions of her own cousin, Mary, Queen of Scots, and one of her favourite courtiers, Robert Devereux, Earl of Essex.

This book aims to show Elizabeth I, her life and legacy in mini-chapters through surviving artifacts and buildings associated with England's iconic queen and those that served and defied her. They provide a snapshot and an insight into her world and represent the various stages of her enthralling but turbulent life.

Paul Kendall
Folkestone, 2022

# Acknowledgements

I thank Lee. B. Spitzer for kindly allowing me to use his image of the Martyrs' Cross in this volume. I am grateful to Eddie O'Gorman (www. spanisharmadaireland.com) for his assistance and TudorHistory.org for their kind help. I also extend my thanks to Martin Mace and John Grehan for their continued guidance and help with this project. I am grateful to Robert Mitchell for his assistance with images and thank my partner, Tricia Newsome, for her support.

# 1

# Memorial Commemorating the Birth of Queen Elizabeth I, Royal Naval College, Greenwich

## Elizabeth's Birth at Greenwich Palace

**Greenwich Palace once stood along the banks of the River Thames on the site of the Royal Naval College. A plaque commemorates the births of Elizabeth on 7 September 1533, her father, Henry VIII, on 28 June 1491 and her step-sister, Mary, on 18 February 1516, highlighting the historic importance of this location in relation to the Tudor line.**

At 3 pm on 7 September 1533, Anne Boleyn, the second wife of Henry VIII, gave birth to Princess Elizabeth at Greenwich Palace. Despite the sound of church bells ringing across London in celebration, the birth caused much discord throughout the nation and Europe. There was little rejoicing at court because Henry VIII wanted a son to succeed him and he had abandoned his first wife, Katherine of Aragon, in order to marry Anne and Anne knew that her position was precarious if she could not produce a male heir.

Three days later, on 10 September, Elizabeth was christened at Greyfriars Church close to the palace. Elizabeth spent the first three months of her life in the nursery that had been prepared within Greenwich Palace. She was placed under the care of Lady Margaret Bryan, who was appointed by Henry VIII as 'lady mistress'.[1] This role was defined as a governess, but similar to a nanny, and this was usual practice for royal children during the Tudor period. Lady Bryan was a widow who had previously cared for Princess Mary. A wet nurse was also employed and additional staff to rock the baby's cradle to ensure that she slept soundly. Blanche Parry was among those who would rock her cradle as an infant princess. She would serve Elizabeth for six decades and eventually became Chief Gentlewoman of the Privy Chamber and later Keeper of the Queen's Jewels.

Stone plaque commemorating the births of King Henry VIII, Queen Mary and Queen Elizabeth I at Greenwich Palace which was unveiled in the Grand Square of the Royal Naval College in 2003. (*Author's Collection*)

Greenwich Palace was the site of many prominent events that took place during Elizabeth's lifetime. When Anne Boleyn was unable to provide a son for Henry, she was arrested at Greenwich Palace on trumped up charges of treason and conveyed to the Tower of London on 2 May 1536. Elizabeth's brother, Edward VI, died at

Detail of the plaque commemorating the births of King Henry VIII, Queen Mary and Queen Elizabeth I at Greenwich Palace. (*Author's Collection*)

Greenwich Palace on 6 July 1553. King Philip II of Spain, who was married to Queen Mary, arrived at Greenwich on 20 March 1557 to gain support from the English in a war against France.

Elizabeth would spend the summer months at Greenwich Palace during her reign. Here she was close to the royal dockyards at Deptford and Woolwich. During summer 1559 she was able to visit Woolwich Dockyard to attend the launching of the galleon named *Elizabeth* in her honour on 3 July. It was from the windows of Greenwich Palace on 7 June 1576, that Elizabeth, with ladies of the court, waved farewell to Sir Martin Frobisher, sailing with the ships *Michael* and *Gabriel*, at the start of his expedition to Greenland in search of the North-West Passage.[2]

Elizabeth signed the death warrant of her cousin Mary, Queen of Scots at Greenwich Palace on 1 February 1587. During Christmas 1594, Shakespeare performed two comedies in front of Elizabeth at the palace. Thomas Platter, a Swiss tourist, was given access to the royal palaces during September 1599. He recalled visiting Greenwich Palace and Elizabeth's chambers, including 'the field room, overlooking the Thames … in the said chamber which formed a bay overlooking the river, was also a charming canopy with numerous cushions and feather plumes under it, where the queen sits in her magnificence'.[3]

# 2

# Portrait of Henry VIII

## Elizabeth, Heir to Henry VIII

**Elizabeth's position as successor to Henry VIII was secured through the Act of Succession, 1533. Four years later, Hans Holbein the Younger painted the original portrait of the king in 1537, but the version seen here was the work of an unknown artist, possibly from his workshop, and completed between 1537 and 1547.**

The portrait depicts Henry VIII as a large, intimidating person. His eyes look intently towards the artist, commanding unconditional obedience and exuding confidence and omnipotence. His legs astride, Henry VIII stands confidently with his right hand on his hip, with a pose demonstrating his assertiveness and gravitas as he upholds his right to the throne. The strong image it portrays made it ideal for diplomatic purposes, to send as political gifts to establish and maintain relationships at home and abroad, as well as deter anyone who thought of challenging his rule. Such portraits of the sovereign were commissioned by wealthy courtiers and nobleman to display in their great halls to show their allegiance and loyalty to the king. It is believed that this well-known image of Henry VIII was indeed commissioned by a wealthy courtier, intent on affirming support for the king. The image is similar to his stance in the Whitehall Mural which shows Henry VIII with his parents and Jane Seymour. It was painted by Hans Holbein the Younger in 1537 but was destroyed in a fire in 1698 at Whitehall Palace, where the painting hung. The Mural was reproduced in an oil painting by Remigius van Leemput for Charles II. The courtier who commissioned this painting of Henry VIII may have had access to the Whitehall Mural. It is the image that transformed Henry into an iconic king.

This portrait was painted after the period during which he had evolved into a tyrant. His twenty-four-year marriage to Katherine of Aragon had produced one daughter, Mary, and Henry VIII desperately wanted a son, an heir to ensure

Portrait of Henry VIII. (*Courtesy of the Walker Art Gallery*)

stability and the survival of the Tudor dynasty. Besotted by Anne Boleyn, his failed attempts to seek an annulment from the Pope incited Henry VIII to take matters into his own hands by severing ties with the Vatican, abandoning Catholicism and establishing the Church of England. As Supreme Head of the Church of England Henry could divorce his first wife and marry Anne Boleyn with the hope that she would provide him with a son.

Although Anne Boleyn gave birth to Princess Elizabeth, the nation did not favour the king's second marriage. There was still significant support for Queen Katherine and Princess Mary. Henry was anxious to subdue any opposition to his marriage to Anne and wanted to ensure that Elizabeth was next in the line of succession to the throne. Encouraged by Anne to safeguard her daughter's security, he initiated the Act of Succession, which was passed by Parliament towards the end of 1533, and ratified on 30 March 1534, in his presence. The Act acknowledged Anne as Henry's lawful wife and recognised Elizabeth as his heir apparent. It also relegated Katherine from queen to princess dowager and Princess Mary declared illegitimate and disinherited. The Act meant that it was treason to address Katherine as queen.

The Act not only cemented Elizabeth's position as heir to the throne, but it also brought about the downfall of many people within the country who refused to recognise the Act of Succession by swearing an oath that acknowledged her as the successor of Henry VIII. The Act of Treason passed by Parliament in 1534 made it treason for anyone who refused to swear that oath. High-profile figures such as the former Lord Chancellor, Sir Thomas More and John Fisher, the Bishop of Rochester would not compromise their faith, or allegiance to Queen Katherine and would die at the execution block because they would not swear that oath. It marked the beginning of a reign of terror that saw Henry VIII behaving like a tyrant.

Elizabeth's position as heir to the throne lasted only three years. Her life in the years that followed before her own accession to the throne was turbulent and precarious. On 8 June 1536 the Second Act of Succession was authorised by Parliament, which disinherited Elizabeth as Henry's successor and declared her illegitimate, which meant that for a year Henry VIII did not have a legitimate heir until the birth of his son, Edward, in 1537. The Third Act of Succession during July 1544 restored the Princesses Mary and Elizabeth as heirs to the throne, but stopped short of reversing their illegitimacy.

# 3

# Old Palace, Hatfield

## Childhood Home of Princess Elizabeth

**Construction of the Old Palace at Hatfield was completed during 1497 for Cardinal Morton, Bishop of Ely and minister of Henry VII, grandfather of Elizabeth. The building formed a quadrangle and only one side, containing the Great Hall, remains. Bricks from the other three sides were used for the construction of Hatfield House, which was built to the east of the Old Palace in 1611. Henry VIII seized the Old Palace during the dissolution of the monasteries and utilised it as a home for his children.**

The Tudor royal court was overcrowded and unhygienic, which was not conducive to raising royal babies. Three months after her birth, during December 1533, the infant Elizabeth was separated from Anne Boleyn and sent to live at the Old Palace, Hatfield, where she would reside at various times prior to becoming queen, as well as spending intermittent periods at Eltham Palace, south London, Ashridge House, near Berkhamsted, and Hunsdon House, close to Harlow. The household at the Old Palace was headed by Sir John and Lady Shelton, uncle and aunt of Anne Boleyn, while Lady Bryan continued to care for Elizabeth. Mary's household was disbanded and sent to Hatfield to serve Elizabeth on 13 December 1533. To her consternation, Mary, who was aged 17, was appointed Maid of Honour to attend upon Elizabeth from 1533 to 1536, but Mary refused to acknowledge her step-sister as heir or recognise Anne Boleyn as queen while her mother was alive, nor would she renounce her Catholic faith. Mary was unhappy with her father's mistreatment of her mother, Katherine, and that he had declared her illegitimate, casting her aside, disinheriting her as heir in favour of Elizabeth.

When Mary arrived at Hatfield she resented her little step-sister, refused to eat at the same table and to accompany her as she was carried around the grounds. Mary justifiably felt bitter towards her father, step-mother and her infant step-sister and remained in her chamber. Henry VIII tried to make her conform to his will and accept the situation by denying her access to her jewels and ordering that no meals be served in her chamber. This compelled Mary to eat in the Great Hall with Elizabeth, but she did not curtsey to the infant and nor did she address her as princess. During March 1534, Anne Boleyn visited Hatfield to ensure that Elizabeth was well cared for. She also used the trip as an opportunity to improve her relationship with Princess Mary and try to reconcile her with Henry VIII, but was not successful in this. It was after this visit that Elizabeth was moved to Eltham Palace.

During her step-sister's reign, Elizabeth returned to the Old Palace in October 1555, but while Queen Mary was sovereign her life was perpetually under threat. She maintained a small household at the Old Palace, to live within her means and not to cause Mary to become jealous. She was surrounded by her close attendants, Blanche Parry and Katherine Ashley, but she was unable to distance herself from the dissension that was tearing the country apart and because of the plots against Queen Mary, Elizabeth and those who worked for her were under suspicion. While she lived at the Old Palace Elizabeth's movements were under scrutiny by her step-sister who was afraid that she would be usurped. The Venetian diplomat, Giovanni Micheli, wrote, 'for everyone thinks it hard that a king's daughter should be so miserably treated. Since Wyatt's rebellion she has never been free; for though she is allowed to live in her house, some twelve miles distant from London, still has many guards and spies about her, who observe all comers and goers.'[4]

Sir Thomas Pope was appointed head of Elizabeth's household in 1556 in order to monitor her. Pope received strict orders that his family should conduct Mass at Hatfield, but Pope conspired with Protestant servants within the household who discretely ensured that Elizabeth could practise her Protestant faith.

Old Palace, Hatfield. (*Stephen G. Roberts/Shutterstock*)

# 4

# Eltham Palace

## Another Childhood Home of Princess Elizabeth

**Eltham Palace had been a royal residence since 1311, when King Edward II took possession after the death of its owner, Anthony Bek, Archbishop of Durham. Surrounded by a moat, it was much larger than Hampton Court Palace. Elizabeth spent her formative years as an infant at Eltham Palace away from court life. The Great Hall and the bridge that crossed the moat, built by Edward IV, are the only parts of the palace that have survived and would have been familiar to Elizabeth during her lifetime.**

Anne Boleyn failed to reconcile with Princess Mary when she visited Elizabeth at the Old Palace, Hatfield, during early March 1534 and later that month, Elizabeth was relocated to Eltham Palace, which was closer to her parents at Greenwich Palace. Elizabeth was a healthy baby and her parents made regular visits to monitor her progress. On 18 April 1534, Sir William Kingston wrote in a letter to Lord Lisle from Greenwich, 'Today the King and Queen were at Eltham, and saw my lady Princess, as goodly a child as hath been seen, and her grace is much in the King's favour as goodly child should be, God save her.'[5] The diplomat Eustace Chapuys reported to Charles V that Henry visited Eltham during July 1534 to see Elizabeth.

During her reign, Elizabeth would visit Eltham occasionally. She made an excursion from Greenwich to Hampton Court Palace during the summer progress of 1559 and ventured into Kent, where she stayed at Dartford and Cobham before heading west and arriving at Eltham on 5 August. She remained there for several days before proceeding to the palaces at Nonsuch and Hampton Court. During stays at Eltham, Elizabeth would hunt in the surrounding forests. Timber for warships being built in Deptford Dockyard in 1586 was sourced from trees felled in the forests close to Eltham Palace.[6]

*Above*: The Great Hall, Eltham Palace was built by Edward IV during the period 1475–80. (*Author's Collection*)

*Right*: Interior of the Great Hall, showing the impressive oak roof. (*Author's Collection*)

Elizabeth appointed one of her favourite courtiers, Sir Christopher Hatton, as Keeper of Eltham Palace. He was succeeded in that role by Lord Cobham in 1592. However, because Elizabeth seldom visited Eltham Palace, it was not well maintained and eventually fell into disrepair.

# 5

# Tower Green

## Site of the Execution of Anne Boleyn

**Three Tudor queens, Anne Boleyn, Katherine Howard and Lady Jane Grey, were executed in private on Tower Green, away from the prying eyes of public spectators and to prevent the risk of civil disorder.**

Anne Boleyn had miscarried on 29 January 1536 and blamed rumours of Henry's affairs in conjunction with the news of Henry's recent accident, when he fell from his horse on the tiltyard at Greenwich Palace, as reasons for losing the child. Instead of comforting Anne after the miscarriage, Henry was more concerned with the prospect of not fathering a male heir and at the time was initiating a romantic relationship with Jane Seymour, lady-in-waiting to Anne Boleyn.

When Henry heard spurious accusations that Anne Boleyn had had sexual relations with several other men at court including her own brother, George, Lord Rochford, he ordered Thomas Cromwell to investigate. After undergoing torture on the rack for 4 hours in the Tower of London on 1 May 1536, the musician Mark Smeaton confessed to Cromwell that he had committed adultery with Anne. On 2 May, Anne was arrested at Greenwich Palace and brought by barge to the Tower of London.

Although Anne Boleyn was flirtatious, she was not disloyal to Henry VIII. On 15 May 1536, Anne was tried in the Great Hall at the Tower of London, found guilty and condemned to death. Any hopes of a reprieve were futile for the king had ordered a swordsman from Calais to conduct the execution. He had commuted her sentence from beheading by axe to decapitation by sword. Death by sword guaranteed a quicker death, requiring just one strike at the neck. An axe could take three strikes before the head was decapitated.

While waiting for her sentence to be carried out Anne Boleyn was informed that on 17 May 1536, Archbishop Cranmer, presiding over a court of ecclesiastical lawyers at Lambeth Palace, pronounced Anne's marriage invalid. Henry purposely delayed the annulment of his second marriage because if the divorce had been passed before the trial, Anne could not have been convicted of adultery and he would have been unable to declare the Princess Elizabeth illegitimate alongside her step-sister, Princess Mary, therefore removing both daughters from the line of succession.

Anne was brought to the scaffold on Tower Green at 8 am on 19 May 1536. After ascending the scaffold, she asked to speak a few words to the onlookers, promising to talk favourably of the king, fearing that any negative lambast would endanger the life of her daughter, Elizabeth. Anne was allowed to address the crowd and then she removed her hood and cloak. One of the ladies in attendance presented her with a linen cap with which she covered her head and ensured that her hair did not obscure her neck, so that the executioner could take clear aim. Another lady covered her eyes with some cloth. As she knelt down, she said the words, 'To Christ I commend my soul, Jesus receive my soul', and then with one strike of the sword the French executioner with precision beheaded Anne Boleyn. Her decapitated body and head were wrapped in white cloth and buried within the chapel of St Peter ad Vincula.

Executed under the orders of her father, Elizabeth was deprived of her mother. Today, a memorial sculptured by Brian Catling commemorates the site on Tower Green where prominent prisoners were executed and serves as a reminder of the trauma that Elizabeth would have felt as a child and throughout the rest of her life as a result of that loss.

The Execution Memorial, looking towards the actual site where Anne Boleyn was executed, in between the entrance to Waterloo Barracks and the White Tower. (*Author's Collection*)

# 6

# Hunsdon House

## Another Childhood Home of Elizabeth

**Hunsdon House was built in 1447 and was used as a residence for the children of Henry VIII. The house was expanded and a moat was installed during his reign. As queen, Elizabeth granted the house to Henry Carey in 1559 when she elevated him to Baron Hunsdon. The house has survived the centuries and is privately owned.**

Elizabeth was living with Mary at Hunsdon House when Anne Boleyn was executed in 1536. She was an infant aged 2 years and 8 months when she lost her mother. The first direct change to her life immediately after her mother's death was that she was no longer a princess and was to be addressed as Lady Elizabeth. Anne Boleyn had ensured that her daughter was well clothed, but as she outgrew her wardrobe, it was no longer replenished. The situation became noticeable when the household at Hunsdon fell into disorder because Henry VIII had neglected the needs of his youngest daughter, probably because of his joy and excitement at his new marriage to Jane Seymour. A regime of austerity at Hunsdon House meant that Lady Margaret Bryan did not possess sufficient funds to clothe Elizabeth. Lady Bryan was devoted to Elizabeth and became very concerned for her welfare given that no clothes were provided for her. In a letter to Thomas Cromwell in early August 1536, Lady Bryan wrote:

> When my lady Mary was born the King appointed me lady Mistress, and made me a baroness; 'And so I have been a m[other] to the children his Grace have had since.' Now, as my lady Elizabeth is put from that degree she was in, and what degree she is at now I know not but by hearsay, I know not how to order her or myself, or her women or grooms. I beg you to be good lord to her and hers, and that she may have raiment, for she has neither gown nor kirtle nor petticoat, nor linen for smocks, nor kerchiefs, sleeves, rails, bodystychets, handkerchiefs, mufflers, nor 'begens'. 'All this his Graces mistake I have driven off as long as I can, that, be my trothe, I cannot drive it no longer.'[7]

Lady Bryan also felt anxious that Elizabeth was allowed to eat rich food and exposed to wine at the same table as the adults in her household and suggested to Cromwell that Elizabeth be served food in her own private chamber. Lady Bryan also referred to Elizabeth teething while at Hunsdon House, highlighting the need for simple food for the young princess to eat. Lady Bryan's letter was effective because Henry VIII provided funds to care for Elizabeth.

Elizabeth spent some of her childhood at Hunsdon House, where she was educated with her brother, Prince Edward, and they were able to play and hunt in the local Hertfordshire forests. Elizabeth and Edward were raised within the Protestant faith, while their elder sister Mary was a devout Catholic. As the royal children grew older, Edward spent more time at court in London while Hunsdon House became the residence of Mary and Ashridge House was assigned to Elizabeth, although she favoured the Old Palace at Hatfield. During her reign, Elizabeth visited Hunsdon House to see her cousin, Lord Hunsdon, during September 1571.

*Right*: Hunsdon House. (*Public Domain*)

*Below*: A limited view of Hunsdon House. (*cc-by-sa/2.0 - © Bikeboy - geograph.org. uk/p/4779820*)

# 7

# The Chapel Royal, Hampton Court Palace

## The Baptism of Prince Edward

The first public engagement that Elizabeth attended was the christening of her younger step-brother, Prince Edward, in the Chapel Royal on 15 October 1537. Cardinal Wolsey began construction of the Chapel Royal during the late 1520s on the site of a chapel patronised by the Knights Hospitaller from 1136. After Wolsey's fall in 1529, Henry VIII took possession of Hampton Court Palace and the old chapel was renovated between 1535 and 1536. One of the main transformations was the installation of an oak, fan-vaulted ceiling, which was carved and painted gold and blue. Droplets descend from the ceiling with carved, gilt images of cherubs playing musical instruments. The royal motto *'Dieu et mon Droit'* ('God and my Right') appears thirty-two times within the design of the chapel and enforced Henry VIII's notion that the Tudor dynasty was endorsed by divine authority. Known as the Chapel Royal at Hampton Court, there is also a Chapel Royal at St James's Palace and the Tower of London. The Chapel Royal was not only a building, but represented a department within the monarch's household known as The Chapel Royal which was an ecclesiastical ensemble of priests, singers and musicians that accompanied the sovereign and served his or her spiritual needs.

Prince Edward, was born on 12 October 1537, and being the only legitimate son of Henry VIII he was immediately proclaimed heir to the throne. Three days later, he was baptised at a midnight ceremony on 15 October. A torchlit procession took place before the ceremony, in which the 4-year-old Elizabeth held the christening robe and was carried into the Chapel Royal. A large platform was constructed in the centre of the chapel, where the font was placed, to enable the guests to witness the occasion which was officiated by Archbishop Thomas Cranmer. Henry VIII was overjoyed at the birth of the son and heir that

The Chapel Royal at Hampton Court Palace, sourced from a plate by W.H. Pyne in 1819, *The History of the Royal Residences*. (*Author's Collection*)

he had yearned for over the twenty-eight years since he had ascended the throne in 1509. The celebrations lasted for less than two weeks because Elizabeth's step-mother, Jane Seymour, died on 24 October as a result of complications from the birth.

As queen, Elizabeth would listen to sermons from the upper gallery of the Chapel Royal. Thomas Tallis, the composer, singer and organist who is regarded as 'the father of English music', joined The Chapel Royal in 1542 and remained in

Both sides of the western entrance to the Chapel Royal are decorated with the painted stone heraldic arms of Henry VIII and Elizabeth's step-mother, Jane Seymour, which are held up by two angels. (*Author's Collection*)

post until his death in 1585. Lupold von Wedel was a German nobleman, soldier, writer and traveller who observed Elizabeth attend a service in the Chapel Royal at Hampton Court Palace during autumn 1584. Wedel wrote:

> This chapel is rather beautifully ornamented. It has a fine organ, mainly of gilt silver with large and small silver pipes. Before the queen marched her bodyguard … They bore gilt halberds and wore red coats trimmed with black velvet. On their coats in front and behind are the queen's arms in beaten gilt silver … then followed the queen in black, because she is in mourning for the Prince of Orange and the Duke of Alençon. On either side of her crisp hair hung a great pearl about as large as a hazel-nut. The common people, who formed two rows on either side of her path, fell upon their knees. The queen's demeanour, however was gracious and gentle and so was her speech, and from rich and poor she took petitions in a modest manner … It being late in the day, there was no sermon, but only singing and prayers.[8]

# 8

# Embroidered Bookbinding,
## *The Mirror of the Sinful Soul*

## A Gift for Katherine Parr

**The bookbinding was embroidered by Elizabeth and its contents translated and
written in her own hand when she was aged 11. Elizabeth presented the book
as a New Year's gift to Katherine Parr, her step-mother, on 31 December 1544.**

Katherine Parr became the sixth wife of Henry VIII on 12 July 1543 when
they married in the Queen's Privy Closet Chamber at Hampton Court
Palace in a ceremony presided over by Bishop Stephen Gardiner and
attended by eighteen people including the king's two daughters, Princesses Mary
and Elizabeth. Katherine proved to be a caring and loving step-mother towards
Elizabeth, Mary and Edward, who remained together at court during 1543.
This embroidered book is a lasting testament to the warm relationship between
Elizabeth and Katherine.

A close bond developed between Elizabeth and Katherine Parr. Although
Elizabeth spent New Year's Eve, 1544 at Ashridge, she sent this book to Katherine
as a gift. The book contained a French poem entitled *Le miroir de l'ame pecheresse*
(*The Mirror of the Sinful Soul*) written by Marguerite de Navarre and translated into
English prose by Elizabeth. The binding of the book cover is believed to have been
embroidered by Elizabeth, with its personal sentiment represented by the initials of
her step-mother, KP, being featured in the design. Elizabeth used a tapestry stitch
in thick, pale-blue silk, interlaced with gold and silver braid.

Inside the book, on the second page, Elizabeth wrote the following
dedication, 'From Assherige [*sic* Ashridge], the last day of the year of our Lord
God 1544 ... To our most noble and virtuous Queen Katherine, Elizabeth her
humble daughter wisheth perpetual felicity and everlasting joy.'[9] The book was
also accompanied with the following letter, dated 31 December 1544, addressed
to Katherine Parr:

Knowing, as the philosopher says, that as an iron instrument grows rusty if not used, so shall the wit of a man or woman wax dull unless occupied upon some study, she has translated this little book out of French rhyme into English prose. It is named 'The Mirrour or Glass of the Sinfull Soul', showing that she (the soul) can do nothing good except by the grace of God, through which she hopes to be saved. Trusts that the file of the Queen's wit will 'rub out, polish and mend (or else cause to mend) the words (or rather the order of my writing) the which I know in many places to be rude'. Meanwhile no other but the Queen shall see it. Prays God to grant her a lucky and prosperous new year, 'with prosperous issue' and years of health and joy. From Assherige [*sic* Ashridge], the last day of the year of our Lord God 1544.[10]

The gift of this book and the accompanying letter provides an insight into the close relationship between Elizabeth and Katherine Parr. The level of detail in the embroidery, the translation and handwriting of the prose shows the love and care invested by Elizabeth in creating this gift. In return Katherine Parr bought matching outfits for Elizabeth, Mary, Edward and herself as New Year's gifts, demonstrating her attempts to unify her husband's family, treating each one of his children as equals. Katherine took a maternal interest in both step-daughters, but she was closest to Elizabeth and played an active and influential role in her education and personal development.

The book entitled *The Mirror of the Sinful Soul*, bookbinding embroidered and words translated from French into English by Elizabeth. (*Author's Collection*)

# 9

# Painting, *The Family of Henry VIII*

## Elizabeth and Mary Restored to the Line of Succession, 1544

**It was not until Henry VIII married his sixth wife, Kathrine Parr, that Elizabeth and Mary were restored to their rightful places in the royal household and to the line of succession during spring 1544, behind their step-brother, Prince Edward. During July 1544, the Third Act of Succession restored Mary and Elizabeth to the line of succession but did not reverse the declaration of their illegitimacy. This painting, produced by an unknown artist *c.* 1545, celebrated the reconciliation of Henry VIII with his children.**

The painting shows Henry VIII seated beneath a canopy of state, Jane Seymour, his third wife who had died eight years previously, and his three heirs, Edward, Mary and Elizabeth. Remarkably, his wife at the time, Katherine Parr, was not featured in the image. Henry places a reassuring arm across the shoulders of Edward. It was painted in Whitehall Palace; the garden can be seen through the arches and the King's Beasts, carved in wood, placed on columns. A wooden fence painted in the Tudor colours of green and white was also depicted in the painting. The two figures passing the archway belong to the king's household and the man on the right is Will Somers, the king's jester. The artist is unknown, but it is thought that the artist was influenced by Hans Holbein. Henry is presenting his family and reaffirming the strength of the Tudor dynasty in confirming the succession through his children. Elizabeth sat for the painting and used it as an opportunity to express her secret allegiance to her mother Anne Boleyn. Henry VIII ordered that all traces of Elizabeth's mother, including ciphers bearing the entwinned initials of Henry and Anne that had been portrayed in stone, glass and wood within the royal palaces, be removed after her execution. He did not want to be reminded of his second wife, however Elizabeth wore Anne's 'A' pendant around her neck

*The Family of Henry VIII* features, left to right, a member of the royal household, Princess Mary, Prince Edward, King Henry VIII, Jane Seymour, Princess Elizabeth and the court jester, Will Somers. (*Courtesy of TudorHistory.org*)

to show that she still thought of her mother and it is discretely featured within the painting, which was displayed at Whitehall Palace.

A year before this painting was believed to have been produced, Katherine Parr invited Elizabeth to attend upon her at court when she acted as regent while Henry was fighting in France during the siege of Boulogne between July and September 1544. It provided Elizabeth with an insight into court life where she could observe her step-mother conversing with courtiers and ambassadors and make important decisions of state. Katherine Parr would inspire Elizabeth, as throughout her life she had seen her father take the commanding role as sovereign, with his wives relegated to the side lines. This was the first time that Elizabeth saw a fellow female performing the role of sovereign and assert herself in a male-dominated environment, with powerful male courtiers bowing to a woman. This must have made a distinct impression on the 11-year-old Elizabeth and would have influenced her when she eventually became sovereign.

Despite being responsible for killing her mother, annulling the marriage which resulted in her illegitimacy and forfeiture of her right to ascend the throne for eight years from 1536 to 1544, Elizabeth was fond of and respected her father. Elizabeth was aggrieved that she had been declared illegitimate and that her mother's honour had been compromised, given that she had insisted that Henry VIII marry her before they shared a bed. Venetian ambassador Giovanni Macheli wrote of Elizabeth:

She is proud and haughty; for in spite of her mother, she holds herself as high as the Queen [Mary] and equally legitimate, alleging in her own behalf that her mother would not cohabit with the king save as his wife and that with authority of the Church, after sentence given by the Primate of this realm; so that even if she were deceived having acted in good, she contracted a valid marriage and bore her child in lawful wedlock. Even supposing she be a bastard, she bears herself proudly and boastfully through her father, whom she is said to resemble more than does the Queen.[11]

Although Elizabeth was proud to refer to herself as the daughter of Henry VIII, she was not ashamed of her mother and was proud of her Boleyn lineage. She maintained friendships with the Boleyns and would later promote them within her court. She adopted the falcon, her mother's emblem, for her own emblem and wore a jewelled ring that contained an image of herself and her mother, which features later in this book.

# 10

# *Prayers and Meditations* of Queen Katherine Parr, Cover Embroidered and Translation by Princess Elizabeth

## Elizabeth's Gift to Henry VIII

Elizabeth gave a translation of Katherine Parr's *Prayers and Meditations* to her father on New Year's Day, 1546. This gift demonstrated her needlework skills and her abilities as a fluent linguist in several languages. Katherine was an independent thinker and the publication of *Prayers and Meditations* on 29 May 1545 made her the first Queen of England to have a book published. She revelled in debating theological matters and was an advocate of religious reform. It was an inspired choice of gift because Elizabeth was simultaneously honouring her father and step-mother.

The cover of *Prayers and Meditations* was embroidered by Elizabeth. She intertwined the initials of Henry and Katherine in the centre, with the Lion of England below it. In each corner, she stitched a white rose, the emblem of her grandmother, Elizabeth of York, and namesake. The book contained 117 pages in which Elizabeth had written in her own hand translations of the work in Latin, French and Italian. Along with the book, Elizabeth sent a letter which she had written from Hertford Palace. Elizabeth began her letter by addressing her father with respect: 'To the most illustrious and most mighty King Henry the Eighth, king of England, France and Ireland, Defender of the Faith, and second to Christ, supreme head of the English and Irish Church, Elizabeth, his majesty's most humble daughter, wishes all happiness, and begs his blessing'.[12]

It must be remembered that Elizabeth was aged 12 when she composed this letter and it demonstrates her strongly developed intellect and ability to articulate her thoughts. Her address to her father shows her appreciation, value and respect for the sovereign and head of the nation's church. She praised the merits of Katherine Parr in writing the book and recommended that her father read it. She wanted to please her father as a daughter and wanted him to be proud of her. Elizabeth's letter continued:

Which work, since it is so pious, and by the pious exertion and great diligence of a most illustrious queen has been composed in English, and on that account may be more desirable to all and held greater value by your majesty, it was thought by me a most suitable thing that this work, which is most worthy because it was indeed a composition by a queen as a subject for her king, be translated into other languages by me, your daughter … Wherefore I do not doubt that your fatherly goodness and royal prudence will esteem this inward labour of my soul not less than any other mark of honour and will regard this

*Prayers and Meditations* of Queen Katherine Parr, cover embroidered and translation by Princess Elizabeth. (*Courtesy British Library*)

divine work as more to be esteemed because it has been composed by the most serene queen, your spouse, and is to be held in slightly greater worth because it has been translated by your daughter.[13]

Mary had resolutely stood by her mother when Henry mistreated Katherine, which placed her in direct confrontation with him and made it difficult for them to reconcile. Elizabeth did not take the same stance in regard to Anne Boleyn and seems to have disregarded his awful treatment towards her, as demonstrated in this letter when she refers to his 'fatherly goodness'.[14] Although inside she may have felt pain and sorrow for the brutal death of her mother, apart from wearing a pendant bearing the letter A in the family portrait discussed in the previous chapter, Elizabeth concealed her bereavement and sense of the loss from the world and did not let it interfere with her relationship with Henry in order to secure her own position at court, which demonstrates how politically astute she was at such a young age. If her father was capable of ordering the murder of his mother, he was capable of committing such an abhorrent act against his daughter, so Elizabeth knew how to placate her father for her own survival.

# 11

# Portrait of Princess Elizabeth, *c.* 1546

## A Painting by William Scrots

**This portrait was listed in the inventory of the property inherited by Edward VI from his father in 1547 and it is thought that it was painted specifically for Henry VIII.**

Given that her position was uncertain and her life was under threat, Elizabeth dressed in clothes that were plain and unassuming prior to her accession. She appears demure in this portrait, holding a book, presenting the young princess as scholarly, intelligent and articulate. She began studying for 3 hours a day from the age of 5 and fully embraced learning.

Elizabeth studied mathematics, astronomy, geography and history and was also proficient in several languages including French, Flemish, Italian, Spanish and Latin. The ability to speak fluently in several languages was a skill that would benefit her when she became queen, enabling Elizabeth to receive foreign ambassadors in their own tongue and read letters from abroad without the need for an interpreter or translator. It was through reading the works of the great philosophers in their native language that she developed her way of thinking that would equip her for when she became sovereign. Twelve years after this portrait was painted, the Venetian diplomat Giovanni Micheli wrote that Elizabeth:

> … is esteemed to be no less fair in mind than she is in body. Albeit, in face she is pleasing rather than beautiful; but her figure is tall and well proportioned. She has a good complexion, though of a somewhat olive tint, beautiful eyes, and above all, a beautiful hand, which she likes to show. She is of admirable talent and intelligence, of which she has given proof by her behaviour in the dangers and suspicions to which she has been exposed.[15]

It was during the year that this portrait was painted that Elizabeth was separated from her brother for whom she had developed a close bond of affection, when she was sent to live at Hatfield, while he resided at Hertford Palace. The siblings were close and Elizabeth pledged that they would continue to correspond through letters. At the request of her brother, she sent him a portrait of herself. Although this was not the portrait, however, it was probably similar and the accompanying letter, dated 15 May 1547 from Hatfield, provides an indication of how she missed him. She wrote, 'I shall humbly beseech your Majesty, that when you shall look on my picture, you will witsafe think, that as you have but the outward shadow of the body afore you, so inward mind wisheth that the body itself were often in your presence.'[16]

Portrait of Princess Elizabeth painted *c.* 1546 and attributed to William Scrots. (*Google Art Project*)

# 12

# Tomb of Henry VIII

## Death of Elizabeth's Father

**Henry VIII spent his final days at Whitehall Palace where he suffered a further bout of fever on New Year's Day, 1547. Henry rallied and was well enough to receive the French and Spanish ambassadors on 17 January. At 2 am on 28 January 1547, Henry VIII died at Whitehall Palace. He was buried at St George's Chapel, Windsor Castle.**

Due to the secrecy surrounding his illness and passing, the exact cause of death was difficult to ascertain, but it was believed that he died from septicaemia. The Privy Council informed Elizabeth and Edward that their father had died, and they consoled each other. After being embalmed and placed in a lead coffin, the remains of Henry VIII were laid in state in Whitehall Palace. During the afternoon of 7 February 1547, from 2 pm to 6 pm, at Leaden Hall and St Michael's in Cornhill alms amounting to 1,000 marks were distributed to the poor in accordance with his last will with 'injunctions to pray for his soul'.[17] His will had also decreed that 'common beggars, as much as may be, avoided'.[18] Each man, woman and child who was present in those locations were given a grote. According to Charles Wriothesley, 21,000 people received these alms. Church bells within the City of London and the suburbs rang throughout the day and night in honour of Henry VIII, and a requiem mass for his soul was held in every church throughout England.

Charles Wriothesley recorded that on the '14th day of February, the corpse of King Henry the Eighth was solemnly with great honour conveyed in a chariot, with his image lying on it, toward Windsor, and rested that night at Syon, where was a rich hearse made of wax of nine stories high'.[19]

The king's remains arrived at Windsor on 15 February 1547 where they were received by the Dean of Windsor and the Eton College choir before being taken to Windsor Castle. His wish was to be 'laid in the choir of his college of Windsor,

*Above*: St George's Chapel, Windsor Castle. (*Courtesy of Aurelien Guichard*)

*Left*: Grave of Henry VIII, Jane Seymour and Charles I. (*By AloeVera95 (Fotografia scattata personalmente) [CC BY-SA 4.0 ( https:// creativecommons.org/ licenses/by-sa/4.0)], via Wikimedia Commons*))

midway between the stalls and the high altar, in a tomb now almost finished in which he will also have the bones of his wife, Queen Jane'.[20]

Henry VIII stipulated in his last will that he wanted his son Edward to succeed him as sovereign, but he did not appoint a protector to act as regent in the event that Edward ascended the throne before he was 18. The government was given authority to act in that capacity but soon after the death of Henry VIII, it appointed Jane Seymour's brother and the boy's uncle, Edward Seymour, Duke of Somerset, as Lord Protector and Governor until the young king reached 18 years of age. A provision was made in the will that in the event that Edward died Mary was designated next in the line of succession followed by Elizabeth. After that the line of succession passed to Henry's younger sister, Mary, Duchess of Suffolk and then her eldest child, Lady Jane Grey.

Katherine Parr was designated guardian of Elizabeth, who was granted an income of £3,000 (the equivalent of £824,000 in 2017), and a provision of £10,000 (the equivalent of £2,746,987 in 2017) as a marriage dowry on the condition that the marriage was approved by her brother, Edward.

The remains of Henry VIII were laid in the nave of St George's Chapel at Windsor Castle next to Jane Seymour. Consideration was given to constructing an elaborate monument to contain his remains in July 1567, but the plans were abandoned during Elizabeth's reign.

# 13

# Plaque Commemorating Henry VIII's Manor House at Chelsea

## Occasional Home of Elizabeth

**Although Elizabeth was bequeathed an annual income, being aged 14, she was deemed too young to live alone and resided with Katherine Parr at Manor House, Chelsea during 1547–8. A plaque commemorates this royal home in Chelsea Mews, London. During her reign, Elizabeth would occasionally stay at Manor House, using it as resting place when travelling between London and Richmond.**

K atherine Parr inherited Manor House at Chelsea after the death of Henry VIII. The house was set in the countryside along the banks of the River Thames. She invited Elizabeth and Mary into her household there. Elizabeth decided to live with Katherine and Lord Admiral Thomas Seymour, the brother of Edward Seymour. Thomas resented his brother's status as the Lord Protector and had ambitions to advance his own position within the royal family. He made an audacious attempt to marry Elizabeth a month after the death of Henry VIII. Elizabeth refused his advances. Seymour was not confident that the Privy Council would agree to a marriage with the princess, so he diverted his attention to her step-mother and her father's widow, eventually marrying Katherine Parr during mid-April 1547.

Mary declined Katherine's invitation to live at Manor House because Thomas Seymour sought her help to influence Katherine to marry him. She was also concerned about Elizabeth's reputation if she remained there and offered her a home at New Place in Essex. Elizabeth elected to stay with Katherine Parr explaining to Mary that the 'Queen having shown me so great affection, and done me so many kind offices, I must use much tact in manoeuvring with her, for fear of appearing ungrateful for her benefits'.[21]

Given that Katherine had been in a relationship with Seymour prior to her marriage to Henry VIII, Elizabeth and Mary were not pleased that Katherine Parr had married Seymour so soon. They considered that the union was disparaging to the memory of their father. Despite resenting her step-mother's decision to remarry, Elizabeth lived with her at Manor House for a further year.

Although Thomas Seymour had married Katherine, it did not stop him pursing Elizabeth at Manor House. This was an alarming situation for Elizabeth because Seymour was her step-father and her guardian. He would abuse that position of trust. Katherine Ashley, governess to Elizabeth, produced a written statement confirming Seymour's unsolicited attention towards Elizabeth while at Manor House and that his behaviour was not welcomed by Elizabeth:

After he was married to the queen, he would come many mornings into the said Lady Elizabeth's chamber before she was ready, and sometime before she

Plaque marking the site of King Henry VIII's Manor House in Chelsea. (*Author's Collection*)

did rise; and if she were up he would bid her good morrow, and ask how she did, and strike her upon the back or on the buttocks familiarly ... and if she were in her bed, he would pull open the curtains and bid her good morrow, and make as though he would come at her; and she would go further in the bed, so that he could no come at her.[22]

On other occasions Seymour was reputed to have forced Elizabeth to embrace him and slashed her dress with his sword. His behaviour towards her could be construed as sexual abuse. Katherine Ashley had inadvertently facilitated opportunities for Seymour to be alone with Elizabeth, but when his behaviour escalated to an unacceptable level, she decided to warn Katherine Parr about his conduct. Katherine initially dismissed any notion of impropriety between Elizabeth and her husband. She realised that this was not the case when she found Seymour embracing Elizabeth and mistakenly believed that Elizabeth requited his advances, which resulted in her feeling betrayed by her husband and her step-daughter. Despite protesting her innocence, Katherine asked Elizabeth to leave Manor House and in June 1548, she went to stay at Theobalds Palace, Cheshunt, Hertfordshire, the home of Katherine Ashley's brother-in-law.

The abuse experienced by Elizabeth at the hands Seymour at Manor House would further impact upon her view of men and foster her distrust of marriage. As a 14-year-old adolescent she had endured a man, who was thirty-four years older than her and who recently married her step-mother, enter her bed to force himself physically upon her. Seymour abused his position within that house and also betrayed his wife, who was pregnant with his child; his behaviour also caused friction between Elizabeth and Katherine Parr. Elizabeth probably lost trust in men from an early age.

# 14

# Katherine Parr's Tomb

## The Death of Katherine Parr

**Elizabeth's step-mother died as a result of complications following childbirth on 5 September 1548. Katherine was buried at St Mary's Church, Sudeley Castle, Gloucestershire. She is the only English queen buried on private land.**

Katherine Parr also left Manor House, Chelsea, in June 1548 and stayed at Sudeley Castle for her period of confinement before giving birth. She was feeling anxious because of her husband's behaviour towards Elizabeth and false rumours that Elizabeth was carrying his child. It was dangerous for Katherine to be expecting a child at the age of 36 during the Tudor period, it being risky for both mother and baby. Although Katherine felt disappointment that in her view she had found her husband in an inappropriate position with her step-daughter, she found it in her heart to forgive Elizabeth, although the situation was not instigated by Elizabeth. They remained firm friends, regarded each other with affection and continued to exchange letters with each other which Elizabeth signed as 'your humble daughter'.[23] On 31 July 1548, Elizabeth wrote:

> Although your highness letters be most joyful to me in absence, yet considering what pain it is for you to write your grace being so great with child and so sickly your commendation were enough in my lords' letter. I much rejoice at your health with the well liking of the country, with my humble thanks that your grace wished me with you till were weary of that country, your highness were like to be cumbered if I should not depart till I were being with you, although it were in the worse soil in the world ... your presence would make it pleasant.[24]

On 30 August 1548, Katherine Parr gave birth to a baby daughter named Mary. A few days after the birth Katherine became ill with a fever. In the presence of her husband she said to Lady Elizabeth Tyrwhytt, 'My Lady Tyrwhyt [*sic* Tyrwhytt], I am not well handled, for those that be about me careth not for me, but stand laughing at my grief.'[25]

Katherine Parr died on 5 September 1548 and her burial at Sudeley was the first Protestant royal funeral. In her will, Parr, bequeathed half of her jewels to Elizabeth. However, she was no longer around to protect Elizabeth, who once again found herself in jeopardy thanks to the intrusive advances of Thomas Seymour who pursued her with increased vigour. Access to the princess was initiated by her governess, Katherine Ashley, and other members of her household who allowed themselves to be manipulated by Seymour for their own personal gain. Despite being much older than Elizabeth, Seymour was intent on marrying the king's sister in an effort to usurp his brother's regency, however it would lead to his execution in March 1549.

Elizabeth was implicated in Seymour's treacherous scheme to seize the throne. She was held as a prisoner at the Old Palace, Hatfield, under the custody of Sir Robert Tyrwhytt and her household was arrested and interrogated to ascertain if Elizabeth had had direct involvement in the plot. Spies from the Privy Council observed Elizabeth when she was informed that Seymour had been executed to see if she revealed any emotion. She responded with serenity, commenting that 'this day died a man with much wit and very little judgement'.[26]

Katherine Parr's tomb at St Mary's Church, Sudeley Castle. (*Elvis Vaughn/Shutterstock*)

# 15

# Statue of Edward VI, St Thomas's Hospital, London

## Elizabeth's Step-Brother Ascends the Throne

**Edward was 9 years old when he succeeded Henry VIII. At his coronation Edward wore decorative clothing that mirrored the style of his father. He wore gowns made of cloth of gold which were bejewelled and lined with sable. Jewels were removed from caps worn by Henry VIII and sewn into the bonnets worn by Edward. He might be a boy, but the clothes were chosen for reasons of politics over fashion and to portray an image of power and authority. This statue was erected to commemorate him as founder of St Thomas's Hospital in 1551.**

The coronation of Edward VI took place at Westminster Abbey on 20 February 1547. The ceremony was conducted by Thomas Cranmer, Archbishop of Canterbury and was adapted to suit the boy king, reducing it from 12 to 7 hours and changing the coronation oath to reflect the reformation of the Church.

A regency had to be established because Edward VI was a child and too young to govern. His uncle, Edward Seymour, Earl of Hertford and later Duke of Somerset was appointed Protector who would govern England until Edward became an adult. Seymour led a campaign against the Scots in 1547 because they had renegaded on a promise to betroth Mary, Queen of Scots to Edward. This campaign, part of the Anglo-Scottish War known as the 'rough wooing', resulted in Seymour defeating the Scots at the Battle of Pinkie Cleugh on 10 September 1547 on the banks of the River Esk near Musselburgh, but there was no peace agreed until March 1551.

The reformation would continue through Edward's reign and would lean towards promoting Protestant worship. The first *Book of Common Prayer* was introduced in 1549 which aimed to bring unity for all across England. It replaced Latin services with English sermons, but its introduction caused revolts in Devon and Cornwall. Roman Catholic statues of saints, images and stained-glass windows were removed

Statue of Edward VI, St Thomas's Hospital, London. (*Courtesy of Chris McKenna*)

from churches. In 1552 Archbishop Thomas Cranmer produced a revised *Book of Common Prayer* that would align with Protestant churches in Southern Germany and Switzerland and provide a template for worship within the Church of England for the next 400 years. Compulsory attendance at church services every Sunday was declared, non-compliance to be punished with six months' imprisonment and on the third offence permanent confinement. This law could not be enforced because many people were disillusioned with the new service and refused to attend, and these offenders received a verbal reprimand.

Although Elizabeth spent less time with her brother after his accession, she maintained a good relationship with him. Their letters are affectionate in tone and in one particular correspondence, written on 2 February 1548, Elizabeth gives an insight into their warm bond. Elizabeth wrote:

> To the most illustrious and most noble King Edward the Sixth. Of your love towards me no more numerous or illustrious proofs can be given, king most serene and illustrious, than when I recently enjoyed to the full the fruit of a most delightful familiarity with you. Which truly when I recall (and I do recall it daily) I seem plainly, as it were, to be present with you and to be enjoying the humaneness of your conversations. What is more, when to my mind there come your innumerable favours to me.[27]

On 1 October 1549, the Privy Council was concerned that Seymour had mismanaged the governing of the country, fighting unnecessary wars, causing civil unrest and taking treasures from the young king. Seymour took Edward to Windsor Castle, where it was believed the king had been taken prisoner by his uncle. Seymour was arrested eleven days later, while Edward was brought to Richmond Palace. Seymour was released from the Tower of London in February 1550 and restored to the Privy Council, which was led by John Dudley, Earl of Warwick, also known as the Duke of Northumberland. Seymour was arrested for treason in October 1551 and accused of trying to overthrow Dudley. Seymour was executed on 22 January 1552.

# 16

# Letter Written by Princess Elizabeth to her Brother, King Edward VI

## Elizabeth's Concerns for Her Brother's Health

**At various times during their childhood Elizabeth resided with Edward at the Old Palace, Hatfield, and Hunsdon House, near Harlow. Elizabeth was caring and attentive towards her younger sibling. When he became King of England, they were separated, but they continued their affectionate relationship through letters. Edward suffered ill health and Elizabeth was worried about his well-being.**

This letter was written by Elizabeth on 21 April 1552, fifteen months before Edward's death, and reveals her feelings towards him and her concerns. Elizabeth addressed the letter 'To the most noble Kind Edward the Sixth' and wrote:

What cause I had of sorry, when I heard first of your Majesties sickness. All men might guess but none but myself could feel, which to declare were or might seem in point of flattery, and therefore to wrote it I omit. But as the sorrow could not be little, because the occasions were many, so is the joy great to hear of the good escape out of the perilous diseases. And that I am fully satisfied and well assured of the same by your grace's hand, I must needs give you, my most humble thanks, assuring your Majesty that a precious jewel at another time could not so well have contented as your letter in this case hath comforted me. For now, do I say with Saint Austin that a disease is to be counted no sickness that shall cause a better health when it is past that was assured afore it came. For afore you had them every man thought that that should not be eschewed of you that was not scaped of many, but since you

Letter written by Princess Elizabeth from Hatfield House to King Edward VI, dated 21 April 1552. (*Courtesy of Houghton Library, Harvard University*)

have had them, doubt of them is past and hope is given to all men that it was a purgation by these means for other worse diseases which might happen this year. Moreover, I consider that as a good father that loves his child dearly doth punish him sharply, so God, favouring your Majesty greatly, hath chastened you straightly, and as a father doth it for the further good of his child, so hath God prepared this for the better health of your grace. And in this hope, I commit your Majesty to his hands, most humbly craving pardon of your grace that I did write no sooner, desiring you to attribute the fault to my evil head and not to my slothful hand. From Hatfield this 21 of April.

Your Majestie's most humble sister to command Elizabeth.[28]

A year after Elizabeth wrote this letter, Edward VI continued to suffer from poor health during February 1553 and by June it was clear he was suffering from tuberculosis and that this was terminal. Edward opposed Mary's succession to the throne on the grounds of legitimacy and religion. Edward and his Council were concerned that if his step-sister succeeded him, the country would return to Catholicism and reverse the English reformation. He did not favour Elizabeth succeeding him because of the issue of male inheritance. Edward decided to discard his father's wishes and bequeath the Crown to the male heirs of his cousin, Lady Jane Grey, who was aged 16. He was encouraged by John Dudley, Duke of Northumberland, who had succeeded Somerset as Lord Protector, and who had a vested interest in such a scheme because Lady Jane Grey was his daughter-in-law and had married his son, Lord Guildford Dudley. During June 1553, Edward was resolute and produced a document entitled 'My Devise for the Succession', in which he changed his decision slightly to name Lady Jane Grey and her male heirs as his successors. Within a month of writing this document Edward VI, aged 15, died on 6 July 1553 at Greenwich Palace. He had reigned for six-and-a-half years. Mary and Elizabeth were once again removed from the line of succession. The death of Edward was kept secret for several days while the Privy Council decided how to proceed. Lady Jane Grey was not told that she was his successor until three days after his death on 9 July. The funeral of Edward VI was delayed for four weeks while the constitutional crisis was resolved and after Mary I asserted and claimed her right to the throne, she discussed with her ministers the format of funeral rites. The funeral took place on 8 August 1553 when the English *Book of Common Prayer* was used for the first time at the funeral of a sovereign. Edward VI was buried beneath the original altar of Henry VII's Lady Chapel at Westminster Abbey.

# 17

# Portrait Medal of Mary Tudor

## Queen Mary I Ascends the English Throne

**It is believed that Prince Philip of Spain commissioned the Italian medalist Jacopo Nizolla da Trezzo to produce this medal during 1554 to commemorate his marriage to Mary and praise her good government. An image of Mary based on her portrait painted by Anthonis Mor depicts her wearing an elaborate brocaded gown and jewel with a large pearl, a gift from Philip known as the La Peregrina, which was later owned by the renowned actress Elizabeth Taylor four centuries later. The reverse of the medal celebrated the positive aspects of her reign, bringing peace to the realm and reconciliation with the Vatican in Rome. The figure symbolises Peace and sets ablaze the weapons of war, while the cowering figures in the background represent the people of England in the midst of a storm.**

Princess Mary refused to acknowledge Lady Jane Grey as her brother's successor to the throne. As soon as Lady Jane was proclaimed Queen of England, Mary raised an armed force and headed to London to seize the Crown. Elizabeth initially avoided any involvement in the struggle for the Crown by declaring that she was ill. She was careful not to declare her allegiance for fear of misplacing that support to the losing party, which could result in imprisonment or death.

As Mary and her forces descended upon London, a thousand armed horsemen rallied to Princess Elizabeth, who disregarded her illness, and forced her into making a decision as to who to support and she eventually ordered them to support her step-sister. Elizabeth met Mary at Wanstead Palace where they rode into London together and Lady Jane Grey was overthrown.

Queen Mary was the first female English sovereign for four centuries, since Matilda, who controlled England for seven months in 1141, and her coronation took place on 1 October 1553 in London. She was introverted and lacked the

Portrait medal of Queen Mary I by Jacopo Nizolla da Trezzo, an Italian medallist employed at the Spanish court, produced in 1554. Obverse side. (*Courtesy of Metropolitan Museum of Art, New York*)

Allegory of Mary Tudor's reign. Reverse side. (*Courtesy of Metropolitan Museum of Art, New York*)

charisma and gravitas of her father, Henry VIII. Mary was unable to engage with her subjects. She felt awkward and uncomfortable as the crowds cheered her along the procession route to Westminster Abbey and she was too reserved and distant to acknowledge a group of children who sang a song in her honour.

During her reign, Mary reversed Protestant reforms introduced during the reign of Edward VI and restored the Roman Catholic rites in the English Church. She attempted to reinstate the roles of abbots, monks and priors and tried to get the assets that were taken from them during the reformation returned to them. This proved to be a futile and impossible scheme because those who were given lands by Henry VIII were reluctant to part with them. She sanctioned the persecution and execution of Protestants within her realm which resulted in her initial popularity with her subjects diminishing. It also caused division with her sister Elizabeth, who could never be safe while her sister was queen. Soon after the coronation there was discord between Mary and Elizabeth due to their religious beliefs. Elizabeth was a Protestant and her persistent refusal to attend Mass irritated Mary and the Privy Council who were intent on restoring the papacy to England. Mary regarded Elizabeth as a potential threat to her rule.

During October 1553 the Spanish ambassador brought to Queen Mary a written proposal from Emperor Charles V suggesting a marital union with his son, Prince Philip of Spain. A treaty was agreed to determine the conditions of the marriage on 10 January 1554, which permitted the Spanish prince to adopt the title of King of England and Ireland, while the marriage lasted, but in order to ensure that England would remain independent of the Spanish Empire, Mary would have full autonomy when governing England. Although measures were in place to restrict Philip's influence in making decisions within the English court, concerns were aroused amongst English noblemen regarding Mary's intended marriage. They feared that English values, identity and sovereignty would be compromised if the heir to the Spanish, Netherlands and Milan throne was to become Mary's husband and they were fearful that the reformation, instigated by Henry VIII, would be reversed and that Mary and Philip would promote and enforce Catholicism in England. Protestant factions within the English nobility were preparing to obstruct the marriage and its implications for England by usurping Mary from the throne and installing Elizabeth as sovereign. Sir Thomas Wyatt raised a small force in Kent and marched into London to depose Mary in January 1554 but this was crushed.

# 18

# Steps of Whitehall Palace

## Elizabeth's Departure for the Tower of London

In 1939 excavations for a new government building on Victoria Embankment revealed the river wall of the Tudor Whitehall Palace, together with the terrace that projected 70ft into the River Thames and was 280ft long and known as Queen Mary's steps, built by Sir Christopher Wren in 1691 for Mary II in front of the Tudor river wall. It was constructed on the site of the old Tudor terrace that enabled state barges to disembark members of the royal family to access the state apartments of the palace. There were two curved flights of steps at each end of the terrace and here we are concerned with the northern stairwell. Princess Elizabeth left Whitehall Palace from this site on a barge bound for the Tower of London to be imprisoned for her alleged involvement in the Wyatt Rebellion in 1554.

Although the Wyatt Rebellion was crushed, Elizabeth, who was residing at Ashridge House in Hertfordshire, was implicated in the attempt to overthrow her half-sister. Elizabeth was taken to Whitehall Palace on 24 February 1554, where she remained under house arrest for four weeks. While Elizabeth was at Whitehall Palace, Wyatt and his fellow rebels were being interrogated in the Tower of London. Wyatt confessed under torture that he had written to Elizabeth and that she sent a messenger with her verbal reply, which was non-committal regarding the revolt. He also signed a confession that Elizabeth was involved, but before being executed on the scaffold he retracted that statement on 11 April 1554.

On 15 March, Elizabeth was questioned by Stephen Gardiner, Bishop of Winchester and nineteen members of the Privy Council, who accused her of supporting the Wyatt Rebellion. After proclaiming her innocence and loyalty to Queen Mary, she was implicated in the rebellion led by Sir Peter Carew in the West Country, which supported Wyatt's Rebellion. Elizabeth was resolute and would not incriminate herself before the Privy Council, which warned her that she should prepare to be sent to the Tower of London for further interrogation.

During the following morning, Henry Radclyffe, 2nd Earl of Sussex arrived at Whitehall Palace to convey Elizabeth to the Tower of London. He advised her that a barge was ready. Elizabeth's was aware that her life was in jeopardy and she insisted that she be taken to her sister so that she could pronounce her innocence of the treason carried out in her name. Her request for a personal audience was refused, but the Earl of Sussex permitted her to write a letter to Queen Mary to reassure her that she was not involved in the plot. On 16 March 1554, in desperation Elizabeth wrote a letter, completely aware that her life depended upon it. She drew lines on the blank part of the second page of the letter to prevent anyone from writing anything, such as a false confession, which would incriminate her. The letter is known as the Tide Letter because it is believed that Elizabeth deliberately wrote it as slowly as possible in order to wait for the high tide of the River Thames at noon, which would render it impossible for a barge to transport her beneath the narrow arches of old London Bridge. The next low tide was at midnight and it was considered too dangerous to make the passage from Whitehall Palace along the River Thames and to navigate between the arches of London Bridge in the dark, so her imprisonment

The steps of Whitehall Palace at Victoria Embankment, London. (*Author's Collection*)

in the Tower of London was delayed by one day. Simon Renard, the Burgundian diplomat, wrote on 22 March 1554:

> It was only because no one would take charge of Elizabeth, that it was decided to conduct her to the Tower last Saturday, by river and not through the streets; but it did not happen that day, because when the tide was rising Elizabeth prayed to be allowed to speak to the Queen, saying the order could not have been given with her knowledge, but merely proceeded from the Chancellor's hatred of her. If she could not speak to the Queen, she begged to be allowed to write to her. This was granted, and while she was writing the tide rose so high that it was no longer possible to pass under London bridge, and they had to wait till the morrow.[29]

Mary did not respond to Elizabeth's letter, instead she rebuked the officers for the delay in transferring her to the Tower of London. These steps are on the site of where Elizabeth was transported by barge from Whitehall Palace to imprisonment in the Tower during the morning of 17 March 1554.

# 19

# Model of the Medieval London Bridge (St Magnus the Martyr Church, London)

## Elizabeth's Journey to the Tower of London

**The old medieval bridge that spanned the River Thames during the Tudor period was built between 1176 and 1209. It was positioned 30yd east of the current bridge. The Church of St Magnus the Martyr was located at the northern end of the bridge, where this model of the bridge is on display.**

London Bridge was supported by twenty piers which were reinforced by twenty stone arches. Wooden piles, made of elm, were driven into the riverbed in an elliptical shape, and masonry was constructed above them. Houses and shops were built upon the bridge. There was a chapel dedicated to St Thomas Becket built in the middle of the bridge. On the approach from Southwark, pedestrians would cross two arches before reaching a stone gate, which was fortified. After crossing a further four arches, pedestrians would reach another strongly fortified tower, where there was a drawbridge that could be raised for tall ships to pass. Thomas Platter described the bridge when he visited London in 1599, 'The bridge across the river is of squared stone … On this same bridge are as aforesaid many tall handsome merchant dwellings and expensive shops, where all manner of wares are for sale, resembling a long street.'[30]

When the bridge was overcrowded, there were instances when people were crushed to death or fell into the Thames, and there were numerous fires in the houses on the bridge which resulted in people being burned to death. There were risks associated with passing through the arches beneath the bridge, due to the narrowness of the arches which acted as a dam against the river tides. This would cause the water to rush at great force against the piers and between the arches at speed resulting in the water level falling to 6ft and creating perilous whirlpools.

It was upon the battlements on this fortification that the heads of traitors were stuck on pikes and displayed as a warning to Londoners and visitors of the consequences of treachery. The heads would be boiled and tarred to ensure that birds did not peck at them. The tradition continued during the reign of Elizabeth I, as reported by German visitor Paul Hentzner, who counted thirty heads placed upon spikes when he visited London in 1598.[31] A year later, Thomas Platter saw numerous heads on stakes on the medieval bridge when he visited London in 1599:

> At the top of one tower almost in the centre of the bridge, were stuck on tall stakes more than thirty skulls of noble men who had been executed and beheaded for treason and for other reasons. And their descendants are accustomed to boast of this, themselves, even pointing out to one their

A section of the model of the Old London Bridge which was created by David T. Aggett, a Liveryman of The Worshipful Company of Plumbers, in 1987. Though depicting the bridge as it would have appeared *c.* 1400, it had not changed much by the reign of Elizabeth I. The heads of traitors who had been executed were placed upon pikes on the battlements of the gatehouse to London Bridge, which also included a drawbridge, which can be seen here on the left. (*Author's Collection*)

ancestors' heads on this same bridge, believing that they will be esteemed the more because their antecedents were of such high descent that they could even covet the crown, but being too weak to attain it were executed for rebels; thus, they make an honour for themselves of what was set up as a disgrace and an example. Just as only recently in Basel the young earl of Suffolk, grandson to the Duke of Norfolk, in order to raise the honour of his family, showed that he was so well connected that his forefathers' heads too were on the tower of London Bridge for having coveted the English crown and so were executed.[32]

During her journey from Whitehall Palace to imprisonment in the Tower of London Elizabeth passed under the old medieval London Bridge on Palm Sunday, 17 March 1554, when most Londoners were attending church services. Five years later on 12 January 1559, she made the same journey as sovereign, passing under the bridge at 2 o'clock in the afternoon at the still of the ebb tide of the River Thames.

After the defeat of the Spanish Armada the ensigns of eleven Spanish galleons were displayed at St Paul's Cathedral on 8 September 1588. On the following day they were transferred to London Bridge where they were hung facing Southwark for the citizens of London to view.[33]

Old London Bridge. (*Author's Collection*)

# 20

# Traitor's Gate

## Elizabeth's Arrival at the Tower of London

Traitor's Gate is situated beneath St Thomas's Tower which was built in the 1270s during the reign of Edward I. It was used as an access point from the river and as a royal residence. During the Tudor period this gateway became known as Traitor's Gate and symbolised Henry VIII's reign of terror as it was how political prisoners accused of treason entered the Tower of London for imprisonment. Sir Thomas More, Bishop John Fisher and several priests who had refused to acknowledge Anne Boleyn as queen and swear the oath of succession in April 1534, recognising Elizabeth as next in the line of succession, were among those unfortunate souls that entered through these gates by barge from the River Thames. The majority of prisoners of the state including Elizabeth passed through Traitor's Gate on their arrival at the Tower of London.

On 17 March 1554, Elizabeth's journey by barge from Whitehall Palace to the Tower of London took place while the citizens of London were attending church services for Psalm Sunday. This afforded her some privacy and also prevented her supporters from lining the banks of the River Thames. It was raining as she arrived at Traitor's Gate and she was reluctant to enter via this entrance. She protested, declaring that she was not a traitor, but the lords who accompanied her were not sympathetic to her pleas. As she stepped onto the stairs at Traitor's Gate she said, 'Here landeth as true a subject, being prisoner, as ever landed at these stairs, and before Thee, O' God. I speak it, having no other friend but Thee alone.'[34]

As she ascended the steps from Traitors Gate into the fortress Elizabeth was astounded to see a line of warders. She was told that this was customary when prisoners arrived, but she requested that they be dismissed. It was reported that these warders 'kneeled down and with one voice prayed God to preserve her'.[35] The following day they were discharged because they had showed this respect towards Elizabeth.

Before she was escorted to her cell she sat on a stone in the pouring rain. She was urged to rise, but she replied, 'Better sit here than in a worse place: for God knoweth whither you will bring me.' When she turned and saw an usher weeping, she chided him with the words, 'You ought rather to comfort than dismay me, especially for that, I know my truth to be such that no man shall have cause to weep for my sake.'[36]

Elizabeth must have felt a sense of foreboding and fear as she entered the Tower of London through Traitor's Gate. It was the place where her mother had been imprisoned, tried for treason and executed. Elizabeth's chances of freedom looked remote and death was a real possibility while under suspicion of treason against Queen Mary.

*Above*: Traitor's Gate. St Thomas's Tower was built by King Edward I between 1275 and 1279. He was able to berth his royal barge within this water gate, inside the Tower of London. (*Author's Collection*)

*Right*: Traitor's Gate, as seen from outside the walls of the Tower of London. (*Author's Collection*)

# 21

# The Bell Tower

## Elizabeth's Imprisonment in the Tower of London

**The Bell Tower is the second oldest tower within the Tower of London and stands in the south-western corner of the fortress. It is called the Bell Tower because it is surmounted by a small wooden turret which contains the bell which was rung to signal the curfew or raise the alarm within the fortress. Elizabeth was imprisoned within the Bell Tower for two months between 17 March and 19 May 1554.**

During the fifth day of her imprisonment Elizabeth was interrogated. She was asked questions about her connections with Sir Thomas Wyatt and other insurgents, to which she replied protesting her innocence and denying knowing about or receiving any communications about the recent revolt.

Mary insisted that Elizabeth practise Catholicism and Mass was forced upon her while she was incarcerated within the Bell Tower. Sir John Gage, Constable of the Tower, treated her harshly. Initially, for the first month, she was placed in solitary confinement, not permitted visitors and forbidden to take exercise outside the walls of her cell until it affected her health. Then she was allowed to walk in the queen's garden escorted by the constable, the lieutenant and a guard. There was dissension on the streets of London and demonstrations of support for Elizabeth were taking place while she was held captive inside the Tower of London. Simon Renard, a Burgundian diplomat, wrote, 'A letter has been scattered about the streets, as seditious as possible and in favour of the Lady Elizabeth, and yet another, in which nothing was written but the words: "Stand firm and gather together, and we will keep the Prince of Spain from entering the kingdom."'[37]

Sir Thomas Wyatt was beheaded on Tower Hill on 11 April 1554, while Elizabeth was imprisoned. Despite Wyatt's declaration on the scaffold which exonerated Elizabeth from involvement in the rebellion, she remained detained within the Tower of London. However, some restrictions were eased while Mary and her

The Bell Tower. (*Author's Collection*)

Privy Council decided her destiny. Antoine de Noailles, French ambassador to the English court, wrote on 17 April 1554 that, 'Madame Elizabeth, having since her imprisonment been very closely confined, is now more free. She has the liberty of going all over the Tower, but without daring to speak to anyone but those who are appointed to guard her. As they cannot prove her implication (with the recent insurrection), it is thought she will not die.'[38]

The cell within the Bell Tower, Tower of London, where Elizabeth, the future Queen of England, was incarcerated during 1554. (*Author's Collection*)

Elizabeth feared that she would suffer the same fate as her mother, Anne Boleyn, and was resigned to the prospect of being executed. She even contemplated requesting to be executed by sword as opposed to the axe because death was swifter by this method. There was not sufficient evidence to convict Elizabeth of treason, but Mary was reluctant to give her liberty and ordered that she be held under house arrest. On 19 May, on the eighteenth anniversary of the death of her mother, she was released from the Tower of London without charge. People congregating on London Bridge cheered as she passed beneath it, mistakenly believing that she had been freed. Although she was released from the Tower of London, Elizabeth remained a prisoner and was sent to the royal manor at Woodstock, Oxfordshire, where she was placed in the custody of Sir Henry Bedingfield.

# 22

# Queen Mary's Chair

## The Marriage of the Future King Philip II of Spain and Queen Mary I

**Queen Mary's Chair in the Lady Chapel, Winchester Cathedral, is a leather and wooden chair that was used during the lavish wedding ceremony of Queen Mary I and Philip of Spain, which took place at Winchester Cathedral on 25 July 1554.**

Mary's first priority as queen was to find a suitable husband and produce an heir to secure her throne. When she saw a portrait of Prince Philip of Spain painted by the Italian artist Titian during September 1553, she was enamoured with his handsome appearance and attracted to his Spanish lineage. Philip shared the same nationality and faith as her mother, Katherine of Aragon, as well as being heir to the throne of Spain and the Holy Roman Empire. He would eventually become a very powerful man. He also had conceived a son from a previous marriage so he was fertile and hopefully could conceive with Mary to produce an heir.

The marriage union was agreed during January 1554. Philip arrived at Southampton with an entourage of 4,000 attendants on 20 July 1554. He was reputed to have drawn his sword in his hand when he first set foot on English soil, a gesture that did not bode well for the future, indicating his willingness to rule by fear. However, Spanish diplomats attempted to allay those fears and interpreted this gesture as his intention to defend the nation. Three days later he arrived at Winchester where he stayed at the Dean's House and during the evening he met Queen Mary in person for the first time at nearby Wolvesey Castle. Mary could understand some Spanish but could not converse in the language so Philip attempted to speak English. It is believed that they were able to communicate in French. Mary was smitten by the appearance of her groom, although Philip was not so impressed. Mary was aged 37 and eleven years older than her future husband.

QUEEN MARY'S CHAIR.

*Left*: Queen Mary's Chair in the Lady Chapel, Winchester Cathedral. This leather and wooden chair was used during the lavish wedding ceremony of Queen Mary I and Philip of Spain, which took place at Winchester Cathedral on 25 July 1554. (*Author's Collection*)

*Below*: Portrait Medal of Philip II of Spain by Jacopo Nizolla da Trezzo produced in 1555. The reverse side shows the image of Queen Mary, the same design used in the medal produced in 1554.

She looked older than her years and had lost most of her teeth by the time she was 20. The marriage was not based on love but motivated by political union between England and Spain.

On the night before the wedding, Emperor Charles V gave the crown of Naples to his son, Philip, so that he would become a king and be of equal status to Queen Mary. The wedding ceremony took place in Winchester Cathedral on 25 July 1554. Although Philip was a king, he was not treated as such in England and certainly not as an equal to Mary. At the wedding banquet she was served food on gold plates, while he was served with silver plates. While he resided in England Mary occupied chambers reserved for the sovereign, but Philip stayed in quarters set aside for the queen's consort.

Philip was never crowned King of England, but it was hoped that the union would improve Anglo-Spanish relations and raise hopes of a Catholic heir. However, the people of England were fearful of a Spanish occupation and therefore suspicious. There was dissension between Spanish courtiers and their English counterparts inside the court of Queen Mary and when they came into contact with the people on the streets.

Immediately after the wedding, Mary believed that she had conceived, but after her period of lying in at Hampton Court Palace in April 1555 there was no baby. Mary was distraught and believed that she was being punished by God. Philip left Mary in England while he governed the Netherlands for seventeen months. He remained with Mary for a further four months during which time she incorrectly thought that she was pregnant once again.

# 23

# Martyrs' Cross

## Execution site of Prominent Protestants, Broad Street, Oxford

**A cross marks the site where Archbishop Thomas Cranmer and other Protestant martyrs were burnt at the stake. It serves as a reminder of the religious persecution that took place during the reign of Queen Mary and of the danger that Elizabeth endured during those dark days.**

The reign of Queen Mary was a dangerous period for those of the Protestant faith, including Elizabeth. Mary affirmed to the Privy Council on 22 August 1553 that although she was a committed Catholic, she would not compel others to adopt the faith. However, her attitude changed when at her third Parliament on 3 October 1554 the statute for the burning of heretics was restored. Known as 'Bloody Mary', she regarded Protestants as heretics who threatened her position as sovereign and they were hunted down and punished. Many were either burned at the stake or died in prison during her reign which promoted the revival of Catholicism between 1554 and 1558. During this period 300 people died at the stake with a third of those executions taking place in London. The remaining individuals were burnt outside London, at sites such as the Martyrs' Cross in Oxford. It has been argued that these deaths were unnecessary because many of the martyrs had acknowledged both Mary as queen and Catholicism.

Reformers such as Archbishop Thomas Cranmer were arrested for treason during September 1553 and committed to the Tower of London. Guarded by 400 soldiers, Cranmer was brought to the Guildhall with Lady Jane Grey and her fellow supporters on 13 November 1553 when they were tried 'for having levied war against the queen, and conspired to set up another in her room'.[39] They all pleaded guilty and were condemned to death. They were returned to the Tower of London, where they were kept under less severe restrictions and there was hope that Queen Mary would grant them clemency. The situation changed after the failure of the Wyatt Rebellion, and so long as Lady Jane Grey was alive, she would remain a threat to Queen Mary. She was executed on 12 February 1554. Cranmer languished in the Tower of London until he was transferred to the Bocardo, the prison in Oxford, in April 1554, where he was to be brought before divine scholars. Mary disliked Cranmer because he was a leading advocate of Protestantism in England and he was complicit in supporting Henry VIII in annulling his marriage to her mother, Katherine of Aragon, and for his support for Elizabeth's mother, Anne Boleyn. Cranmer was tried in St Mary's Church, Oxford, but he denied being guilty of treachery or heresy. His fate was determined by papal law in the Vatican and while he waited for their verdict, Cranmer watched from the tower of the Bocardo the execution of fellow bishops Hugh Latimer and Nicholas Ridley, who were burned at the stake at Martyrs' Cross, Broad Street, on 16 October 1555.

The Vatican decided to remove Cranmer's title of Archbishop of Canterbury as punishment in December 1554. Disturbed by witnessing the deaths of Ridley and Latimer, Cranmer recounted his Protestant faith and accepted Catholicism, declaring in writing his acceptance of the Pope as the supreme head of the Church of England. Despite canon law dictating that all recanting heretics be reprieved, Queen Mary was not convinced of his change in faith. She wanted to make an example of him, settle old scores and ordered his execution.

Martyrs' Cross, Broad Street, Oxford. The cross marks the spot where Cranmer, Ridley and Latimer were burnt at the stake in 1555. (*Copyright © 2014 Lee B. Spitzer. All rights reserved. Used with consent*)

It was here on Broad Street that Cranmer was executed on 21 March 1556. On that day he withdrew his recantations so that he could die a heretic. A stake was planted in the ground and a raised platform constructed so that the prisoner could be seen by the crowd. Faggots of wood were placed beneath the platform around the stake. When he arrived, he knelt on the floor and prayed to God before removing his outer garments down to his shirt in preparation for death. He ascended the platform and was tied to the stake with an iron chain before the wood was set alight. It was reported that:

When the wood was kindled and the fire began to burn near him, stretching out his arm, he put his right hand into the flame, which he held so steadfast and unmoveable, (saving that once with the same hand he wiped his face,) that all men might see his hand burned before his body was touched. His body did so abide the burning of the flame with such constancy and steadfastness, that standing always in one place without moving his body, he seemed to move no more than the stake to which he was bound; his eyes were lifted up into heaven, and he oftentimes repeated 'his unworthy right hand', so long as his voice would suffer him; and using often the words of Stephen, 'Lord Jesus, receive my spirit', in the greatness of the flames he gave up the ghost, in the sixty-seventh year of his age.[40]

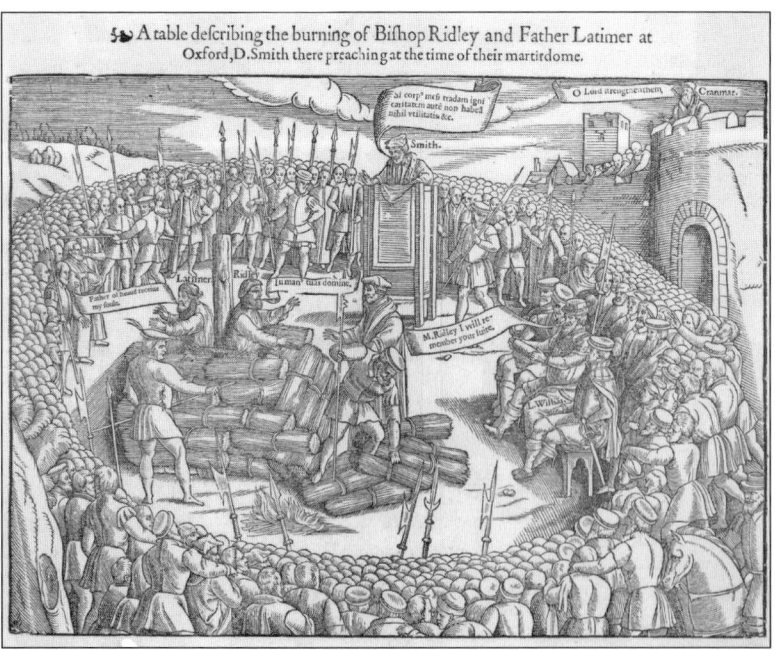

Hugh Latimer and Nicholas Ridley martyred by being burnt at the stake, John Foxe's *Foxe's Book of Martyrs*, 1563 edition. (*Author's Collection*)

# 24

# Hampton Court Palace

## Reconciliation Between Queen Mary and Elizabeth

Cardinal Wolsey began rebuilding Hampton Court Palace in 1515, a project that took a decade to complete. Situated 10 miles south-west of London and connected by the River Thames, the palace was designed to accommodate his large entourage, as well as to welcome and entertain important guests such as monarchs, politicians and foreign dignitaries. Its construction was influenced by European palaces and would match the prestige of Wolsey. After Wolsey's fall from grace in 1529, Henry took complete possession of Hampton Court Palace and it was inherited by his children, Edward, Mary and Elizabeth.

Hampton Court Palace was where Queen Mary reconciled with Elizabeth during July 1555. Mary's husband, Philip, who was now King of Spain, would become Elizabeth's saviour from imprisonment with the plan to arrange a marriage between her and a foreign prince. Elizabeth would be closely supervised and removed from England. Emmanuel Philibert, the Duke of Savoy, who belonged to Philip's entourage, was considered to be an appropriate suitor, however he had to return home to defend his land. If Elizabeth was to marry the Duke of Savoy, she could no longer be kept captive. Bedingfield was ordered to bring Elizabeth from Woodstock to Hampton Court Palace. Courtiers knelt and kissed the hand of Elizabeth when she arrived, much to the dismay of Mary.

Mary realised that she would have to restore Elizabeth to favour, but wanted to accomplish this on her own terms, where she was superior and her sister was in a state of submission, making Elizabeth beholden to the queen. In order to do this, Elizabeth was placed in solitary quarters during her first two weeks at Hampton Court Palace. Bishop Stephen Gardiner, Lord Chancellor visited Elizabeth at the end of the two-week period, requesting that Elizabeth make submission to the queen on the guarantee that she would receive clemency. Elizabeth was resolute and declared she was not guilty of any wrongdoing against her sister and that

there was no evidence that she had committed treason. She would rather remain imprisoned than admit to treason that she had never committed or was willing to be tried in a court of law. Mary sent Gardiner to give Elizabeth an opportunity to confess any offence against her. Elizabeth responded, 'Nay, it may please her to punish me as she thinketh good.' Gardiner retorted, 'Well, you must tell another tale before you are set at liberty.'[41] Elizabeth held her ground and would rather be held a captive with truth and honesty instead of being free and suspected by the queen.

Elizabeth was left in solitude for a further week, until she was summoned to the queen's chamber at 10 o'clock in the evening, where she found Mary sitting on a chair like a judge. This was the first time that the two sisters had met in two years. Elizabeth knelt before her and prayed to God to preserve her as a true subject and hoped that Mary would regard her as such, irrespective of ill-foundered rumours that she might have heard within the confines of the court. Mary said, 'You will not confess your offence, but stand stoutly in your truth; pray God it may so fall out.' Elizabeth replied, 'If it doth not, I request neither favour or pardon at your Majestie's hand.' Mary responded, 'Well, you stiffly persevere in your truth. Belike you will not confess but that you have been wrongfully punished.' Elizabeth replied, 'I must not say so, if it please your Majesty, to you.' Mary asked, 'Why, then, belike you will to others?' Elizabeth answered, 'No, I have borne the burden and must bear it. I humbly beseech your Majesty to have a good opinion of me, and think me to be your true subject, not only from the beginning hitherto, but for as long as life lasteth.'[42] These words spoken by Elizabeth reconciled her with Mary. Bedingfield and his soldiers were ordered to stand down and Elizabeth was allowed to live

*Above*: Hampton Court Palace. This is the Base Court looking towards the Anne Boleyn Gatehouse and the Great Hall (to the left). (*Shutterstock*)

*Below*: The ceiling of the Great Hall in Hampton Court Palace. The Great Hall was primarily used as a dining room for the royal household, including courtiers and servants. Henry and Elizabeth did feast within this hall on state occasions when there was dancing and merrymaking, but usually they took their daily meals within the privacy of their own private chambers. (*Plus One/Shutterstock*)

freely at Hampton Court Palace until October 1555, when she was permitted to return to her childhood home at Hatfield.

During her reign, Elizabeth returned to Hampton Court Palace and was recorded as residing here during 1559, 1570, 1573 and 1579 and during Christmas 1572, 1575 and 1593. Thomas Platter, a visitor from Switzerland, visited Hampton Court Palace in September 1599 and was shown the throne room, known as the Paradise Chamber, where Elizabeth conducted affairs of state. He described the 'Paradise Chamber, where the ceiling is adorned with very beautiful paintings and an extremely costly canopy or royal throne, from which amongst other precious stones, pearls, large diamonds, rubies, sapphires and the rest shine forth, like the sun amongst the stars. Beneath this the queen is accustomed to sit in the magnificence, upon a very stately chair covered with cushions.'[43]

Elizabeth used the Great Hall to welcome foreign dignitaries and for entertainment purposes. Banquets and dances were held here and it was also a venue where she would watch plays performed for her amusement. She contracted smallpox while in residence at the palace in 1562 and for a period she was reluctant to return. Elizabeth was not fond of Hampton Court Palace and much preferred the privacy of her other residences at Richmond Palace and Windsor Castle.

# 25

# Queen Elizabeth's Oak Tree, Hatfield

## The Start of Elizabeth's Reign

On 22 July 1985, Queen Elizabeth II planted an oak tree on the site of the original oak tree in the grounds of Hatfield House, where her predecessor, Elizabeth I, learnt of her accession on 17 November 1558. This date was added to the calendar of festivities celebrated by the Church of England. It was known as Queen's Day or Ascension Day and was unprecedented because no such day had been designated for her predecessors.

Aware that Queen Mary's health was failing during summer 1558, Elizabeth maintained a low profile at the Old Palace, Hatfield, and made plans for her eventual accession. Elizabeth surrounded herself with people who she could trust. Sir William Cecil was giving her guidance. He ensured that she did not need to rely on an individual or another country for protection and would govern independently. Count de Feria had an audience with Elizabeth on 10 November to establish good relations with his master, Philip II of Spain, prior to her accession and offer her support, which she graciously declined. Count de Feria wrote that, 'to great subtlety she adds very great vanity. She has heard great talk of her father's mode of action, and means to follow it. I have great fear that she thinks ill in the matter of religion, for I see that she inclines to govern by men who are suspected heretics.'[44]

By November 1558 it was apparent that Queen Mary was terminally ill. Parliament urged the Privy Council to encourage Mary to acknowledge her sister as successor. Mary concurred on the provision that Elizabeth paid her debts, retained Mary's privy councillors and did not interfere with the Catholic Church in England. Elizabeth would ignore her sister's wishes, but in the meantime accepted these conditions and prepared to assemble her court at Hatfield. Two days before her death, Mary sent Jane Dormer, her favourite Maid of Honour, to deliver the Crown jewels to Elizabeth at Hatfield.

*Above*: The oak tree planted by Elizabeth II in 1985 to commemorate the spot, in the grounds of Hatfield House, where Elizabeth I first learned she was queen. (*Courtesy of www.picturesofengland.com*)

*Below*: Plaque at the oak tree planted by Elizabeth II, Hatfield House. (*Courtesy David Sands*)

Queen Mary died on 17 November 1558 at 6 o'clock in the morning at St James's Palace, London, while her husband, Philip II, was in Brussels. Two hours after her death, Parliament was summoned and the Privy Council invoked the Act of Succession, passed by her father in 1544 which dictated that Elizabeth would succeed as Queen of England, France and Ireland and Defender of the Faith. Once Parliament had broken up that morning, the proclamation of Elizabeth was read in the Palace of Westminster.

Later that day, news reached Elizabeth that her sister had died and that she had been proclaimed queen. Elizabeth was cautious and wanted verification that the news was true and sent Sir Nicholas Throckmorton to London. Before he returned, lords from the Privy Council dashed to Hatfield to confirm the news to Elizabeth. When they arrived at the Hatfield estate, it is alleged that they found Elizabeth sitting under an oak tree reading a book. They addressed her as sovereign. Among them was Robert Dudley, who was mounted on a white steed. After dismounting he paid homage on his knees to the queen. It was reported that, 'though well prepared for the intelligence she appeared at first amazed and overpowered at what she had heard, and, drawing a deep respiration, she sank upon her knees and exclaimed: "It is the Lord's doing, it is marvellous in our eyes."'[45]

Elizabeth later confided to French envoys Chasteau and Bellievre that she shed tears when she learnt of the death of Mary. While London rejoiced at the demise of her sister, Elizabeth did not join them and remained at Hatfield as a mark of respect.

# 26

# The Great Hall, Old Palace, Hatfield

## Elizabeth's First Council of State

**The Great Hall within the Old Palace, Hatfield, was where Elizabeth ate as an infant and it was recorded that 'in Shrovetide, 1556, Sir Thomas Pope made for the Lady Elizabeth, all at his own costs, a great and rich masque in the great hall at Hatfield; where the pageants were marvellously furnished'.[46] The first six days of her reign were spent at the Old Palace. Elizabeth spent 18 and 19 November 1558 forming her Privy Council. It was in the Great Hall that she convened her first Council of State as sovereign with the Privy Council on 20 November 1558.**

The Privy Council is a formal body of advisers to the sovereign comprising senior politicians and former members of the House of Commons and House of Lords appointed by the monarch. Its origins date back to the thirteenth century and its role is to advise the monarch on the conducting of duties, including the exercise of the Royal Prerogative and other protocols assigned to the sovereign by Acts of Parliament.

The first decision of her reign was to appoint Sir William Cecil as her Principal Secretary who would lead the Privy Council. Elizabeth trusted the high-minded and reliable Cecil. He would serve as secretary for the following fourteen years, when in 1572 he eventually became Lord Treasurer. He would remain a member of Elizabeth's Privy Council and exert a strong influence upon her until his death in 1598. After Cecil took the oath in the Great Hall at the Old Palace, Hatfield, Elizabeth addressed him with the following words, which was a summary of his duties and the standards that she expected from him:

I give you this charge that you shall be of my Privy Council and content yourself to take pains for me and my realm. This judgement I have of you that you will not be corrupted with any manner of gift, and you will be faithful to the state, and that without respect of my private will you give me that council that you think best. And if you shall know anything necessary to be declared to me of secrecy, you shall show it to myself only, and assure yourself I will not fail to keep taciturnity therein, and therefore herewith charge you.[47]

The Great Hall was where Elizabeth ate as an infant and where she convened the first Privy Council meeting of her reign. (*Courtesy Paul Hudson via Wikimedia Commons*)

Elizabeth then addressed the lords of Queen Mary's Privy Council in her first speech in which she acknowledged that, as sovereign, she had been anointed by God. She also used the opportunity to announce that she would reduce the Privy Council from forty-four to nineteen councillors. Elizabeth believed that good-quality advice from a smaller number was far more effective and valued than advice from a larger number of advisors. Twenty-nine members of her sister's Privy Council who were devout Catholics and therefore unlikely to support her Protestant agenda were dismissed. In order to allay concerns within the Catholic community and to ensure that her Privy Council included experienced men, Elizabeth retained a small number of her sister's Privy Council who, despite their Catholic faith, had supported her father during the creation of the new Church of England in his reign and who were able to adapt and support Elizabeth as she steered the nation in the direction of Protestantism.

Amongst the inner circle of her Privy Council, those who were devout Protestants, she ordered the restoration of the Protestant religion. Then with the entire Privy Council she turned her attention to the defence of the realm, ordering that the ports should be closed and the Tower of London should be garrisoned with trusted, loyal soldiers. Since Mary depended upon her husband, Philip II, for defence, England was ill prepared to defend itself independently. To remedy this Elizabeth ordered the procurement of munitions and gunpowder, which had to be brought from Germany and the Low Countries. She ordered that peace initiatives towards the French should continue. Elizabeth remained at Hatfield until 23 November 1558, when she began her journey to London.

# 27

# Charterhouse, London

## Elizabeth's Preparations for Entering London

**Charterhouse was a Carthusian priory built in 1371, situated north of the walls of the City of London. During 1558, it was the home of Lord Edward North, a former privy councillor of Queen Mary. Elizabeth had dismissed Lord North from the Privy Council at Hatfield and she lodged at Charterhouse prior to entering London as sovereign.**

E lizabeth left Hatfield for London on 23 November 1558, escorted by 1,000 noblemen and ladies of the court. The people of London ventured from outside the city walls to welcome her. Before arriving at Highgate, Elizabeth was received by a procession of bishops who knelt before her and pledged their allegiance to her. She offered each of them her hand to kiss except for Edmund Bonner, Bishop of London, who was known as 'Bloody Bonner' for his involvement in the persecution of heretics during the reign of Queen Mary, acts for which she was abhorred. Elizabeth was then escorted to Charterhouse by the Lord Mayor and aldermen from the City of London.

Elizabeth stayed at Charterhouse for five days while the Tower of London and Whitehall Palace were being prepared and the streets of London were gravelled before her first entry into London as sovereign. Charterhouse was a monastery before the dissolution and was chosen for its size – it could accommodate her retinue – and close proximity to the City of London. While at Charterhouse she held court and met her Privy Council in the Great Chamber. In this room she made a gesture to cement peace and harmony within England by ordering the release of all prisoners incarcerated for their religious beliefs, both Protestants and Catholics, on 24 November. Elizabeth left Charterhouse on 28 November for the Tower of London.

Lord North died on 31 December 1564 and Charterhouse passed to his son Roger, Lord North. He sold it the following year to Thomas Howard, 4th Duke of

Charterhouse. (*Author's Collection*)

Charterhouse depicted in 1770 when it served as a hospital. (*Public Domain via Wikimedia Commons*)

Norfolk, who used it as his London residence and from which time it was known as Norfolk House. He lived here until 1569 when he was committed to the Tower of London for attempting to marry Mary, Queen of Scots without the permission of Elizabeth. He returned to Charterhouse in 1570, where he received Roberto Ridolfi, the international banker from Florence, who was plotting to assist Catholics

Model of Charterhouse.
(*Author's Collection*)

in England to usurp Elizabeth, facilitate a Spanish invasion of England and place Mary, Queen of Scots on the English throne. Known as the Ridolfi Plot, Ridolfi sent Charles Bailey with a document to Norfolk that detailed plans of the invasion and forty individuals who supported her claim in ciphers. This coded document was found concealed under the tiles on the roof of Charterhouse along with a letter discovered under a mat in his chamber, which implicated Norfolk in the plot against Elizabeth that led to his arrest and execution. Elizabeth permitted the Norfolk family to continue to own Charterhouse by passing it to the duke's second son, Lord Thomas Howard.

# 28

# Medieval London Wall, Cripplegate

## Elizabeth Enters London for the First Time as Sovereign

**Cripplegate is one of the gates of the City of London. The origins of its name are uncertain. 'Crepel' was an Anglo-Saxon word meaning a covered passageway, but there is also a theory that it was named after the disabled citizens who begged in the vicinity.**

While Elizabeth was preparing her administration and formulating policy at the Old Palace, Hatfield, and at Charterhouse, the people of London rejoiced at the prospect of the accession of the young queen and felt optimistic about the beginning of a new reign. Apart from the Catholic bishops and priests, Londoners celebrated Elizabeth's accession. Henry Machyn, a London resident and diarist, wrote that on 17 November 1558, 'the same day, at afternoon, all the churches in London did ring, and at night, did make bonfires and set tables in the street and did eat and drink and made merry for the new Queen Elizabeth'.[48] However, the people of the City of London had to wait a further eleven days before Queen Elizabeth entered London.

On 28 November Elizabeth left Charterhouse to formally take possession of the Tower of London. Crowds departed from the walls of the City of London to line the route from Charterhouse to Cripplegate as she was transported in a chariot. She was welcomed by the Lord Mayor of London with a brief speech at the gates of Charterhouse before entering London through Cripplegate, where some of the London wall remains. Built on Roman foundations, the upper structure was constructed during the thirteenth century and it formed a defensive perimeter around the capital. Dressed in a riding gown of purple velvet, it was here that she mounted on horseback. On either side were her Sergeant-at-Arms, her guard and Lord Robert Dudley, her Master of the Horse. Elizabeth entered through Cripplegate accompanied by the Lord Mayor bearing the sceptre and the Garter King of Arms. Lord Pembroke rode immediately in front of Elizabeth carrying the Sword of State.

Elizabeth wanted to proceed to the Tower of London via a different route to the one she would take for her coronation so that the people of London could have the opportunity to see her. Elizabeth engaged with the people as she rode from Cripplegate through the London streets. Sir John Hayward wrote that, 'she graced every person either of dignity or employment'.[49] Elizabeth was aware of the importance of keeping her subjects on her side and she made efforts to connect with everyone. The procession then proceeded from Cripplegate along the London wall to Bishopsgate, then down Leadenhall, Gracechurch Street and Fenchurch Street to the Tower of London.

A bastion that formed part of the medieval London wall at Cripplegate, situated next to the Museum of London. The base was constructed during the Roman occupation, the wall above it is medieval and the brickwork that lines the interior dates from the nineteenth century. (*Author's Collection*)

# 29

# Queen's Stairs, Tower of London

## Elizabeth's Return to the Tower of London as Sovereign

**Important visitors such as kings, queens and high-ranking officials arrived at Queen's Stairs to enter the Tower of London. Eizabeth's mother, Anne Boleyn, arrived here in 1533 and was welcomed by Henry VIII before her coronation. Elizabeth maintained the royal traditions of her ancestors and before her coronation she stayed one night at the Tower of London arriving by these steps, known as Queen's Stairs, on 12 January 1559.**

Elizabeth's last visit to the Tower of London was as a prisoner when she entered via Traitor's Gate in 1554. Four years later she arrived as queen to take possession of the fortress. On 28 November 1558, Elizabeth reached the Tower of London for the first time as sovereign from the city through the Byward Tower. Elizabeth commented that, 'some have fallen from being princes of this land, to be prisoners in this place; I am raised from being a prisoner in this place, to be prince of this land'.[50] She remained in the Tower of London until 5 December when she moved to Somerset House in the Strand and went on to spend Christmas at Whitehall Palace.

Elizabeth returned to the Tower of London a month later. On 12 January 1559, prior to her coronation, Elizabeth departed from Whitehall Palace in a barge leading a flotilla of vessels conveying the Mayor of London, alderman and various dignitaries eastwards along the River Thames and disembarking at the Queen's Stairs at the Tower of London. Il Schifanoya, the Mantuan envoy, reported:

> At 2 p.m., the flood-tide then serving to pass under London Bridge, her Majesty, accompanied by many knights, barons, ladies, and by the whole Court, passing through the private corridor, embarked in her barge, which was covered with its usual tapestries, both externally and internally, and was towed by a long galley rowed by 40 men in their shirts, with a band of music, as usual when the

Queen goes by water. Her Majesty having passed the bridge, in sight of the Tower, some pieces of artillery were fired; she landed at the private stairs, and, entering by a little bridge, was seen but by very few persons.[51]

Queen's Stairs can be seen today as well as the little bridge referred to by Il Schifanoya which leads into the Byward Tower opposite the stairs. In 1533, Anne Boleyn used the same steps before her coronation in 1533 and was welcomed by Henry VIII who led her across the same bridge into the Byward Tower.

Staying at the Tower of London was part of the coronation process during mediaeval times. On 13 January Elizabeth appointed her Knights of the Bath, but she was most sparing in the distribution of these honours. During her stay at the

Queen's Stairs. Anne Boleyn arrived here on 29 May 1533, two days before her coronation at Westminster Abbey. Her daughter, Elizabeth, used the same steps as queen to enter the Tower of London on 12 January 1559 before her coronation. (*Author's Collection*)

Tower of London the superstitious Elizabeth consulted with her newly appointed scientific advisor, Dr John Dee, to produce an astrological chart to select the most suitable date for the coronation. The renowned mathematician and astrologer recommended Sunday, 15 January 1559 as an auspicious date. Dee had predicted that Mary would die prematurely, but given her frail health, that could have been determined without prophecy.

Before she left the Tower of London on 14 January 1559, she attended morning service in St John's Chapel within the White Tower, which was primarily a place reserved for the sovereign and members of her court to worship. Built in about 1078, it is one of the oldest churches in London. The Knights of the Bath kept vigil in this chapel and joined Elizabeth during the service before she was escorted from the Tower of London to Westminster for her coronation.

An artist's impression of Queen's Stairs and Postern Gate at the Tower of London. (*Information Panel at Queen's Stairs/ Author's Collection*)

# 30

# Drawing of the Coronation Procession

## A Powerful Spectacle

**This image is from a document held at the College of Arms that depicts Elizabeth's coronation procession on 14 January 1559. Elizabeth recognised at the beginning of her reign that if she was to command respect, she would need to be seen by her subjects. A procession was the ideal vehicle for visually demonstrating her power and authority, dressed in jewels and silk, while attended upon by her noblemen.**

The second part of the coronation process involved the procession from the Tower of London to the Palace of Westminster on the day proceeding the coronation. On 14 January 1559, Elizabeth made her triumphant entry into the City of London, carried on a canopied litter, covered with gold cloth, through the streets to be paraded before her people. Although there were reservations expressed by misogynistic elements within the court who felt uneasy and uncomfortable that the country would be ruled again by a woman, in contrast to her sister, Elizabeth was loved and respected before she ascended the throne. She was beautiful, charming, charismatic and possessed gravitas, but above all she represented hope, stability and peace after the turbulent, brutal regime of Queen Mary. Elizabeth was warmly welcomed by the people of London, who waited to see her on a cold, wintery day.

The route passed through Cornhill, Cheapside and the old medieval St Paul's Cathedral, continuing along Ludgate Hill, Fleet Street and then along the Strand to Westminster. Wooden barricades lined the route of the procession from behind which merchants, traders and residents could view the spectacle. The multitude of people lining the route and the foul weather rendered the condition of the streets muddy, so sand and gravel was spread outside each house and shop. Ambrose Dudley, performing his role as Master of the Horse, and his brother, Lord Robert Dudley, followed the litter bearing Elizabeth. Behind them came the Lord Chamberlain and the lords of the Privy Council. Il Schifanoya was among those persons who witnessed the pageant:

> The number of horses was in all 1,000, and last of all came her Majesty in an open litter, trimmed down to the ground with gold brocade, with a raised pile, and carried by two very handsome mules covered with the same material, and surrounded by a multitude of footmen in crimson velvet jerkins, all studded with massive gilt silver, with the arms of a white and red rose on their breasts and backs, and laterally the letters E. R. for *Elizabetta Regina* wrought in relief, the usual livery of this Crown, which makes a superb show. They were uncovered (*scoperti*), and without anything on their heads. The Gentlemen-Pensioners of the Axe walked at the sides, with hammers in hand, and clad in crimson damask, given them by the Queen for livery, all being on foot and bareheaded. Her Majesty was dressed in a royal robe of very rich cloth of gold, with a double-raised stiff pile, and on her head over a coif of cloth of gold, beneath which was her hair, a plain gold crown without lace, as a princess, but covered with jewels, and nothing in her hands but gloves.[52]

After leaving the Tower of London Elizabeth passed under several triumphal arches that were erected in her honour along the route through the City of London from Cheapside towards St Paul's churchyard and along the north facade of St Paul's Cathedral towards Ludgate.

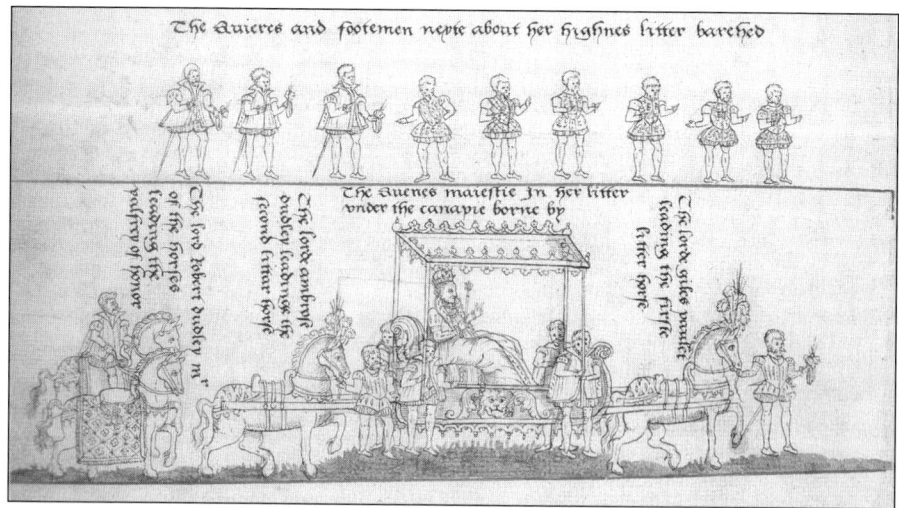

Drawing of the coronation procession. (*Public Domain/College of Arms*)

# 31

# Statue of Elizabeth I

## Triumphant Queen

**This is the only known surviving statue carved during Elizabeth's lifetime and the oldest outdoor statue in London which stands above the entrance to the vestry of St Dunstan in the West Church in Fleet Street. The statue was carved in about 1586 and once stood on the western facade of Ludgate, the western entrance to the City of London. Elizabeth passed through Ludgate during her coronation procession through the City of London into Fleet Street towards Westminster on 14 January 1559. Ludgate was damaged during the Great Fire of London in 1666 and demolished a century later in 1760.**

Elizabeth's procession was welcomed by a fanfare of music as it approached Ludgate. After moving through Ludgate, the coronation procession proceeded into Fleet Street, passing the City of London School where scholars read her an oration.

The statue of Elizabeth overlooks Fleet Street and the route of her coronation procession. The procession took longer than planned because Elizabeth allowed her coach to stop on numerous occasions to listen to petitions and acknowledge the affection demonstrated by her citizens along the route. Elizabeth set a precedent at the start of her reign by engaging with all elements of society, ensuring to be seen by as many people as possible. She was the first English sovereign to establish what is known today as the royal walkabout, a tradition that was not repeated by successive monarchs until George V ascended the throne in 1910. Sir John Hayward wrote:

> She cheerfully received not only gifts from persons of worth, but nosegays, flowers and rose-marie branches, and such like presents, offered unto her from very mean persons, insomuch as it may truly be said, that there was never a courtesy nor cost cast away that day upon her. It is incredible how often she

caused her coach to stay, when any made offer to approach unto her, wither to make petition, or whither to manifest their loving affection.[53]

Later that afternoon Elizabeth arrived at Whitehall Palace where she spent the night before her coronation. The following morning she was taken by barge from Whitehall Palace to Westminster Hall from where her procession to Westminster Abbey began.

After Ludgate was demolished in 1760, the statue was given to the Church of St Dunstan in the West which is located on the north side of Fleet Street, along the route Elizabeth took during her coronation procession from the City of London to Westminster. The original church was constructed between 988 and 1070. The quick actions of the Dean of Westminster prevented its destruction in 1666 during the Great Fire of London when he organised forty scholars from Westminster with buckets of water to extinguish the flames. The church fell into decay and was rebuilt in 1831 and still stands today, together with the statue of Elizabeth.

Statue of Queen Elizabeth I, Church of St Dunstan in the West, Fleet Street, London. (*Author's Collection*)

# 32

# The Coronation Chair

## Coronation of Elizabeth I

**The Coronation Chair was made on the order of King Edward I to enclose the Stone of Scone, which had been taken from Scotland and transferred to Westminster Abbey. It was built of oak and completed in 1301. This throne was used during the coronation of thirty-eight English monarchs including the coronation ceremony of Elizabeth I on 15 January 1559. Her predecessor, Queen Mary I, refused to sit in the Coronation Chair during her coronation because she believed that it was tainted by her Protestant brother and requested that another chair be sent by Pope Julius III from the Vatican.**

Elizabeth's coronation ceremony took place at Westminster Abbey on 15 January 1559. Protocol dictated that the Archbishop of Canterbury performed the coronation service, but the incumbent, Reginald Pole, had died on 17 November 1558, the same day as Mary, and his successor had not been appointed. Nine other bishops had also died during the previous year and a successor had yet to be found. Those bishops already in position were reluctant to conduct the ceremony because they were fearful that Elizabeth would not abide by a Catholic ceremony. On 13 December 1558, two days before Mary was buried at Westminster Abbey, Elizabeth walked out of a requiem mass held for her sister. Nicholas Heath, Archbishop of York, was asked but he refused to conduct the service. Eventually, Owen Oglethorpe, Bishop of Carlisle, was coaxed into administering the coronation ceremony on the proviso that Elizabeth would take the Catholic oath that had been taken by previous monarchs. The service conducted in Westminster Abbey was spoken partly in Latin and partly in English. The Litany was read in English and the Gospel and Epistle both in English and Latin. It was the last occasion on which the service was conducted in Latin in England, although only in part.

The Coronation Chair, Westminster Abbey, on which Elizabeth I sat as she was crowned on 15 January 1559. (*Copyright Dean and Chapter of Westminster*)

Elizabeth wore the same coronation robes that were used during the coronation of Mary I in 1553, however, Mary wore the robes and kirtle, which was a garment, a bodice, that supported the bust, loose, while Elizabeth requested that the bodice be altered so it was tighter fitting. Il Schifanoya, the Mantuan envoy, attended the coronation of Elizabeth and reported:

On Sunday, 15th January, mass was sung for the coronation in Westminster Abbey, which was decorated with the handsomest and most precious tapestries that were ever seen, they having been purchased by Henry VIII ...

The Queen was received under the canopy by the Archbishop and another Bishop, they having previously perfumed her with incense, giving her the holy water and the pax, the choristers singing; ... they proceeded to the church, the Queen's long train being carried by the Duchess of Norfolk, after whom followed the Lord Chamberlain, upon purple cloth spread on the ground; and as her Majesty passed, the cloth was cut away by those who could get it. Then followed the duchesses, marchionesses, countesses, etc., dragging their trains after them, going two by two, and being exquisitely dressed, with their coronets on their heads, and so handsome and beautiful that it was a marvellous sight.

On her Majesty's arrival at the church, all the bells in London ringing, she ascended the lofty tribune erected between the high altar and the choir, being thus exhibited to the people, of whom it was asked if they wished her to be their crowned Queen? Whereupon they all shouted 'Yes'; and the organs, fifes, trumpets, and drums playing, the bells also ringing, it seemed as if the world were come to an end. Descending from the tribune, the Queen placed herself under her royal canopy; and then the choristers commenced the mass, which was sung by the Dean of her Chapel, her Chaplain, the Bishops not having chosen to say mass without elevating the host or consecrating it, as that worthy individual did; the Epistle and Gospel being recited in English.

After the Epistle, the Bishop of Carlisle commenced the coronation according to the Roman ceremonial, neither altering nor omitting anything but the outward forms, which were not observed as in Italy; the English having no Masters of the Ceremonies, except the Kings-at-arms, and still less caring about formalities.[54]

# 33

# Westminster Hall

## Coronation Banquet

**The Palace of Westminster was at the epicentre of government and had been the principal residence of the monarch since construction was completed in 1099 during the reign of William Rufus until most of it was destroyed by fire in 1512, except for Westminster Hall.**

Before the coronation ceremony in Westminster Abbey, Elizabeth was presented with the crown, sceptre and associated symbols of royal power and they were displayed on the King's Table at a coronation breakfast in Westminster Hall. This symbolised the sovereign taking possession of the kingdom and was applauded by the lords. It was a tradition that had been followed for 300 years by seventeen monarchs including Henry V, Richard III and Henry VIII.

After being crowned in Westminster Abbey, Elizabeth and her court returned to Westminster Hall to celebrate the coronation at a lavish banquet. Il Schifanoya described her entrance into Westminster Hall, 'her Majesty carrying in her hands the sceptre and orb, and wearing the ample royal robe of cloth of gold. She returned very cheerfully, with a most smiling countenance for everyone, giving them all a thousand greetings, so that in my opinion she exceeded the bounds of gravity and decorum.'[55]

As Elizabeth adjourned to divest herself from her heavy robes the banquet was being arranged, four long tables were laid in Westminster Hall, divided in the centre to accommodate the waiting servants who were dressed in red liveries. At each table 200 guests were seated including titled noblemen and women, aldermen, sheriffs and the Mayor of London.

Elizabeth was attended by two noblemen during the banquet. Il Schifanoya confirmed:

... after 3 p.m., when the Queen commenced washing her hands, the water and the napkin were given her by the noblemen who had waited on her

Majesty as server and as carver, viz., William Lord Howard of Effingham, Lord High Admiral, and the Earl of Sussex [Henry Ratcliffe], the former carving, and the latter placing and removing the dishes, both of them serving on their knees.[56]

After the second course of the banquet was served, Sir Edward Dimmock, her champion, entered the hall mounted on a horse, dressed in steel armour with his spear on his thigh. He cast down his gauntlet and offered to fight anyone who challenged her right to be sovereign of the realm. No one answered the challenge, all accepting Elizabeth as sovereign. As he rode out of Westminster Hall, Elizabeth took a gold cup containing wine and drank a toast to her champion. She thanked him and gave him a silver-gilt cup. The celebrations lasted until 1 am the following morning when Elizabeth was transported by royal barge the short distance along the River Thames from Westminster to Whitehall Palace.

Westminster Hall hosted the banquet celebrating the coronation of Elizabeth I in 1559. (*Gimas/Shutterstock*)

# 34

# Engraving Depicting Elizabeth I Opening Parliament

## Elizabeth's Relationship with Parliament

**Elizabeth summoned thirteen Parliaments during her forty-five-year reign, which were convened when the queen wanted to pass laws and raise income through increasing taxes. The first opening of Parliament during her reign took place on 25 January 1559.**

Six days after her coronation, on 21 January 1559, Elizabeth attended Parliament for her first parliamentary session and conveyed her immediate aims for the initial stages of her reign through the Lord Keeper, Sir Nicholas Bacon. These were to restore stability, prosperity and peace to the realm. Concerns for national security were raised as Calais had fallen to the French and the English navy and coastal defences were in a poor state and needed to be strengthened. Elizabeth returned to Parliament on 30 January to propose that religion should be reformed and all laws recently passed revoked and also to request money. This parliamentary session lasted until 8 May 1559.

Reforming religion was a challenge because of the 402 Members of Parliament in the Lower Chamber a quarter were of the Catholic faith and had served under Queen Mary. Also, the lords and bishops sitting in the House of Lords were predominantly Catholic and were resistant to bills that championed the establishment of a Protestant Church of England. However, ten bishops had recently died and their positions were still vacant, while a number of the remaining bishops were ill. Therefore, there was a Catholic minority within the House of Lords. After lengthy debate two measures were agreed, the Act of Supremacy and Act of Uniformity, which were passed by Parliament on 3 April 1559 to form the Elizabethan Settlement of Religion. The Act of Supremacy restored the law passed during Henry VIII's reign in 1534 and repealed by Queen Mary in 1555, which gave ecclesiastical autonomy to the sovereign and abolished papal authority from the Vatican. However, Elizabeth was not comfortable with being anointed Supreme Head of the English Church, but preferred to be known as Supreme Governor of the Church of England to prevent further money being paid to the Pope.[57] She also wanted to leave the bishops to administer the Church free from royal or political interference and in her role as Supreme Governor she was acting as a guardian protecting the English Church during the period of transformation until the bishops were in a position to manage their religious institutions. The Act of Uniformity aimed to unify the country, by introducing the English Book of Common Prayer with the instruction that the order of prayer be changed to make the Protestant book acceptable to Catholics in England, with priests permitted to wear the same vestments worn during the reign of Queen Mary. It also decreed that it was mandatory for all persons to attend church once a week, non-compliance being punishable by a fine. After these Acts had been passed through Parliament, Protestantism became the official religion of the nation, which meant that England and its Church were completely independent from the Vatican and has been since 1559. In May 1559, six months after Elizabeth's accession, the English service was ordered to be conducted in all churches. The Count de Feria wrote to the Spanish king, 'the Catholics are very fearful of the measures to be taken in this Parliament'.[58]

However, the number of fanatical Protestants and Catholics were in the minority in England and the popularity of the Pope in the country had declined. Elizabeth brought stability to the nation. All people wanted was to attend religious services in a language which they could understand. Clergymen in England complied with the new legislation, because out of 9,400 clergy, only 192 refused the oath of supremacy.[59] Those that refused the oath either fled the country or were imprisoned in the Tower of London, then later placed under house arrest in their homes.

The Treasury would generate income through repossessing all religious houses under royal control and the restoration of the First Fruits and Tenths Act which was a tax on religious institutions which were requested to pay a proportion of their income in the first year and then a tenth of annual earnings thereafter.

On 6 February 1559, Parliament petitioned Elizabeth to marry and produce an heir to secure the line of succession and ensure stability. King Philip II of Spain, the widower of her sister had proposed marriage to Elizabeth to ensure that Catholicism prevailed in England in January 1559, but after considering the proposal for a month she politely declined on the premise that the Pope would not allow her to marry her brother-in-law and that England was strong and able to defend its interests at home and internationally. She maintained amicable relations with him because he was a powerful ally who helped to restore peace between France and England in April 1559.

QUEEN ELIZABETH IN PARLIAMENT

A. L.ᵉ Chancellor. B. Marquises, Earles &ᶜ. C. Barons. D. Bishops. E. Iudges. F. Masters of Chancery. G. Clerks. H. Speaker of ẏ Comōns. I. Black Rod. K. Serieant at Armes. L. Members of the Commons house. M. S.ᵗ Francis Walsingham Secretary of State.

This engraving depicts Queen Elizabeth opening Parliament during the latter part of her reign, as it shows Sir Francis Walsingham, Secretary of State standing on her right. (*Courtesy of Metropolitan Museum of Art, New York*)

The queen's response to Parliament's petition for her to marry was to address the House of Commons on 10 February 1559, when she asserted, 'I have already joined myself in marriage to a husband, namely, the kingdom of England.'[60] The statement concluded, 'As for me, it shall be sufficient that a marble stone shall declare that a queen, having lived and reigned so many years, died a virgin.'[61]

Although Elizabeth was not contemplating marriage, thirty Members of Parliament and twelve lords discussed who might be considered eligible to marry the queen at a meeting held on 16 February, but the outcome was not recorded. Towards the end of the parliamentary session, the Speaker represented the privy councillors and a deputation of thirty members from the House of Commons who insisted that the line of succession be settled and that the queen choose a consort for marriage.

At the very start of her reign, Elizabeth declared that she would never marry, she would not surrender herself or her possessions to another man. She saw her father mistreat her mother and step-mother, Anne Boleyn and Katherine Howard, which resulted in their executions and Seymour betrayed her step-mother, Katherine Parr, and also attempted to take advantage of Elizabeth, which caused scandal that tainted her character within the court. She had also seen her sister, Mary, concede some authority to her husband, Philip of Spain, in contravention of the clauses agreed that were meant to prevent such a situation before their marriage. Elizabeth understood the consequences of marriage in Tudor times, when men dominated the world and women were regarded as possessions, including their bodies and wealth, to be owned by the husband irrespective of the fact that she might be a sovereign. Elizabeth was also afraid of pregnancy and childbirth because she had seen two step-mothers, Jane Seymour and Katherine Parr, die as a result of complications from giving birth. She saw the pressure exerted on her sister, Queen Mary, to produce an heir, resulting in her inability to conceive and the humiliation of experiencing phantom pregnancies. Elizabeth was never going to submit to marriage or motherhood. During the early years of her reign, her Privy Council did not take Elizabeth's reluctance to marry seriously, but, like her father, Henry VIII, they knew the importance of an heir to ensure security, stability and to prevent a civil war on the scale of that which took place between the Houses of York and Lancaster in the previous century.

Although the question of marriage had not been resolved, Queen Elizabeth's first session of Parliament passed twenty-four public statutes and seventeen private measures by the time it was dissolved on 8 May 1559.

# 35

# The Tudor Royal Coat of Arms of Elizabeth I

## Elizabeth Demonstrates Her Authority

**The coat of arms in St Catherine's Church, Ludham, Norfolk, is a rare example that was introduced in every English church during the reformation and served as a visual symbol of the sovereign as the Supreme Governor of the Church of England.**

The reformation introduced by Henry VIII brought radical changes to religion, the appearance of churches and the way parishioners worshipped during the Tudor period. To ensure that congregations across the country conformed to the doctrines of the newly created Church of England, existing Catholic images were removed and to enforce upon the minds of the parishioner that Henry VIII was the supreme head of that religion, the Royal Coat of Arms were displayed upon the chancel arch facing the congregation in every English church from 1536. Coats of arms were removed from churches when Mary I became queen in 1553, but Elizabeth restored that Protestant practice when she ascended the throne and ordered that the royal arms be displayed in all churches to replace idolatry symbols depicting the crucifixion of Christ. The coat of arms was a visual reminder that the sovereign had overall control of the English Church.

The arms displayed in the north aisle of St Peter's Church in Berkhamsted are from the Elizabethan era. Painted on canvas on an oval panel, it was mounted in a larger frame years after the Tudor dynasty had ended together with a short poem attached to the arms which celebrated the reign of Elizabeth:

This mighty Queen is dead and lives, and leaves the world to wonder.
How she a maiden Queen did rule, Few Kings have gone beyond her.

The coat of arms of Queen Elizabeth was formed upon the shield of Henry IV, with a red cross dissecting four quarters. Three fleur-de-lys (representing France) are depicted in two of the quarters, and three lions (representing England) are pictured in the other two quarters. The shield is supported by the English Royal Lion and the Welsh Dragon. Two mottos are displayed on the coat of arms, in Latin '*Honi soit qui mal y pense*' (translated, 'Shame on whomsoever would think badly of it') and in French the motto of the Order of the Garter, '*Dieu et mon Droit*' (translated, 'God and my right'). A crown and rose surmounts the coat of arms. All these heraldic components asserted the right of Elizabeth as Queen of England, Wales and France. English monarchs laid claim to the French throne up to 1800.[62]

*Right*: The coat of arms of Elizabeth I facing the chancel at St Catherine's Church, Ludham, Norfolk. (*Michael Garlick; www.geograph.org.uk*)

*Below*: Elizabeth's coat of arms displayed in St Peter's Church, Berkhamsted. (*Author's Collection*)

# 36

# Upnor Castle

## Elizabeth Defends the Nation

**Upnor Castle was an Elizabethan artillery fort built in Kent between 1559 and 1567 to protect Chatham Dockyard and Tudor warships moored in the River Medway. It was redeveloped between 1599 and 1600. The construction of Upnor Castle was ordered during the first year of Elizabeth's reign. Sir Richard Lee, the military engineer, was instructed to design the fortifications at Upnor, but because he was also involved in work strengthening the defences of Berwick on the Anglo-Scottish border, the work was managed by his deputy, Humphrey Locke, and Richard Watts, former Mayor of Rochester and victualler to the navy. Stone from derelict buildings within Rochester Castle was used to construct Upnor Castle.**

The main building of Upnor Castle was built into the western embankment of the River Medway and was protected by towers and a curtain wall. A triangular gun battery, armed with twenty cannon, projected into the river and could fire north and south along the river.

Towards the end of Elizabeth's reign there existed concerns that Philip II would send a second Spanish Armada and steps were made to prepare the defences along the River Medway and these involved Upnor Castle. Lord Admiral Charles Howard wrote to Secretary of State, Sir Robert Cecil, during February 1596:

> I send you intelligence [of the designs of the enemy] brought by Abraham Van Harwyke and Quester. If they have such a design, it will be practised at spring tides. I wish the Queen would send Sir W. Raleigh to guard the ships at Chatham; three or four good ships should lie at Quinborough. Upnor Castle should be well garrisoned or pulled down, for if they surprised it, they would beat the ships terribly with the ordnance. I wish fifty trained men were put in to defend it. My Lord Chamberlain should give orders to the deputy lieutenants about it.[63]

In 1596 the Calendar of State Papers confirmed that wages were paid to eighty men who were garrisoned at Upnor Castle. On 10 November 1596 the following orders were issued pertaining to the defence of the River Medway in the event of an assault upon Chatham Dockyard:

> Orders for the safe-guarding of the Medway. A ketch is to ride without Sheerness, and on sight of any enemy's vessel, to give notice to the Aid which rides within Sheerness. The Aid is then to prepare to meet the enemy, and to fire three guns, whereupon a pinnace riding at Oakamness is to speed up the river towards Chatham, giving alarm all the way up, to Chatham, Upnor Castle, the beacons of Chatham and Barrow Hill, and the four sconces and borders of the river on each side. On this the Bear, riding against St. Mary's creek mouth, is to shoot three pieces of ordnance to continue the alarm, which the Mary Rose, riding against Rochester Bridge, is to take up, and shoot three pieces of ordnance, on which all the country within hearing is to repair to

Upnor Castle. (*Courtesy of Phil Pead*)

This plaque is fastened to the entrance of Upnor Castle on Upchat Road near the junction with Upnor Road and is next to the gates of Upnor Castle House. The plaque shows Queen Elizabeth I standing in front of Upnor Castle during a thunderstorm. (*Courtesy of Marathon; www.geograph.org.uk*)

Chatham church and Upnor Castle, on directions of the deputy lieutenants of the shires. Those places that cannot be warned by shots and beacons are to be warned by hoblers sent from Rochester by the deputy lieutenants; the Mayor of Rochester is to send notice to Sir John Leveson, Thos. Walsingham, Mr. Style, Mr. Mayor of Maidstone, Mr. Lennard, and Mr. Rivers, and each of these captains to give notice to the rest. With note on 12 Nov., that these five captains with 1,080 men are to repair to Upnor Castle, and there be distributed in the five ships next the chain; and that four others named are to repair to Chatham church, with 540 men more.[64]

Upnor Castle failed to prevent Dutch ships from entering the River Medway to burn and capture anchored English vessels in 1667, but it stands as an example of a fortification built during the reign of Elizabeth.

# 37

# Elizabethan Town Walls, Berwick-upon-Tweed

## Defending the Scottish Border

**Skirting the north-eastern perimeter of Berwick-upon-Tweed and measuring 6m in height, stand the Elizabethan town walls. Constructed using limestone in earthen bulwarks, this was the first example of arrow-headed bastions built in Britain.**

Berwick-upon-Tweed had been under Scottish control for three centuries before 1296 when it was captured by Edward I, who ordered these fortifications be built to strengthen the town's defences. Possession of the town was passed back and forth between the English and Scottish before the English captured it in 1482. In 1558, encouraged by her mother, Mary of Guise, Mary Stuart, Queen of Scots married Francis, the French Dauphin, which cemented Scottish-French relations. Canon law decreed that Elizabeth was illegitimate, which precluded her from the throne. Mary Stuart, great-grand-daughter of Henry VII, was a Catholic and considered to have a stronger legitimate claim to the throne of England. Calais had fallen to the French during that same year, and the French perceiving England to be weak, encouraged Scotland to attack England's northern bastion at Berwick-upon-Tweed. Before her death, Queen Mary I ordered Sir Richard Lee, military engineer, to reinforce the town's defences by replacing its medieval walls with a bastioned fortification system, which had first been adopted by Italian engineers in Verona. Bastions are artillery emplacements used as platforms with projecting walls, which enable defenders to fire artillery towards an advancing enemy on each side. After Mary's death, construction of the defences accelerated and intensified. Labourers were sought from across the nation to strengthen the Berwick defences. On 17 January 1559, Elizabeth signed a 'warrant to issue money for payment of 200 labourers, to be levied in Gloucester and Worcester, for service at Berwick'.[65]

Within weeks, English soldiers, equipped with supplies of ammunition and ordinance, were sent to northern border towns including Berwick-upon-Tweed to defend against a Scottish attack. Sir William Cecil laid down stringent orders, authorised by Elizabeth, for the soldiers and residents, who lived within the ramparts of Berwick. The long list included:

> … soldiers not taking the oath to forfeit their wages, stealers and receivers of the Queen's ordnance and stores to suffer death, inter-communing and encouraging desertion to be taken as treason, affrays at any of the gates or the watch hill to be punished with death, any going from the walls after the watchword is given to suffer death, soldiers absent without license to loose double wages, the gates shall be shut at every alarm, and all carts with fodder, straw etc., to be searched under pain of death, no soldier to use any vile occupation, as fishing, every soldier to wear a jacket of the Queen's colours, white and green, watchers neglecting to give warning of every ship and person coming within sight to have their heads struck off at the market cross, no soldier to be in the streets without a bill or axe, no Scottish born person to be of the garrison on pain of death, no soldier to come on the town wall suspiciously by night without the watchword.[66]

It took ten years to build the ramparts and this was completed in 1569 before work on the upper ramparts commenced. Mary, Queen of Scots was imprisoned in England in 1568, the threat of a Franco-Scottish invasion had receded and as it became apparent that Elizabeth would not produce a successor and that James VI of Scotland would eventually succeed her, work to fortify the town stopped. When he ascended the English throne as James I, Berwick-upon-Tweed was the first English town to welcome him as he crossed the border. The Berwick fortifications stand as a prominent reminder of the reign of Elizabeth.

The ramparts of the town wall, with one of the eastern bastions above the low ground to the east of the town, Berwick-upon-Tweed. (*Courtesy of Nilfanion*)

# 38

# Statue of Mary, Queen of Scots, Linlithgow Palace

### Elizabeth's Rival for the English Throne

**Mary, Queen of Scots was Elizabeth's cousin and many Catholics within England looked upon Elizabeth as illegitimate, regarding Mary as the rightful heir to the English throne as the senior surviving descendant of Henry VII through her grandmother, Margaret Tudor. Despite the end of the war with France and Scotland, the arms of Mary, Queen of Scotland and France continued to feature in the arms of England.**

Mary Stuart was born on 8 December 1542 at Linlithgow Palace and was proclaimed Queen of Scotland nine months later on 9 September 1543. Mary married the French Dauphin, Francis, in 1558 when she was aged 16. She had lived in France during her childhood while regents governed Scotland. On 10 July 1558, Francis ascended the throne, which meant that Mary became Queen of France. The coat of arms of Mary Stuart included heraldic emblems of Scotland, France and England. So long as Mary was alive, she would remain a threat to the security of Elizabeth's reign.

England was at war with France and Scotland when Elizabeth ascended the throne in 1558. Her sister Mary's marriage to Philip II of Spain brought England into conflict with France in 1557 which resulted in the French regaining Calais from the English. Acknowledging that her position was precarious, one of the first directives issued by Elizabeth to her privy councillors was to restore peace with these two countries. The Treaty of Cateau-Cambrésis, signed on 7 April 1559, ended the conflict of France and Scotland with England. France no longer supported Mary's claim to the English throne and England agreed that France would retain Calais for eight years and restore it to English rule on conditions that would be impossible for England to fulfil, which meant that despite Mary, Queen of Scots agreeing to the treaty, she continued to bear the heraldic arms of England and obliquely continued her claim to its throne.

*Left*: Statue of Mary, Queen of Scots at her birthplace at Linlithgow Palace. (*Courtesy of Stinglehammer via Wikimedia Commons*)

*Below*: Linlithgow Palace. (*Courtesy of Alex Sanz via Wikimedia Commons*)

When Henry II of France was killed on the tiltyard in a jousting accident on 10 July 1559, the husband of Mary, Queen of Scots succeeded him as King Francis II. Mary became Queen of France which raised alarm in Elizabeth's court that France would resume support of Mary's claim to the English throne. The French Catholic Mary of Guise, mother of Mary, Queen of Scots, was currently ruling as regent in Scotland and intent on the suppression of the reformation and insisting that everyone attend daily Mass and confession. A force of 12,000 French soldiers arrived at Leith on 15 October 1559. Although Mary of Guise was acting as regent until her daughter came of age to rule, Scotland was in effect governed by the French. Protestant Lords in Scotland began to rebel against her rule. Elizabeth was in a dilemma whether to unite in friendship with Mary, Queen of Scots, who held a claim to the English throne, was a devout Catholic and who opposed the religious reforms that Elizabeth wanted to implement or favour the Protestant lords and spiritual leaders who were resisting French attempts to rule Scotland via the regency of Mary of Guise. The prospect of French reinforcements being deployed to Scotland to assist in quelling that rebellion prompted Elizabeth to send support to these Protestant lords. If they were suppressed, then France would be in a position to launch an assault upon English soil from Scotland. Elizabeth sent the English fleet to Leith to obstruct any attempts to land French reinforcements close to Edinburgh. Elizabeth dispatched Thomas Howard, 4th Duke of Norfolk to Berwick to assemble an army to reinforce the English–Scottish border. Norfolk signed the Treaty of Berwick on 27 February 1560 with Scottish Protestant noblemen pledging Elizabeth's support to expel French forces already garrisoned in Leith, led by Mary of Guise, and to prevent further French reinforcements from reaching Scotland.

# 39

# Giant's Brae, Leith

## Siege of Leith

**Giant's Brae is an earthen bulwark at Mount Pelham that protected English artillery during the Siege of Leith in 1560. It is one of two mounds, the other being Lady Fyfe's Brae, which have survived 400 years at Leith Links.**

On 30 March 1560, William Grey, Lord Wilton, led 10,000 English soldiers into Scotland and headed to Leith where they besieged the garrison which was defended by 3,500 French and 500 Scottish soldiers. During the night of 5 April the English army arrived outside Leith. Sir William Cecil reported to English ambassadors in Spain that when it encircled the town during the following day 'fifty French were taken and thirty slain, and of the English ten hurt and slain'.[67] Thomas Howard, 4th Duke of Norfolk received a report that the French casualties were a lot heavier with 'eighty slain and 200 hurt'.[68] By 17 April, 29 English ships commanded by William Winter with approximately 5,000 men were anchored in the Firth of Forth off the coast at Leith.

The English launched an assault upon Leith on 7 May 1560. Captain Vaughan led 1,200 English soldiers from this bulwark at Mount Pelham. The French garrison was strongly fortified behind the bulwarks and the English were unable to penetrate the defences of Leith. Cecil referred to the earthen bulwarks at Leith in a report to Montague on 12 May 1560:

> … the army remained two full months and the town of Leith besieged, and it is hoped that it will be won either by famine or by assault. The town is very strong, having in it 3,500 very good soldiers, saving by skirmishes many of them be diminished; it is fortified with good walls of earth and sods, and very full of ordnance. The English army is too small, not being above 9,000 men, and the Scots not past 4,000 footmen, whereof many will not come nigh any shot.[69]

On 13 May, French soldiers were exposed as they picked cockles and winkles on the shoreline. Lord Grey ordered his light horsemen to attack them and fifty were slain. By 19 May, English engineers were excavating mines beneath the town walls and earthen works defended by the French garrison at Leith. Mary of Guise, Dowager of Scotland, mentioned the bulwark at Pelham in a letter, 'the enemy have very much advanced the mine, and they count to finish it by Wednesday. They say that they know they are countermined, but that theirs is so deep that they pass under the countermine. They find the fort of Peleric [Pelham] strong, and it is said that they have another mine going towards the mill bulwark.'[70]

During the siege, Mary of Guise died on 11 June 1560, aged 44, at Edinburgh Castle. Her death would facilitate the negotiation of a peace treaty. A truce was agreed on 17 June and Cecil began peace negotiations with the French. He succeeded in gaining a promise from French commissioners for the abandonment of the French king and queen's claim to the English throne and secured the liberty of the Scottish Protestants who had rebelled against the regent. On 6 July 1560, the Treaty of Edinburgh was signed which decreed that both English and French forces withdraw from Leith. Mary, Queen of Scots refused to sign the treaty because it forfeited her right to raise an army against England and her right to the succession of the English throne after the death of Elizabeth. Mary, Queen of Scots was intent on championing her claim and would continue to be a problem for Elizabeth. Her husband, King Francis II, died in December 1560 and Mary, Queen of Scots was Queen of France for only seventeen months. The widowed Mary, Queen of Scots wanted to return to Scotland but Elizabeth refused her passage through England unless she ratified the Treaty of Edinburgh. Mary sailed to Scotland by ship arriving at Leith on 19 August 1561. She sent a deputation to Elizabeth to demand acknowledgment of her right to succeed the English throne, which Elizabeth refused.

Remains of an Elizabethan English artillery battery known as Giant's Brae, which was used during the Siege of Leith in 1560. (*Courtesy of Kim Traynor; www.geograph.org*)

# 40

# Oil Painting, *Elizabeth I and Leicester*

## Elizabeth's Relationship with Robert Dudley

**This painting by William Frederick Yeames, from 1865, depicts Elizabeth receiving Robert Dudley, her favourite and closest confidant. Her cousin, Thomas Howard, 4th Duke of Norfolk, can be seen interrupting proceedings in the background.**

During autumn 1559, European kings and noblemen were vying for the hand of Queen Elizbeth, but she stood resolute and refused to commit to anyone. Despite her resistance to marriage, she had inherited her mother's flirtatious nature and enjoyed the attention of amorous courtiers. Sometimes she behaved with such blatant suggestiveness amongst certain men that the court assumed that she might have been having an affair. Robert Dudley was one courtier who would remain a firm favourite of Elizabeth's for a large part of her reign until his death in 1588.

A close relationship began developing between Robert Dudley and Elizabeth at an early age. Robert and Elizabeth were both born in 1533. Dudley, the son of John Dudley, 1st Duke of Northumberland, was a childhood friend of Elizabeth since they were 8 years old. Dudley became a Member of Parliament in 1553 representing Norfolk. He was jailed in the Tower of London for supporting his father's attempt to place Lady Jane Grey on the throne and remained incarcerated when Elizabeth was imprisoned in 1554. Dudley supported Elizabeth during her sister's reign and his loyalty was rewarded when she appointed him as Master of the Horse on her accession.

Dudley was 6ft tall, handsome, immaculately dressed and well groomed, well educated and excelled in sports such as tennis and jousting. He was the embodiment of the renaissance man which appealed to Elizabeth. However, Dudley was also married to Amy Dudley (née Robsart), but Elizabeth could enjoy the companionship and attention offered by Dudley safe in the knowledge that he would be unable to propose marriage. During their eight-year marriage, Amy saw very little of her husband because Elizabeth demanded that he remain at court. However, despite being married, there was evidence of intimacy between Dudley and the queen. Rumours circulated around the court that Elizabeth and Dudley were conducting an affair.

On 23 April 1559, Elizabeth elevated Dudley to the Order of the Garter, alongside Thomas Howard, 4th Duke of Norfolk and the Marquess of Northampton which caused much consternation within the court. Norfolk and Northampton had received this honour based on merit and their service to the nation. Dudley's father and grandfather had been executed as traitors and it was perceived that Dudley had received the honour based on his good looks and because he was a favourite of

*Elizabeth I and Leicester* by William Fredrick Yeames. (*Museum of Fine Arts of Lyon*)

the queen. When she conferred the Order of the Garter upon Dudley, she tickled his neck and after a tennis match she took Dudley's handkerchief and wiped the sweat from his brow in front of members of her court and household. Elizabeth granted him an annual income and gave him properties at Kew, Knole in Kent and Kenilworth Castle in Leicestershire.

Courtiers and ambassadors talked within the English court about the relationship between Dudley and Elizabeth. On 6 August 1559, the ambassador Baron Caspar Breuner reported to the Emperor Ferdinand I: 'The Master of the Horse is, I hear, married to a fine lady for whom he has had nothing but good; nevertheless, since the queen was crowned, he has never been away from court. Moreover, they dwell in the same house and this it is which feeds suspicion.'[71]

Cecil was concerned that Dudley had much influence over the queen who sought his advice on political matters and about the scandal that their liaison could potentially cause. They would spend days hunting together. It was suggested that if his wife died, Elizabeth would marry Dudley. On 8 September 1560, Amy died when she fell down a staircase and broke her neck. Suspicion surrounded her death, despite a coroner's court concluding that it was death by misadventure. For a while Elizabeth kept Dudley at a distance to avoid any further scandal.

# 41

# Coin Bearing Image of Elizabeth I

## Elizabeth's Restoration of Coinage

**In order to raise income to finance foreign wars and fund his opulent lifestyle Henry VIII introduced the currency debasement policy in 1544. With the principal aim of raising revenue for the Crown, savings in the cost of currency production were made by using less bullion to mint new coins. It meant that the amount of gold and silver used in the production of coins was reduced, and these metals were supplemented with cheaper base metals such as copper as a substitute. Henry became known as 'Old Coppernose' because as the coins wore down copper appeared through the king's image. Although the cost of materials had been reduced by using inferior metals, the value of the currency was maintained at pre-debasement level. This policy caused an increase in prices and public loss of faith in England's coins. Elizabeth endeavoured to restore the coinage and public confidence during her reign.**

The problem of devalued currency was not resolved during the reigns of Edward VI and Mary, which meant that many of the debased coins remained in circulation when Elizabeth ascended the throne. A proclamation recalling all base money from circulation was issued on 28 September 1560. Officers of the Mint received the following directive from the queen on 29 September 1560 'to refine and recoin a certain mass of base money into fine sterling silver of 5s the ounce'.[72]

Such was the urgency to create good-quality money that a warrant was issued to the Lord Treasurer, William Paulet, 1st Marquess of Winchester, 'to deliver certain old plate, gilt and parcel gilt, to the Treasurer of the Mint, to be converted into coin'.[73] A similar warrant was sent by the queen to Winchester 'to deliver in the Mint all unserviceable old plate of gold and other utensils of gold, remaining in his custody, to be coined'.[74] In order to distinguish between old devalued coins and new coins, Elizabeth also ordered 'directions to affix the marks of a

*Above left*: An Elizabeth I sovereign, *c.* 1591–4. (*Author's Collection*)

*Above right*: An Elizabeth I half pound, *c.* 1591–4. (*Author's Collection*)

*Left*: Elizabeth I gold trial plate, 1560. Trial plates were used to verify that coins were actually made of gold or silver. To test the integrity of Mint officials, trial plates were separated and sent to the Mint, Treasury and Goldsmiths' Company. Samples of metal were frequently compared to coins produced at the Mint. If the metal was not the same as the coin, then the Master of the Mint would be questioned. (*Author's Collection*)

greyhound and portcullis on the testons in currency, to distinguish the base from the better sort'.[75]

During December 1560, Elizabeth implemented the restoration of the coinage and ordered the return of all old coins to the Mint, when everyone received the nominal value base coin in the new sterling money. Although the government incurred the expense, it demonstrated that the queen was capable of good will and integrity in doing the right thing for her people. The old coins were melted down in the Mint and re-produced as new coins with higher purity and displaying her image. Elizabeth visited the Tower of London to inspect the Mint on 10 July 1561. She coined pieces of gold with her own hand and distributed these coins to those her attended upon her that day including her cousin, Lord Hunsdon, and the Marquis of Northampton, the brother of Katherine Parr.

The process lasted until October 1561 and produced good-quality coins that were better than coins produced over the previous 200 years in England and superior to coins produced in Europe at that time. The new Elizabethan coins would help boost the economy and raise public confidence.

# 42

# Queen Elizabeth I Smallpox Medallion

## Elizabeth's Illness

**In 1562 Elizabeth I contracted smallpox and a medal was produced to commemorate her recovery. Smallpox was an infectious disease that was prevalent during the Tudor period. The symptoms of smallpox included high temperature, blisters and scabs appearing on the skin, headaches, back pain and sore throat.**

On 10 October 1562, while residing at Hampton Court Palace, Elizabeth was suffering with a high fever but a rash did not appear on her skin until a few days later. She was eventually diagnosed as suffering from smallpox by the German physician Burchard Kranich, known in England as Dr Burcot. Elizabeth discarded his advice and referring to Burcot as a 'knave' ordered his removal from court. Her condition deteriorated to a critical level, her temperature increased, she was unable to speak and lost consciousness. Concerned that the queen was close to death, the Privy Council was summoned to Hampton Court Palace. On 16 October 1562, Bishop Álvaro de la Quadra, the Spanish diplomat at the English court, reported:

> The Queen has been ill of fever at Kingston, and the malady has now turned to small-pox. The eruption cannot come out and she is in great danger. Cecil was hastily summoned from London at midnight. If the Queen die it will be very soon, within a few days at latest, and now all the talk is who is to be her successor.[76]

The queen's servants were dispatched to plead with Dr Burcot to return to the queen's bedside and tend to her. Offended by the queen's initial rebuke, he replied, 'By God's pestilence. Call me a knave for my good will. If she be sick, let her die.'[77]

The servants were enraged by Burcot's response and he was persuaded to return at the point of a dagger. Burcot treated the queen for smallpox by wrapping her body, except for her head, in a red cloth and getting her to drink a potion that he had prepared. The queen slowly responded to the treatment and recovered.

On 17 October 1562, Bishop Álvaro de la Quadra reported that her health had rallied: 'The Queen is now better as the eruption has appeared. Last night the palace people were all mourning for her as if she were already dead.'[78]

Elizabeth requested that Lord Robert Dudley be appointed Lord Protector in the event of her death, but as she recovered this scenario was remote. On 20 October he was appointed to the Privy Council. He would represent her at audiences because she did not want others to see the scars the disease had left on her face. Quadra reported that, 'the Queen protested at the time that although she loved and had always loved Lord Robert dearly, as God was her witness, nothing improper had

*Above left*: An oval gold medal commemorating the recovery of Queen Elizabeth I from smallpox in 1562. (*Courtesy of the Wellcome Collection*)

*Above right*: The reverse side of the oval gold medal commemorating the recovery of Elizabeth I from smallpox. (*Courtesy of the Wellcome Collection*)

ever passed between them'.[79] The queen publicly acknowledged the closeness of her relationship to Robert Dudley in this proclamation and in appointing him to the Privy Council demonstrated her trust in him.

Quadra reported, 'the Queen will not be visible for some time owing to the disfigurement of her face the audiences will be all to him'.[80] On 25 October 1562 Quadra confirmed that the queen 'is now out of bed and is only attending to the marks on her face to avoid disfigurement'.[81] Elizabeth applied white lead make-up to her face to conceal the disfigurement caused by smallpox.

This medallion was produced as a token of thanksgiving for the recovery of the queen from smallpox. Her survival was attributed to divine protection and the Tudor propaganda machine used the queen's recovery to purport the notion that it was an affirmation of the religious direction of the country. The front of the medallion shows an image of Queen Elizabeth, her face clear of scars from smallpox, although this was untrue. The reverse side shows a hand descending from the clouds shaking a serpent from a finger into the fire, which alludes to the biblical story of St Paul being bitten by a snake, but being unharmed, similar to the queen's experience of smallpox.

# 43

# Windsor Castle

## Elizabeth's Refuge from the Plague During 1563

**Elizabeth spent a lot of time at Windsor Castle and regarded it as a safe sanctuary in times of crisis. She spent more money on refurbishing and building at Windsor Castle than her other palaces.**

Windsor Castle had fallen into disrepair by the time that Elizabeth ascended the throne. A series of renovation works took place during her reign. Existing buildings were repaired while new buildings were installed, including a gallery between a tower built by Henry VII and the Upper Ward, which now houses the Royal Library. The north terrace was built during Elizabeth's reign, with the western section raised to afford her more privacy. During the summer the queen enjoyed walking along this open terrace, which had commanding views towards the River Thames and the picturesque Berkshire countryside. Her routine was to walk along this terrace before dinner was served.

Elizabeth regarded Windsor Castle as a place of safety with the knowledge 'that it could stand a siege if need be'.[82] During September 1563, an outbreak of the plague in London compelled Elizabeth to withdraw her court to Windsor Castle and remain there throughout the winter. She spent the time studying under the tutelage of Roger Ascham. Elizabeth shared her father's passion for hunting and devoted time to this activity. Being a woman did not stop her from grabbing life with both hands. Robert Dudley wrote the following letter to the Archbishop of Canterbury sometime before he was elevated to Earl of Leicester in 1564, about the queen hunting in the adjacent forests at Windsor:

> The queen's majesty being abroad hunting yesterday in the forest, and having had very good hap, beside great sport, she hath thought good to remember your grace with part of her prey, and so commanded me to send you a great fat stag, killed with her own hand; which, because the weather was wet, and

the deer, somewhat chafed, and dangerous to be carried so far without some help, I caused him to be parboiled, for the better preservation of him, which, I doubt not, will cause him to come unto you as I would be glad he should.[83]

Elizabeth also used Windsor Castle as a place to welcome and entertain foreign envoys. On 22 April 1564, Elizabeth received French diplomats at the castle to conclude the Treaty of Troyes in which French ownership of Calais, which France had retaken in 1563, was recognised by the English in return for 120,000 crowns, which brought peace between the two nations. On Michaelmas day, 1577, Leicester hosted a banquet in the St George's Hall to discuss the Netherlands revolt against Spain with the French ambassador.

An aerial view of Windsor Castle. (*EQRoy/Shutterstock*)

# 44

# King's College Chapel, Cambridge

## Elizabeth I Visits Cambridge During Her Royal Progress, 1564

**King's College was founded by Henry VI in 1436. Construction of King's College Chapel began five years later when Henry VI laid the first stone on 25 July 1441. No other college had a chapel of such magnitude. Elizabeth visited Cambridge only once during her reign in 1564, and this was the first official royal visit since Henry VIII passed through the town in 1522. King's College Chapel played a pivotal role in welcoming Elizabeth to the campus.**

On 12 July 1564, Sir William Cecil wrote to Edward Hawford, Master of Christ's College and Vice Chancellor of the University of Cambridge, to make preparations, three weeks before the visit. He was advised to consider along with the masters of other colleges where the queen should lodge, sermons to be presented in Latin and English, debates that the queen could attend and ask the Mayor of Cambridge what provisions he would make in order to mitigate against the risk of plague contagion. Sufficient provisions of ale, beer and wine were sent to King's College in advance of the queen's visit and officers of the court visited the town to ensure that there were no recent deaths resulting from the plague.

Elizabeth arrived at Cambridge on 5 August 1564 and was welcomed by academics from the college. It was recorded that:

> ... she alighted from her horse, and asking of what degree every Doctor was offered her hand to be kissed. And then four of the principal Doctors bearing a canopy, she, under the same, entered into the Church, and kneeled down at the place appointed, between the two doors North and South; the Lady Strange bearing the train: and all the other ladies followed in their degrees.[84]

*Above*: King's College, Cambridge. (*Courtesy of Christopher Hilton; www. geograph.org*)

*Left*: The interior of King's College, Cambridge. (*Courtesy of Philip Halling; www. geograph.org*)

The main focus of her visit was attending philosophy and ecclesiastical debates. On several evenings Elizabeth took part in the Evensong ceremony at King's College Chapel and she was reported to have marvelled at 'the beauty of the Chapel, greatly praised it, above all other within her realm'.[85] During one evening at the chapel, Evensong was followed by the performance of the play *Aulularia Plauti* on a stage that was built within the chapel. Elizabeth remained there until midnight before retiring to her lodgings at the King's College Provost Lodge.

On 7 August, Elizabeth attended debates held at St Mary's Church and watched the performance of the play entitled *Dido* in King's College Chapel during the evening. The queen's schedule was replicated the following day and ended with watching *Ezechias* at King's College Chapel. On 9 August Elizabeth rode through Cambridge, visiting the colleges and monuments dedicated to previous English monarchs. She also gave an oration in Latin in St Mary's Church which was well received by the students.

Elizabeth enjoyed her stay at Cambridge and would have remained another day were it not for the fact that the provision of beer and ale that had been procured for the visit had been consumed. She left Cambridge on 10 August 1564. Elizabeth would make a similar visit two years later during the summer progress to visit Oxford and its universities.

# 45

# Abolition of Slavery Memorial, Ponce, Puerto Rico

## Elizabeth's Connection with the Slave Trade

**This is the only memorial in the Caribbean that commemorates the abolition of the slave trade. Slaves were transported to Puerto Rico from Africa from the early sixteenth century until its abolition in 1873.**

John Hawkins was a privateer licensed by the English government to raid enemy merchant shipping, in return for paying a proportion of the bounty earned to the government. During an expedition with three vessels to Hispaniola in the Caribbean in 1562, Hawkins intercepted and captured a Portuguese slave ship containing 300 Africans near Sierra Leone on the west coast of Africa. He would become one of the first Englishmen involved with the slave trade when he transported them across the Atlantic to the Americas to be traded for pearls, leathers, pelts and sugar with Spanish settlers in Santo Dominga. The Spanish and Portuguese authorities complained that their trading monopolies were threatened by English incursions and two of the ships were seized. When Hawkins returned home with these profitable commodities and significant financial returns for investors in London, Elizabeth was impressed by the wealth generated by this voyage and supported Hawkins' further expeditions by leasing him the 700-ton carrack *Jesus of Lübeck* stocked with supplies and munitions.

John Hawkins recognised that the slave trade was a more lucrative business and profitable alternative to trading in gold. He embarked on a second voyage in 1564 to traffic slaves across the Atlantic to be sold to the Spanish colonies in America. Hawkins returned home in 1565 with the profits generated from this ghastly trade from which Elizabeth would receive a return for her investment. Elizabeth acknowledged Hawkins' success and substantial income that he had earned for the Treasury by granting him a coat of arms bearing the image of an African man enslaved. Today, Hawkins' coat of arms symbolises the abhorrent practice of slavery engaged in by the English when privateers and seafarers extended their influence overseas. It signifies Elizabeth's support for an unsavoury episode in English history which profited on the suffering and incarceration of citizens from other continents. Although the maverick seafaring actions of molesting foreign vessels and plundering their wealth by privateers such as John Hawkins and later Francis Drake, Martin Frobisher and Walter Raleigh bordered on piracy, Elizabeth learned that sponsoring these individuals was an effective way of increasing revenue for her Treasury.

Hawkins embarked on a third voyage accompanied by his cousin, Francis Drake, during 1567–8, but this proved to be less lucrative than the previous voyages and resulted in the loss of Elizabeth's ship, *Jesus of Lübeck*, which was captured by the Spanish. Over the course of three voyages, Hawkins was responsible for the transportation of 1,200 captive Africans to slavery across the Atlantic Ocean.

Although Englishmen such as John Lok in 1555 and William Towerson in 1557 had traded in slaves, John Hawkins is regarded as the person responsible for establishing the English slave-trade triangle, which involved trading English merchandise in return for African slaves on the West African coast, trafficking those slaves across the Atlantic to the Americas to be sold in return for goods which would then be sold at a profit in England.

The memorial commemorating the abolition of slavery, Ponce, Puerto Rico. (*Courtesy of Daylayown*)

# 46

# Lochleven Castle

## Mary, Queen of Scots' Island Prison

**Mary, Queen of Scots was imprisoned on the island stronghold in Loch Leven, near Kinross, in 1567. The keep of Lochleven Castle was built during the 1300s. The lower floors contained the kitchens and service areas, while the lord's hall was on the first floor. The rooms that served as a prison for Mary, Queen of Scots were on the second floor.**

On 10 February 1567, Lord Henry Stuart Darnley, the husband of Mary, Queen of Scots, was murdered. The building in which he was residing in at a house at Kirk O'Field, close to Edinburgh, blew up. It was believed that he had escaped from the burning building but then been strangled outside. James Hepburn, the Earl of Bothwell was suspected of having committed adultery with Mary and of being involved with planning Darnley's death. Bothwell, who was a Protestant, was charged with his murder, but his trial collapsed because prosecution witnesses were intimidated and did not attend the hearing. After acquittal he divorced his wife and then married Mary, Queen of Scots. Controversary surrounds the nature of their relationship because Mary and Bothwell had conceived a child and it was rumoured that Bothwell had abducted and raped Mary in order to ensure the marriage and the Crown. The union disturbed Catholic nobles. The forces of these Catholic lords confronted Mary and Bothwell at Carberry Field, outside Edinburgh, on 15 June 1567. No blood was shed on that day and Mary surrendered to the Catholic Lords while Bothwell fled.

On 16 June 1567 the queen was imprisoned in the keep at Lochleven Castle. She suffered a miscarriage while there and on 24 July 1567, Mary, Queen of Scots was forced to abdicate. Her son, who was 13 months old, was proclaimed King James VI with Mary's step-brother, James Stewart, Earl of Moray, appointed regent. Elizabeth was furious that Mary had been usurped and thought that such a substitution on the Scottish throne was unjustified. She immediately wanted to provide assistance to her captive cousin, but Sir William Cecil supported the action of the Scottish lords and dissuaded Elizabeth.

Mary was incarcerated at Lochleven Castle for eleven months until she escaped on 2 May 1568. She gathered support from loyalists, but her army was defeated at the Battle of Langside on 13 May. Three days after her defeat at Langside, Mary, Queen of Scots fled across the border into England on 16 May 1568. She was received by representatives from Elizabeth's court and kept captive in Carlisle Castle for six weeks while her cousin decided what do with her. There was concern amongst Protestants that Mary would inspire a Catholic rebellion against Elizabeth. Despite calls from privy councillors and Parliament to execute Mary, Elizabeth refrained, because she did not want to kill a sovereign, especially when she was her cousin. For the following nineteen years Mary, Queen of Scots was moved around England as a prisoner.

Lochleven Castle. (*Sue Burton Photography/Shutterstock*)

# 47

# Durham Cathedral

## The Rising of the North, November 1569

**The construction of Durham Cathedral began in 1093 and it was here that a revolt took place against Elizabeth's Protestant reign. The Rising of the North during November 1569, also referred to as the Northern Rebellion or the Revolt of the Northern Earls, was a serious attempt made by Catholic noblemen to depose Elizabeth and replace her with the Catholic Mary, Queen of Scots, who was held captive in England.**

Thomas Percy, 7th Earl of Northumberland and Charles Neville, 6th Earl of Westmorland were devout Catholics who had written to Pope Pius V in October 1569 lobbying his support and requesting Elizabeth's excommunication. On 14 November 1569 they rallied 6,000 armed men and led them to Durham Cathedral where they desecrated the English Bible and the Book of Common Prayer and ordered the reinstatement of the Latin Mass to be performed as part of church services. This action was a serious challenge to the rule of Elizabeth and the English Church, so severe and divisive it nearly plunged England into civil war. Spanish diplomat Guerau de Espés reported to Philip II: 'The earls of Northumberland, Westmorland, and Cumberland, with 5,000 men and 400 horses entered the city of Durham, where, after having pulled down the wooden table used by the heretics in the cathedral, they had mass performed with great ceremony, and now intend to go to York with a similar object'.[86]

Guerau de Espés' report was inaccurate because the Earl of Cumberland had refused to join the rebellion, but his description of the acts carried out in Durham Cathedral was correct. Reminiscent of the revolt that took place during the reign of Henry VIII in 1537, known as the Pilgrimage of Grace, the Catholic rebels marched south from Durham towards York, behind the banner of the Five Wounds of Christ. When they learned that Thomas Radclyffe, 3rd Earl of Sussex was marching northwards with a force of 10,000 men, the rebels abandoned plans to capture York and dispersed across the border into Scotland, before the only battle was fought at Naworth during February 1570 where rebel forces commanded by Lord Leonard Dacre were defeated. Mary, Queen of Scots was sent to Coventry from her imprisonment at Tutbury Castle, but had she had joined forces with Northumberland and Westmoreland's forces then civil war might have erupted in England.

A total of 600 insurgents were executed in reprisal for the revolt, with 300 hung in Durham and executions in many other northern towns and villages. On 9 February, Guerau de Espés wrote that 'the people are being hanged in the north daily'.[87]

The Rising of the North was a serious threat to Elizabeth's reign, but loyalty from northern noblemen ensured that the rebellion dissipated and did not escalate.

Durham Cathedral, built between 1093 and 1133, was the starting place for the Rising of the North in 1569. (*Attila Jandi/Shutterstock*)

# 48

# Tomb of Pope Pius V

## Elizabeth's Excommunication

**Pius V was appointed Pope during December 1565 and was a strong advocate for confronting Elizabeth's Protestant reign in England. After the Rising of the North had been suppressed in early 1570, Pope Pius V issued a bull which excommunicated Elizabeth I and declared her a heretic and tyrant on 27 April 1570.**

The Pope denounced the queen:

> Elizabeth, the pretended queen of England, the servant of wickedness ... this very woman, having seized on the kingdom and monstrously usurped the place of Supreme Head of the Church in all England, and the chief authority and jurisdiction thereof, hath again reduced the said kingdom into miserable and ruinous condition, which was so lately reclaimed to the Catholic faith and a thriving condition.[88]

Pius V then continued in excommunicating Elizabeth and absolving all her subjects of any oaths and allegiance pledged to her:

> We do out of the fulness of our power, declare the afore said Elizabeth, as being a heretic and a favourer of heretics, and her adherents, in the matters aforesaid to have incurred the sentence of excommunication, and to be cut off from the unity of the body of Christ. And moreover, we do declare her to be deprived of her pretended title to the kingdom aforesaid, and all dominion, dignity and privilege whatsoever; and all the nobility, subjects and people of the said kingdom sworn unto her, to be forever absolved from any such oath and all manner of duty of dominion, allegiance and obedience; and we also do by authority of these presents absolve them, and do deprive the said Elizabeth of her pretended title to the kingdom.[89]

The Pope then ordered the people of England to disobey orders given by Elizabeth and disregard the laws of the kingdom. The bull of excommunication signalled the last time a Pope attempted to depose a reigning sovereign. He was sanctioning any attempt to achieve that aim, be it through assassination or rebellion, but Pope Pius V's action was badly timed because English Catholics felt dispirited after the recent failure of the Rising of the North. The papal bull did incite Catholic resistance when John Felton fastened a copy of Pope Pius's bull on the gates of the home of the Bishop of London on 25 May 1570. Three months later, on 4 August, Felton was arrested and tortured on the rack in the Tower of London. He was tried at the Guildhall for fixing the Pope's bull to the Bishop of London's home and found guilty. On 8 August 1570 Felton was taken from Newgate Prison to St Paul's churchyard where he was hung. Antonio de Guarás, the Spanish ambassador, wrote:

> They executed today the gentleman who nailed the pope ban on the bishop's door. He remained firm saying that all that the declaration contained was sacred. They quartered him with great cruelty whilst he was still alive. The day and the hour of the execution were unusual ones, for fear of the people. It took place before the bishop's house.[90]

The tomb of Pope Pius V at Santa Maria Maggiore, Rome. (*Courtesy of Sonofgroucho*)

The bull of excommunication caused division within England and Protestants became less tolerant of their fellow citizens who practised the Catholic faith. Catholics were excluded from Parliament in spring 1571 and a bill was passed that would make attendance at Sunday services and twice-yearly Communion mandatory for everyone across England irrespective of their faith.

The papal bull also encouraged other Catholic European nations to consider invading England to restore the Catholic religion by force. Local men in towns and villages were recruited into militia for home defence in the south and south-eastern counties, while the English fleet was mobilised. However, the French King Charles IX and Spanish King Philip II were disappointed that Pope Pius V did not consult with them before excommunicating Elizabeth, because at that time they had no desire to embark on a war with England. Pope Pius V died two years after excommunicating Elizabeth in 1572 and was buried at Santa Maria Maggiore in Rome.

# 49

# Frieze Sculpture of Elizabeth I

## Royal Exchange

**The Royal Exchange was opened by Queen Elizabeth in 1571 and granted a Royal Charter. The frieze sculpture of Elizabeth I was taken from the facade of the Royal Exchange after a fire and brought to Hatfield House in 1855.**

London became a major commercial centre during the Elizabethan era. Its inhabitants were employed in commerce, trading with other nations and the River Thames enabled ships from the Netherlands, France and Germany to use London docks to disembark goods and load others in exchange for exportation. In January 1564, Thomas Gresham offered to finance the building of an exchange where merchants in London could assemble and trade. Gresham was a wealthy merchant and regarded as the father of English banking. He represented Elizabeth in Antwerp and procured goods from Europe for the English court and secured loans on behalf of the Crown. On 7 June 1566, Gresham laid the first stone on a site at Cornhill, which had been cleared for the purpose of building the Exchange. The design was inspired by the Bourse, the world's oldest financial exchange in Antwerp. By 22 December 1568 sufficient progress had been made to enable merchants to meet within its walls. Construction was completed in November 1569.

Elizabeth opened the centre in January 1571 and named it the Royal Exchange. It would become London's first centre for trading stocks and it succeeded in becoming an important trading centre in northern Europe. The Royal Exchange was a place of business but was also a venue for recreation. Elizabeth had granted it a licence to sell alcohol at its inauguration. Citizens would walk around its precincts in the evening and football was permitted to be played inside until it was forbidden in 1576. The queen allowed music concerts to be performed at the Royal Exchange freely for everyone to enjoy. The building remained the property of Sir Thomas Gresham until his death in 1579 when he bequeathed it to the

A frieze sculpture featuring Elizabeth that originally adorned the facade of the second London Royal Exchange which replaced the building destroyed in the Great Fire of London in 1666. The frieze can be seen in the grounds of Hatfield House. (*Image © Acabashi, Creative Commons CC-BY-SA 4.0, Wikimedia Commons*)

Byrsa Londinensis *vulgo* the Royal Exchange

The original Royal Exchange in an engraving by Wenceslaus Hollar. (*Public Domain via Wikimedia Commons*)

City of London. Thomas Platter visited the London Royal Exchange twenty years later in 1599. He wrote:

> The exchange is a great square place like the one in Antwerp, a little smaller though, and with only two entrances and only one passage running through it, where all kinds of fine goods are on show; and since the city is very large and extensive merchants having to deal with one another agree to meet together in this palace, where several hundred may be found assembled twice daily, before lunch at eleven, and again after their meal at six o'clock, buying, selling, bearing news, and doing business generally.[91]

The building that Elizabeth opened in 1571 burnt down during the Great Fire of London on 6 September 1666. The Royal Exchange was rebuilt and opened three years later. This frieze featuring Elizabeth I was sculptured by James Bubb and adorned the facade of this building, however it suffered a similar fate when it burnt down in 1838. The frieze was relocated to Lime Walk in the grounds of Hatfield House in 1855. A third Royal Exchange building was constructed and opened by Queen Victoria in 1844. It continued to trade until 2001 when the building was renovated and transformed into a shopping mall.

# 50

# Map of Elizabethan London

## A Thriving Metropolis

**This map of London was first published in a work that featured the cities of the world entitled *Civitates Orbis Terrarium*, by Georg Braun, published in six parts between 1572 and 1617. It reflects the topography of London that would have been familiar to Elizabeth. The city measured approximately 1 square mile and 200,000 people lived in it.**

L ondon was the epicentre of government, law, commerce and royalty. In 1520 its population was approximately 50,000, but towards the end of Elizabeth's reign it began to rise and reached 200,000 by 1600. In 1580, Elizabeth expressed concerns about the increase in population and the expansion of the city and forbade the building of new residential houses within 3,000 paces of the gates of London and stipulated that there should be one family per house. The penalties for non-compliance included imprisonment and forfeiture of the materials used to construct such dwellings.

The city was defended by the Tower of London and a wall that was first built by the Romans and modernised over the centuries. St Paul's Cathedral is seen with its spire; however, it had been destroyed by lightning eleven years earlier in 1561. The nave of St Paul's Cathedral was known as 'Paul's Walkway' and was used as an indoor marketplace. Cheapside, which ran from the north of St Paul's Cathedral to the Royal Exchange, was home to many shops including goldsmiths.

The port of London enabled merchant vessels to bring in produce and goods exported from other nations, including the New World in America. On 31 December 1563, the River Thames froze which allowed Londoners to skate and play football on the ice. André Hurault de Maisse, the French ambassador, arrived in London by ship from Rochester on 2 December 1597 and commented that:

This river is very wide and one of the fairest that can be seen, being flat on either side thence up to London. One passes Greenwich, the Queen's house by the river bank, which is small but fair. From thence to London, it is a magnificent sight to see the number of ships and boats which lie at anchor, insomuch that for the two leagues you see nothing but ships that serve as well for war as for traffic.[92]

On 8 March 1587, Elizabeth wrote a letter to the Mayor of London informing him that intelligence had been received that a foreign power was preparing for war with England and called upon the City of London to provide 10,000 armed men. These men were raised from the twenty-six wards within London and would take part in the defence of England against the Spanish Armada the following year. The City of London also financed and supplied sixteen large ships and four pinnaces with crew to accompany four galleons from Elizabeth's fleet led by Sir Francis Drake on the pre-emptive attack upon the Spanish port at Cádiz. They departed from Plymouth on 12 April 1587 and during the night of 29 April attacked Spanish ships in Cádiz.

The bear baiting rings in Southwark can be seen and Shakespeare's Globe Theatre, although built in 1599, also features on this map. Westminster was a separate village and community outside the City of London that focused upon government and is seen on the left of the map.

A map of Elizabethan London. (*British Library/Public Domain*)

# 51

# The Rack

## Ridolfi Plot

Thomas Howard, 4th Duke of Norfolk was implicated in the Ridolfi Plot and was sent to the Tower of London on 7 September 1571 on suspicion of treason. Eight days later Elizabeth issued a warrant that permitted the torture of two men named Barker and Bannister, serving the Duke of Norfolk, to extract information about the plot. Ciphers were found in the roof tiles of Norfolk's London home at Charterhouse. Those ciphers related to Charles Bailey who carried code letters from Ridolfi to the English conspirators concerning a plot to usurp the queen. Bailey had revealed the contents of those letters while tortured on the rack. The rack was used as an instrument of torture during the reign of Elizabeth I for the purpose of extracting confessions through dislocation of joints, severing of tendons and reducing the resolve of a prisoner through extreme pain and disablement. This replica, displayed in the Tower of London, was similar to the rack used to interrogate prisoners with Elizabeth's sanction.

The rack was a commonly used instrument of torture during the Tudor period to obtain declarations of guilt from prisoners. It comprised an iron frame containing three wooden rollers. An interrogator could operate the rack by pulling a wooden lever, causing the ropes that were connected to the other rollers at the head and foot of the rack to pull in opposite directions. The central roller had an iron ratchet and teeth, which stabilised the rack, held it in position and kept the prisoner stretched.

The prisoner was placed on the frame with his or her hands raised open and tied to the upper rollers of the rack. The feet were tied in a similar way to the lower roller. The device then pulled the feet and hands in opposite directions causing excruciating pain to the prisoner. By pulling hard on the wooden levers, the torturer lifted the prisoner's body off the ground using the ropes and pulled apart the limbs of the body, causing dislocation of the arms and legs.

The replica of the rack on display at the Tower of London. (*Brian Kenney/Shutterstock*)

A warrant sanctioning torture was written in the hand of William Cecil, Lord Burghley and signed by Elizabeth on 15 September 1571. The warrant was addressed to Sir Thomas Knight, member of the Privy Council, and Dr Thomas Wilson and stated:

By the queen. Right trusty and well beloved, we greet you well, and finding in traitorous attempts lately discovered that neither Barker nor Banister, the duke of Norfolk's men, have uttered their knowledge in the under proceeding of their master and of themselves, neither will discover the same without torture, foreasmuch as the knowledge hereof concerneth our surety and estate, and that they have untruly already answered, we will and by warrant hereof authorise you to proceed to the further examination of them upon all points that you can think by your discretions meet for knowledge of the truth. And if they shall not seem to you to confess plainly their knowledge, then we warrant you to cause them both, or either of them, to be brought to the rack, and first to move them with fear thereof to deal plainly in their answers. And if that shall not move them, then you shall cause them to be put to the rack and to … the taste thereof until they shall deal more plainly, or until you shall think meet. And so, we remit the whole proceeding to your further discretion, requiring you to use speed herein, and to require the assistance of our lieutenant of the Tower.[93]

The rack was not required because Barker and Laurence Banister (Norfolk's legal councillor) revealed what they knew about the Ridolfi Plot in return for a pardon. Knight and Wilson reported to William Cecil, Lord Burghley that they had obtained as much information as they could. Banister knew little, but Barker was involved in the plot, 'the common doer, chosen for zeal than wit'.[94] By 20 September Barker was revealing the content within the coded letters.[95] The details obtained from Barker's testimony indicated that Norfolk was aware of the Ridolfi Plot and helped to condemn him.

# 52

# Tower Hill, London

## Execution Site

**Thomas Howard, 4th Duke of Norfolk, the queen's cousin, was executed on 2 June 1572 for allegedly collaborating with Roberto Ridolfi and Mary, Queen of Scots against Elizabeth I. He became the first peer of the realm executed for treason during the reign of Elizabeth I.**

Elizabeth was disappointed that Norfolk had supported Catholic insurgents in the Rising of the North in 1569. She was displeased when she heard rumours from ladies of her court that he had proposed marriage to Mary, Queen of Scots without her knowledge. He argued that by marrying Mary he would ensure a stable succession, but his scheme was conducted in secret which alarmed Elizabeth. Norfolk was imprisoned in the Tower of London for nine months as a consequence and was released after confessing his involvement in the Rising of the North and pleaded for mercy. After Pope Pius V had excommunicated Elizabeth and incited Catholics in England to usurp the English throne, Roberto Ridolfi, a banker from Florence, who resided in London, devised a plan to usurp Elizabeth in 1571. The plan involved assisting Norfolk and other Catholic noblemen to rise against Elizabeth, rescue Mary, Queen of Scots and proclaim her Queen of England. During July 1571, Norfolk was implicated in the plot when a coded letter using ciphers from Ridolfi and a letter from Mary, Queen of Scots was found in between two tiles on the roof of his home, Norfolk House, formerly known as Charterhouse, and a letter found under a mat in his chamber. In September 1571, John Lee, an English spy operating in Flanders, heard rumours that Norfolk was involved in a plot and advised Lord Burghley and that he should be arraigned. Norfolk was arrested and dispatched to the Tower of London. Norfolk was tried at Westminster Hall for imagining and compassing the death of the queen on 16 January 1572. He was found guilty on thirteen counts of treason and condemned to death. The sentence was not carried out because Elizabeth dithered as she was reluctant to

The site of the scaffold is commemorated by this memorial garden at Tower Hill, which is north-west of the Tower of London. (*Author's Collection*)

sanction the death of her cousin, despite his disloyalty and his popularity. Twice she signed his death warrant, but then revoked it. Coerced by her councillors, Elizabeth eventually signed the Duke of Norfolk's death warrant a third and final time on 31 May 1572, demonstrating that she was as ruthless and brutal as her father, Henry VIII.

At 8 am on 2 June 1572, Howard was led from the Tower of London and taken to Tower Hill for execution. This was the first time that the scaffold had been used here for eighteen years and it had to be strengthened and raised. Alexander Nowell, Dean of St Paul's, was at Howard's side to provide him with spiritual comfort. William Camden heard Howard's speech from the scaffold in which he said:

I acknowledge that my peers have justly judged me worthy of my death, neither is it my meaning to excuse myself. That I have treated with the Queen of Scots I freely confess and that in matters of great consequence, without consulting my sovereign; which I have ought to have done; for which I was cast into the Tower. I was afterwards set free, upon my humble submission, and giving my faith that I would have no more to do with her. Yet I confess I did the contrary, and this troubleth my conscience. But at the Communion Table (as is commonly reported) I neither promised nor swore it. Ridolpho [*sic* Ridolfi] I never talked with but one and that not to the prejudice of the queen. For many men know I had dealing with him for money matters upon bills and bonds. I found him to be a man who envied the tranquility of England, and of a prompt and ready wit for any wicked design. Two letters from the

Bishop of Rome I saw, to which I attended to not; nor yet to the Rebellion in the North. I have not been addicted to Popery since the time that I had any taste of religion, but have always been averse from Popish Doctrines and embraced the true religion of Jesus Christ, and have put my whole truth in the blood of Jesus Christ my redeemer and blessed saviour. Yet can I not deny but I have had among my servants and familiars some that have been addicted to the Popish religion. If I have thereby offended God, the Church or the Protestants, I beseech God and them to forgive me.[96]

Two psalms were read and Norfolk said in a loud voice, 'Into thy hands I commend thy spirit.' After speaking privately to Sir Henry Leigh and Dean Nowell, the executioner asked for forgiveness, which Norfolk granted. He was offered a handkerchief to cover his eyes, but he refused saying, 'I fear not death.'[97] Norfolk then knelt and prayed with Nowell. William Camden witnessed the execution and later wrote that Norfolk 'then stretching forth his neck upon the block in an instant his head was cut off at one stroke, and was showed by the executioner as a lamentable spectacle to the sorrowing and weeping people'.[98]

Mary, Queen of Scots denied all knowledge of the Ridolfi plot, however, a letter written and signed in her hand supporting an invasion of England had made her complicit. Elizabeth realised that she would always remain a threat to her rule and concluded that she should never be released from imprisonment.

Plaque at Tower Hill commemorating the execution of Queen Elizabeth's cousin, Thomas Howard, 4th Duke of Norfolk. It also lists Edward Seymour, Duke of Somerset and Sir Thomas Wyatt who were executed here before Elizabeth ascended the throne. (*Author's Collection*)

# 53

# Interior of the Chapel of St Peter ad Vincula

## Burial Place of the Queen's Cousin and Mother

A chapel has existed within the precincts of the Tower of London on the site of the Chapel of St Peter ad Vincula for over a thousand years and this was a place of worship before the construction of the White Tower. The chapel was renovated during the reign of Henry III in 1240. It was then demolished and rebuilt in 1286 on the orders of Edward I. When this chapel was destroyed by fire in 1512, it was rebuilt in 1520 during Henry VIII's reign.

The Chapel of St Peter ad Vincula, which stands to the north of Tower Green, is Tudor in origin. After his execution Thomas Howard, 4th Duke of Norfolk was buried close to the altar. His remains are buried close to Elizabeth's mother, Anne Boleyn, and her step-mother and cousin, Katherine Howard. Sir Thomas More and John Fisher, Bishop of Rochester, who championed the cause of Katherine of Aragon and opposed the marriage of Anne Boleyn to Henry VIII, are also buried within this chapel.

The interior of the Chapel of St Peter ad Vincula. (*Wang Sing/Shutterstock*)

# 54

# Ruins of Old Gorhambury House

## Royal Progresses

**The villa at Gorhambury was built on land that once belonged to the Benedictine Abbey of St Alban's. Its name was derived from Robert de Gorham who was elected abbot of the house in 1151. Henry VIII seized this property during the dissolution of the monasteries in 1540 and passed ownership to Sir Ralph Rowlet, who later sold it to Sir Nicholas Bacon, who transformed it into a luxurious Elizabethan residence between 1563 and 1568. Part of the house was built using bricks from the dissolved abbey.**

Elizabeth embarked on royal progresses every year. These saw her touring various parts of the country for political purposes in order to assert herself as sovereign, to allow her people accessibility, to be seen by her subjects outside London and to remind them and local nobles who governed the country. Elizabeth wore fine silks and opulent jewellery and was accompanied by an entourage of loyal courtiers to demonstrate her power, authority and gravitas to the people. She would stay at the country estates of nobleman who would spend extravagant amounts of money on entertaining her with banquets, pageants, jousting tournaments and all manner of spectacles.

Sir Nicholas Bacon was the brother-in-law of William Cecil and was a practising Protestant. He was appointed Lord Keeper of the Privy Seal when Elizabeth ascended the throne in 1558 and was knighted during the same period. Bacon officiated over the House of Lords when Elizabeth opened her first Parliament in 1559 and served in the role until 1571.

Bacon entertained Elizabeth on four occasions at Old Gorhambury House, the first visit taking place in 1572. The ruins of the building that enclosed the central courtyard are all that remain of Old Gorhambury House on the private estate of Lord Verulam. They represent a small part of a large country house of a Tudor nobleman. Each room was sumptuously decorated and supplied with water through pipes. The classically designed entrance porch, flanked by Doric pillars, still stands and was the principal feature of Bacon's home. The porch once led to the great hall, which was used by Bacon for dining and entertaining important guests such as Elizabeth, and the fireplace and windows are still visible. The chapel lay to the left of the great hall.

Elizabeth returned to visit Sir Nicholas Bacon at Gorhambury on 18 May 1577 and stayed for five days. It cost Bacon £600 (the equivalent of £123,000 in 2017) to entertain the queen during that period.[99] Anyone entertaining the queen also had to provide for her entire entourage during each visit and this was an expensive affair. During this visit to Gorhambury House Elizabeth was reputed to have said to Bacon, 'My Lord, what a little house you have gotten.' Bacon replied, 'Madam, my house is not too little for me, but your majesty has made me too big for my house!'[100] The queen's comment encouraged Bacon to extend his home and by the time of her next visit he had built a long gallery, adjacent to the chapel. Bacon died at Old Gorhambury House in 1579 and was buried in the crypt of St Paul's Cathedral, but his tomb was destroyed during the Great Fire of London in 1666.

The ruins of Old Gorhambury House, near St Albans, Hertfordshire. (*Author's Collection*)

# 55

# Coat of Arms of Elizabeth I, Sandwich

## Royal Progress to Kent

**The coat of arms of Elizabeth I are displayed on the King's Arms public house on Strand Street, Sandwich, in Kent. Elizabeth stayed in the great house opposite this pub called the King's Lodging between 31 August and 2 September 1573, during her royal progress that passed through Kent.**

Preparations were made in advance of the queen's arrival in Sandwich. Two jurors from the village were sent to London to purchase a gold cup costing £100 (the equivalent of £24,000 in 2017) which was presented as a gift to her during the visit. The streets were cleaned and all the dung and filth removed. Residents of Sandwich were ordered to repair their buildings and, in particular, those in Strand Street, where the queen was to stay. The townspeople were asked to decorate their homes in black and white, Elizabeth's key colour scheme, and 200 people were also asked to wear black-and-white clothing. Scaffolds were erected in Strand Street where children would sit spinning yarn. Butchers were ordered to dispose of offal outside the village to reduce any foul smells during the royal visit and local brewers were instructed to ensure there were sufficient supplies of good beer available. The Lord Warden also requested that a hundred men from Sandwich be armed and sent to Dover Castle to provide security for the queen during that part of her progress before her visit to Sandwich.

On 31 August 1573, John Gylbart, the Mayor of Sandwich, and nine jurors received Elizabeth, who was on horseback, at Sandown and escorted her to Sandwich at 7 pm. They arrived at the bridge in front of Sandown Gate where gilt lions and dragons, symbols that form part of Elizabeth's coat of arms, were placed on eleven posts on the bridge and her arms were hung from the gate. Elizabeth rode into town until she reached the house of Mr Manwood in Strand Street which

Henry VIII and Elizabeth I stayed at the King's Lodging at Sandwich during their royal progresses in Kent. (*Author's Collection*)

Queen Elizabeth's coat of arms emblazoned on the side of the King's Head public house, Sandwich. (*Courtesy of the Carlisle Kid; www.geograph.org.uk*)

is known as the King's Lodging. Her father, Henry VIII, had stayed in the same house on two occasions during his reign.

During the following day, Elizabeth watched militia from Sandwich cross the River Stour in two boats and assault a wooden fort that had been built on the other bank. On 2 September, the wife of the mayor, her sisters and the juror's wives prepared a banquet for the queen, comprising 161 dishes presented on a table measuring 28ft in length, in the village schoolhouse. Elizabeth had to pass through Mr Manwood's garden and the adjacent garden in order to enter the school. Elizabeth felt safe and at ease in the company of the villagers from Sandwich because she ate the food without it first being tested for poison. She also requested that some of those dishes be reserved so that they could be brought to her lodging to eat later that evening.

As she departed from Sandwich for her next destination, Canterbury, on 3 September, schoolchildren were spinning yarn on the scaffolds in Strand Street before the queen, which pleased her. Opposite the grounds of the King's Lodging is a pub called the King's Arms which displays Elizabeth's coat of arms.

# 56

# Old Palace, Canterbury

## Birthday Celebrations

**After visiting Sandwich, the next stage of Elizabeth's summer progress in 1573 took her to Canterbury. Elizabeth arrived at Canterbury on 3 September 1573 and stayed for fourteen days. Her host, Matthew Parker, Archbishop of Canterbury mentioned that she lodged at St Augustine's Abbey. She attended services at Canterbury Cathedral and Parker held a feast at the Old Palace to celebrate her fortieth birthday.**

P rior to visiting Dover and Sandwich and before proceeding to Canterbury, Elizabeth was received by Matthew Parker, Archbishop of Canterbury during her summer progress in 1573 on Folkestone Down. Parker had served as chaplain to her mother, Anne Boleyn, and before her execution she asked him to supervise Elizabeth's spiritual welfare. Parker had been reluctant to accept Elizabeth's offer to succeed Reginald Pole as Archbishop of Canterbury in 1559. Parker was defrocked during the reign of Mary I because he had married. Elizabeth and William Cecil, Lord Burghley overlooked this matter and believed that his moderate views made him a suitable candidate to take on the role as England's religious leader. Parker relented to pressure and accepted the position of Archbishop of Canterbury.

Parker left the queen at Dover for his country home at Bekesborne, while she stayed at Dover and Sandwich, but later returned to Canterbury to welcome her to the city at Canterbury Cathedral. Parker wrote that he:

> … went to Canterbury to receive her Majesty there. Which I did, with the Bishops of Lincoln and Rochester, and my Suffragan, at the West door, where, after the Grammarian had made his Oration to her upon her horseback, she alighted. We then kneeled down, and said the Psalm *Deus misereatur* in English … The Quire, with the Dean and Prebendaries, stood on either side

Old Palace, Canterbury. (*Courtesy of Tony Hisgett; www.wikimedia.org*)

of the Church, and brought her Majesty up with a Square-song, she going under a canopy, born by four of her Temporal knights, to her traverse placed by the Communion board; where she heard Even-song, and after departed to her lodging at St. Austins [St Augustine's Abbey], wither I waited upon her. [101]

While she resided in St Augustine's Abbey, Archbishop Matthew Parker welcomed Elizabeth for feasts at his home, the Old Palace, which formed part of Canterbury Cathedral. These banquets were hosted in the Great Hall which was refurbished for Elizabeth's visit and had been where her father, Henry VIII, had entertained Emperor Charles V in 1520, before he proceeded to meet King Francis I of France on the Field of Cloth of Gold. The visit to Canterbury coincided with Elizabeth's fortieth birthday and Archbishop Parker held a feast in her honour which was attended by noblemen. Elizabeth sat in a marble chair covered with a cloth of gold. Parker wrote about the hospitality that he provided for Elizabeth and her court at the Old Palace, Canterbury:

> From thence I brought certain of the Council, and divers of the Court, to my house to supper, and gave them fourteen or fifteen dishes, furnished with two mess at my long table, whereat sat about twenty … And so her Majesty came every Sunday to church, to hear the Sermon; and upon one Monday it pleased her Highness to dine in my great hall, thoroughly furnished, with the Council, Frenchmen, Ladies, Gentlemen, and the Mayor of the Town, … her Highness sitting in the midst, having two French Ambassadors at one end of the table, and four Ladies of Honour at the other. And so, three mess were served by her Nobility at washing, her Gentlemen and Guard bringing her dishes. [102]

Elizabeth enjoyed her visit at Canterbury so much that she extended her stay to two weeks.

# 57

# Execution Site, Smithfield

## Tudor Punishments

**Smithfield was situated outside the walls of the City of London and was used as a place of execution for centuries. William Wallace was hung, drawn and quartered here in 1305 and many traitors found guilty of treason met their end here during the reigns of Henry VIII and Mary I. Further blood was shed here in the name of religion during Elizabeth's reign and would tarnish her legacy.**

John Stow remembered the executions that were carried out during the reign of Mary I. He recalled:

> What things have been done at Smithfield! I was thirty years of age when Queen Mary burned her martyrs. There had been burnings before her time, but she outdid them all … she was ill-advised: she thought to make the people go back to the old religion through fear. She might have led them back through love. I have seen the burning of those stubborn folk. Old and young, men and women, nay children, have I seen standing in the faggots, praying aloud while the flames mounted up and licked their hands and their faces. Mostly they died quickly, being smothered with the smoke; but sometimes the flames were blown away, and we saw the blackened body still in agony, and the lips that moved to the end in prayer.[103]

The reign of Elizabeth was just as barbaric as those of Henry VIII and Mary I. She showed no clemency to those who betrayed her or opposed her authority. In London there were 64 executions between 1563 and 1586 with 228 people put to death as punishment for infringing laws or as a result of religious persecution, many of these carried out at Smithfield. This figure comprised 76 for treason, 71 rebels hanged on two separate occasions, 29 for piracy, 17 for murder, 12 for robbery, 12 for

*Above*: The information panel at the entrance to the park, north of St Bartholomew's Hospital, confirms that 'this open space occupies part of the original "Smethefelde" or "Smoothfeld", which from ancient times was used for jousts, tournaments and executions as well as a market'. (*Author's Collection*)

*Below*: Martyrs executed at Smithfield. (*Author's Collection*)

debasing, clipping or counterfeiting of coinage, 3 for heresy, 3 for military offences, 2 for counterfeiting the queen's signature, 2 for witchcraft and 1 for adultery.[104]

During spring 1575 practising Anabaptists were discovered in Aldgate. This religious sect believed that children should not be baptised, Christians should not take up arms and refused to take oaths or act as magistrates. This congregation, with Dutch origins, was accused of heresy and blasphemy. They were tried at St Paul's Cathedral by the Bishop of London. Fifteen were returned home, while five were condemned to death by burning. However, only two of the sentences were carried out, with Henry Toorwoort and John Weelmaker burned at the stake at Smithfield on 23 July 1575. A chronicler reported that they died 'with great horror, crying and roaring'.[105] The Revd John Foxe appealed to Elizabeth in a letter to refrain from carrying out these executions, imploring her not to tarnish her reign and the reputation of the reformed church, but his petition was ignored. There were 200 Catholics executed during the reign of Elizbeth, a substantial number in comparison to the 308 people executed under the Treasons Act of 1534 during the reign of Henry VIII and the 300 Protestants who were executed during the reign of Mary I.

# 58

# Kenilworth Castle

## Leicester's Building

**Elizabeth visited Robert Dudley, 1st Earl of Leicester at Kenilworth Castle several times during royal progresses and on one occasion stayed for nineteen days, the longest period that she spent at the home of one of her courtiers. Kenilworth Castle was previously owned by John Dudley, 1st Duke of Northumberland, but it was confiscated by Mary I when he was executed for treason for his role in placing Lady Jane Grey on the English throne in 1553. Elizabeth granted Kenilworth Castle to his son and her favourite, Robert Dudley, in 1563. Dudley spent a fortune renovating the palace and gardens to woo the queen. During the 1570s Leicester's Building was constructed and transformed into a residential house specifically to welcome Elizabeth during royal progresses. Since the 1650s the building has stood empty falling into ruin.**

Elizabeth first visited Kenilworth Castle during 1565, when Dudley proposed marriage to the queen, but she refused to give him an answer until Candlemas in February. It is believed that she contemplated the offer but did not accept his proposal. She returned to Kenilworth Castle in 1568.

During 1571, Dudley built accommodation specifically to accommodate Elizabeth and her entourage for their exclusive use and this was known as Leicester's Building. He also ordered the construction of an imposing gatehouse to the castle with the purpose of impressing his royal guest as she entered Kenilworth Castle. Elizabeth saw the work in progress during her visit in 1572. When she returned for her fourth and final visit during summer 1575, she was able to use the completed building.

Elizabeth arrived on 9 July 1575 and was welcomed by the firing of artillery guns and a lavish firework display that lasted for two hours. All the clocks in Kenilworth Castle were stopped at the moment of her arrival, Dudley wanting no one to take account of the time while the queen was in residence at Kenilworth Castle. The days were filled with hunting, pageants, banquets and watching bear baiting. Dudley made a final attempt to woo and persuade Elizabeth to marry him during this visit. The cost of the feast and revelry nearly bankrupted Dudley as a consequence.

Elizabeth was unaware that Dudley had also invited Lettice Knollys, a grandniece of Anne Boleyn, during her visit in 1575 and that Lettice shared Dudley's bed, despite being married to Walter Devereux, 1st Earl of Essex. Lettice had given birth to several children during that marriage, including Robert Devereux, future favourite of Elizabeth. In 1576 Walter died of natural causes in Dublin. In 1578, it is thought that Lettice was pregnant with Dudley's child and they married in secret. Elizabeth was enraged when she discovered that her relative had taken the man that she had loved and regarded as her exclusive possession. Lettice was banished from court and it was five years before Elizabeth forgave Dudley.

Dudley had set a precedent at Kenilworth Castle for those hosting Elizabeth when she visited their homes. The French ambassador, André Hurault de Maisse, wrote that:

> … when she moves into the country, it is ordinarily at the expense of those with whom she lodges, and even then, at her departure must they give her presents, a custom that has been introduced in her time by the earl of Leicester and maintained to such a degree that there is now no one at Court but gives her the like at certain feasts, as on her birthday, her coronation day, and on such occasions.[106]

An aerial view of Kenilworth Castle. (*Shutterstock*)

# 59

# 'Pelican Portrait' of Elizabeth I

## Projecting an Image

**In 1575, it was discovered that Nicholas Hilliard, goldsmith to the queen, was a talented portrait painter when he produced this portrait of Elizabeth, which is known as the 'Pelican Portrait'. Due to increased demand for the queen's portrait, Hilliard diverted his efforts to producing miniatures which were worn by courtiers.**

Elizabeth was popular amongst her subjects from across the social spectrum and her image was reproduced in paintings, engravings and prints. There was high demand from noble families who wished to display her portrait in their homes to demonstrate their allegiance to the sovereign and to garner favour if they were honoured with a visit from her during one of her annual royal progresses. The quality of some of these images was poor and did not reflect the queen's true likeness or how she wanted to be represented. In 1563, the following proclamation was issued relating to artists producing portraits of Elizabeth:

Forasmuch as through the natural desire that all sorts of subjects and people, both noble and mean, have to procure the portrait and picture of the Queen's Majesty, great numbers of painters, and some printers and engravers, have already and do daily, attempt to make diverse manners portraitures of her Majesty in painting, engraving and printing, wherein is evidently shown that hitherto none hath sufficiently expressed the natural representation of Majestie's person, favour, or grace, but for the most part have also erred therein, as thereof daily complaints are made against her Majestie's loving subjects, in so much that for redress hereof of her Majesty hath lately been so instantly and so importunately sued unto by the Lords of her council and others of her nobility, in respect of the great disorder herein used, not only to be content that some special conning painter might be permitted access to her Majesty to take the natural representation of her Majesty whereof she hath been all wise to of her own right disposition very unwilling, but also to prohibit all manner of other persons to draw, paint, engrave or portraiture her Majestie's personage or visage for a time, until by some perfect patron and example the same may be by others followed. Therefore her Majesty, being herein as it were overcome with the continual requests of so many of her Nobility and Lords whom she cannot well deny, is pleased that for their

The 'Pelican Portrait' of Elizabeth I by Nicholas Hilliard. (*Walker Gallery, Google Art Project*)

contentations, some coning person met therefor shall shortly make a portrait of her person or her visage to be participated to others for satisfaction of her loving subjects, and furthermore commandeth all manner of persons in the meantime to forebear from painting, engraving, printing, or making any portraits of her Majesty, until some special person that shall be by her allowed shall have first finished a portraiture thereof, after which finished, her Majesty will be content that all other painters, printers or engravers, that shall be known men of understanding, and so thereto licensed by the head officers of the places where they shall dwell (as reason as it is that every person should not without consideration attempt the same) shall and may at their pleasures follow the said same patron or first portraiture.[107]

The 'Pelican Portrait' was painted in 1575 when Elizabeth was aged 42 and its name derives from the pelican pendant that is attached to her chest. It was her favourite emblem and it is used allegorically to represent the queen as caring, devoted and charitable to her subjects, similar to the nature of the pelican which is renowned for feeding its young from the blood from its breast, a self-sacrificing gesture that would result in the death of the mother. The portrait alludes to Elizabeth acting in a maternal role, being a mother to the nation and putting the interests of the nation above her own.

Hilliard depicted the queen in the style that she favoured and he established the template for how she would be portrayed with smooth skin, concealing her aging years and the scars caused by smallpox, a neutral expression and dressed in majestic clothes. The artist succeeded in producing an iconic image of Elizabeth, which although was a likeness, would be used to project an image of her as stylish, powerful and affluent, a perception that she wished to promote.

# 60

# Replica of the *Golden Hinde*

## Circumnavigation of the Globe and Piracy

**Francis Drake became the first Englishman to circumnavigate the earth in the *Golden Hinde*. Originally named the *Pelican*, after one of Elizabeth's key emblems, on 20 August 1578, during the voyage, Drake renamed the vessel the *Golden Hinde* in recognition of his sponsor, Sir Christopher Hatton, whose emblem featured a hind, a female red deer. A replica of the *Golden Hinde* is berthed at St Mary Overie Dock, London.**

Francis Drake was a privateer who objected to Spanish domination of the New World and its monopoly of plundering the wealth in that region. He actively carried out acts of piracy during voyages, intercepting Spanish merchant ships and pillaging their cargos. Elizabeth encouraged maritime expeditions and privately sanctioned them through financial support for a share of the plunder, on the proviso that if they were caught and her support was compromised, she would disassociate herself from the enterprise. It was a lucrative way of adding to the nation's coffers and a mechanism for waging war without publicly declaring war with Spain. It was effectively state-sponsored piracy. In 1577, Elizabeth, the Earl of Leicester and Sir Christopher Hatton were the principal sponsors of an expedition proposed by Francis Drake, John Wynter and Thomas Doughty to explore the Pacific Ocean along the American coastline, although at that stage there was no plan to attempt to circumnavigate the globe, and to seize Spanish bullion, investing large sums of money to support the venture.

The intention was to engage in acts of piracy against the Spanish, warning Philip II about his influence in the New World and that its resources did not exclusively belong to Spain.

Queen Elizabeth secretly approved this expedition, but in order to ensure that the plan remained a secret Drake told his crew that they were embarking on a diplomatic trading mission to the eastern Mediterranean while their true destination was the

The replica *Golden Hinde*, St Mary Overie Dock, London. (*Courtesy of Tony Hisgett*)

The figurehead of the *Golden Hinde*. (*Courtesy of Tony Hisgett*)

Pacific Ocean. If these men had known the true objective of the expedition and its dangers, they might have been reluctant to have joined the crew.

On 13 December 1577, Drake began the expedition that would eventually circumnavigate the earth from Plymouth aboard the *Pelican* and accompanied by four vessels, the *Elizabeth*, *Marigold*, *Swan* and *Christopher*, crewed by 164 men. The route taken involved sailing along the western coast of Africa to the Cape Verde Islands, where they captured the Portuguese merchant vessel *Santa Maria*, which was renamed the *Mary*. The English flotilla then proceeded across the Atlantic Ocean, reaching Brazil on 5 April 1578.

There was discord between Drake and Thomas Doughty, commander of the *Swan*, especially when Drake took on the role of commander of the entire expedition. The situation deteriorated further when Drake's brother, Thomas, was caught stealing from the plundered cargo of the *Santa Maria*. Matters worsened when Drake demoted Doughty to command the smaller vessel *Swan*. The *Swan* was separated from the other vessels in a storm but when they reunited on 17 May 1578, Drake and Doughty had a fearsome quarrel that was irreconcilable. Drake struck Doughty and ordered his arrest and Doughty was found guilty of mutiny when they reached Puerto San Julian in Argentina and beheaded on 2 July 1578.

Drake continued to sail south along the South American coastline, becoming the first Englishman to pass through the Strait of Magellan to enter the Pacific Ocean. He then proceeded northwards along the west coast of the South and North American continents.

On 1 March 1579, Drake intercepted the Spanish merchant vessel *Nuestra Señora de la Concepción* off the Peruvian coast. Its cargo was silver and gold bullion excavated from Peruvian mines which was being transported to Spain, and it would take six days to unload the valuable hoard onto the English vessels. One important crewman was an escaped African slave named Diego, who could speak fluent English and Spanish and Drake employed as a shipbuilder. When they captured Spanish vessels, Diego was able to communicate false information to the Spanish.

Drake also attacked and plundered another Spanish galleon as well as raiding towns along the coastline. Drake now possessed that bullion too and had a long journey ahead of him to get this wealthy spoil. Drake had seized thirteen Spanish ships during the expedition. In August 1579, Philip II became aware of these actions against Spain, but because he was making a claim for the crown of Portugal, he did not want to embroil Spain in a conflict with England.

Drake was reluctant to return home via the Atlantic Ocean for he feared that the Spanish would be waiting for him and attempt to recover the stolen treasures. There also remained the risk that if captured, Drake would potentially be hung as a pirate. Instead, Drake sailed along the Californian coast in the hope of finding a short route to sail north of the American continent before turning west to cross the Pacific Ocean, which took six weeks. He then sailed across the Indian Ocean to the Cape of Good Hope at the southern tip of Africa, before heading north along the west African coast to reach England. Drake was the first Englishman to complete a circumnavigation of the earth and arrived in Plymouth on 26 September 1580. During the course of the voyage one ship was lost, two ships were scuttled and John Wynter had become separated in his ship and returned to England a year earlier. A total 103 men from the 164 crew had died. Drake's first question was to inquire if Elizabeth was alive, because she would be able to protect him for being tried for the acts of piracy and theft that he had committed against Spanish merchant vessels. Fortunately, Elizabeth was still queen and she treated him as a national hero, but another monarch might have hung him for piracy.

The *Golden Hinde* remained at Deptford Dockyard, berthed in the mast dock as a visitor attraction for the public. It was the first museum ship in the world. In 1599, Thomas Platter, a tourist from Switzerland, visited Deptford after Greenwich Palace and saw the *Golden Hinde* lying in shallow water by the river. He recalled:

> Not far from the said royal palace, upon the shore, we saw the ship of the English captain Drake in which he is said to have sailed round the world. It appears that it was very large and stoutly built of some hundred tons, quite fitted for so long and perilous a voyage, and since it is rotten with age and now decaying, I took a piece and brought it back to Basel.[108]

By 1613 only the lower half of the *Golden Hinde* remained. The ship was dilapidated and visitors had stripped sections of the upper half for souvenirs. By 1650, the wood on the *Golden Hinde* was rotting and it was not feasible to preserve her as an exhibition piece for the nation. It was therefore decided to break her up. In 1668, John Davis, the keeper of the stores at Deptford Dockyard, retained some timber from the *Golden Hinde* which he had made into a chair, which was presented to the University of Oxford. It is on display at the Bodleian Library, Oxford, and is known as the Drake Chair. There are two replicas of the *Golden Hinde* in the United Kingdom and both serve as museums. One is moored at Brixham Quay. The other is berthed at St Mary Overie Dock in London on the south bank of the River Thames and was built between 1971 and 1973. It set sail from Falmouth during the following year and took 164 days to reach San Francisco Bay on 8 March 1975 to commemorate the 400th anniversary of Drake's landing at San Francisco. This replica *Golden Hinde* circumnavigated the world twice during 1979 and 1984. The *Golden Hinde* was brought to St Mary Overie Dock in 1996 and is now a museum.

# 61

# St Mary the Virgin Church, Mortlake and Monument to Dr John Dee

## Dr John Dee, Advisor to the Queen

**The Church of St Mary the Virgin at Mortlake was built in 1543. It has undergone numerous renovations since then and the church tower is all that remains of the original Tudor building. Inside the church there is a monument dedicated to Dr John Dee, the renowned astronomer, alchemist, theologian, geographer and mathematician who served as Queen Elizabeth's scientific advisor throughout her reign. He was also associated with astrology and occult sciences. As mentioned previously, Elizabeth took his advice regarding a suitable day to schedule her coronation and she later sought his counsel about the proposed marriage to Francis, Duke of Anjou and Alençon. Dee lived opposite the church and was buried in an unmarked grave beneath the chancel in 1609.**

England was a small, isolated European nation with a sovereign with no heir who governed a country with limited financial reserves and inadequate military resources. Dee became a strong advocate of English imperialism. He was commissioned by Robert Dudley, Earl of Leicester and Sir Christopher Hatton in 1570 to produce a report on the nation's challenges, its financial position and its social problems. Dee presented a report consisting of a flow chart covering five sheets that were pasted together, entitled *Brytannicæ Republicæ Synopsis*. It detailed various problems and suggested the primary solution was for the nation to expand. He proposed enhancing the navy, maintaining a total strength of fifty vessels, and establishing an empire.

Seven years later, during 1577, Dee wrote *General & Rare Memorials Pertaining to the Perfect Art of Navigation* in which he foresaw the rise of what would become the British Empire, the colonisation of other territories and the exploitation of the

St Mary the Virgin Church tower, Mortlake. (*Courtesy of Mightyhansa; www.wikimedia.org*)

local resources within those territories for the financial benefit of the nation. In order to establish an empire, England had to attain maritime supremacy and Dee recognised the need for English seafarers to improve their navigational knowledge, skills and experience. Dee championed the cause for empire and during November

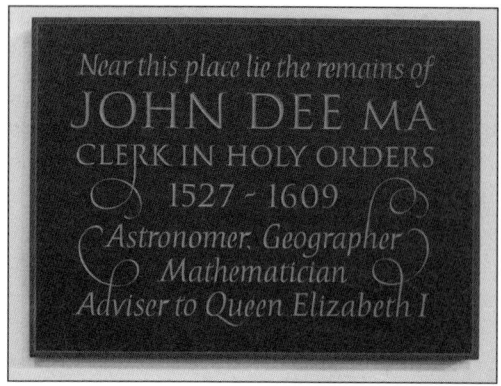

The John Dee Memorial within St Mary the Virgin Church. (*Courtesy of Robert Smith; www.wikimedia.org*)

1577 he advised Elizabeth to challenge the Treaty of Tordesillas, negotiated by Pope Alexander VI in 1494, which designated the rights to colonisation of the New World. The treaty allowed Spain to colonise most of Central and Southern America, while Portugal could claim territory along the eastern coast including Greenland, Newfoundland and Brazil. Dee recommended that Elizabeth should aim to reclaim territory in these regions for England. Dee was respected at court and by Elizabeth. Based on his counsel, she would support English seafarers in discovering new lands for colonialisation and plundering its wealth and Spanish vessels.

Elizabeth visited Dee on numerous occasions at his home, which was situated between London and her palaces at Richmond, Hampton Court and Oatlands. He owned one of the most prestigious private libraries in England and in 1575, the queen accompanied by several nobles paid him an impromptu visit with the intention of viewing his library, but his wife had died and they did not enter. Instead, he spoke to them on his doorstep.

St Mary the Virgin Church has a direct link to Elizabeth because Dee wrote in his diary that Elizabeth called upon him during 1580 by way of the church. Dee wrote:

> Sept. 17th., the Queen's Majesty came from Richmond in her coach, the higher way of Mortlake field, and when she came right against the church she turned down toward my house: and when she was against my garden in the field she stood there a good while, and then came into the street at the great gate of the field, where she saw me at my door making greetings to her Majesty; she beckoned her hand for me; I came to her coach side, she very speedily pulled off her glove and gave me her hand to kiss; and to be short, asked me to resort to her court.[109]

It is reputed that John Dee was the inspiration for Prospero, the protagonist in Shakespeare's play *The Tempest*. Dee died in 1609.

# 62

# Tableau of Queen Elizabeth Knighting Sir Francis Drake

## Elizabeth Rewards One of Her Favourite Courtiers

**This tableau depicting the queen knighting Sir Francis Drake on the deck of the *Golden Hinde* at Deptford in London in 1581 is featured on a statue of Sir Francis Drake which stands in Tavistock, Devon, his birthplace. Elizabeth was delighted with the amount of wealth that Drake brought to England as a result of his expedition around the earth, which was estimated to be worth £750,000 (the equivalent of £153.4 million in 2017). Instead of treating Sir Francis Drake as a criminal, Elizabeth invited him to Richmond Palace to congratulate him on the success of his voyage.**

Elizabeth financially rewarded Drake for the treasures he brought to England. On 24 October 1588, she wrote the following instruction to Edmund Tremayne, Clerk to the Privy Council and Drake's cousin, 'To assist Francis Drake in sending up certain bullion brought into the realm by him, but to leave so much of it in Drake's hands as shall amount to the sum of 10,000l, the leaving of which sum in his hands most secret to himself alone.'[110] The amount awarded to Drake, £10,000 (the equivalent of £2 million in 2017), was a significant sum. After the investors were allocated their share of the returns of their investment, Elizabeth retained the remainder of the spoils of the expedition, which enabled her to pay off the entire national debt. The Privy Council advised Elizabeth to state that the proceeds of Drake's plundering were obtained through trade that did not have any allegiance to Spain. It was also agreed that the passage of Drake's voyage would not be revealed and that publicly it was declared that he did not bring riches back to England because he planned to conduct further expeditions.

Elizabeth invited Drake to court and he became one of her favourite courtiers. At Christmas 1580, he gave Elizabeth a crown set with 5 emeralds and 20,000 crowns, which he had plundered from Peru. The Spanish ambassador,

Bernardino de Mendoza, observed, 'the queen shows extraordinary favour to Drake and never fails to speak to him when she goes out in public, conversing with him for a long time. She says that she will knight him on the day she goes to see his ship. She has ordered the ship itself to be brought ashore and placed in her arsenal near Greenwich as a curiosity.'[111]

On 4 April 1581, Drake brought the *Golden Hinde* to Deptford so that Elizabeth could view the vessel. She arrived from Greenwich Palace by barge along the River Thames. Spectators lined the southern bank to get a glimpse of the queen. Some of those sightseers were standing on a wooden bridge which collapsed because it could not hold the vast numbers of people. Drake welcomed Elizabeth aboard and he showed her charts and items that he had brought home from his passage around the world. He entertained Elizabeth with a banquet and after they had eaten Drake was knighted. Mendoza was incensed that Drake should be rewarded for stealing from Spanish mariners and reported:

On the 4th instant, the queen went to a place a mile from Greenwich (Deptford) to see Drake's ship, where a grand banquet was given to her, finer

A plaque depicting the knighting of Francis Drake at Deptford on the plinth of Drake's statue in Tavistock. Drake was born in Tavistock in 1540. (*Courtesy of Joseph Boehm; www.wikimedia.org*)

than has ever been in England since the time of King Henry. She knighted Drake, and told him she had there a gilded sword to strike off his head. She handed the sword to M. de Marchaumont, telling him she authorised him to perform the ceremony for her, which he did. Drake, has therefore the title of 'Sir' in consideration of the lands he has purchased, and he gave her a large silver coffer, and a frog made of diamonds, distributing 1,200 crowns amongst the queen's officers.[112]

Although Queen Elizabeth is seen in the tableau bestowing the honour upon him, Mendoza was correct in his report, the French diplomat, Monsieur de Marchaumont, was passed the sword to knight Drake. Marchaumont was in London to negotiate a marriage between the French king's brother, Francis, Duke of Anjou and Alençon, and Elizabeth. The queen showed her political astuteness in getting a French diplomat to bestow the honour, a manipulative mechanism to give the impression that France supported Drake's acts of piracy.

# 63

# Tudor Wine Cellar, Whitehall Palace

## Elizabeth's Favourite Palace

Elizabeth entertained French envoys at Whitehall Palace to discuss her proposed marriage to Francis, Duke of Anjou and Alençon during 1581. Wine stored in this cellar was most likely served to them. Whitehall Palace contained 1,500 rooms and was considered the largest palace in Europe during the Tudor period. It stretched along the embankment of the River Thames towards Downing Street to the west and northwards towards Charing Cross. The wine cellar used during the reigns of Henry VIII and Elizabeth I still exists beneath the Ministry of Defence building. Elizabeth abstained from drinking wine because she feared it might cloud her judgement and preferred to drink beer.[113]

The original building was known as York Place and was built in the thirteenth century. When Wolsey was appointed Archbishop of York in 1515, he established his London residence at York Place. After Wolsey's downfall, Henry brought Anne Boleyn to York Place to view the Cardinal's home on 2 November 1529. Elizabeth inherited Whitehall Palace after the death of Queen Mary.

The French ambassador, André Hurault de Maisse, came to Whitehall Palace for his first audience with Elizabeth in December 1597. He arrived by barge and made the following observations:

> The Queen's Palace, called Whitehall is on the banks of the Thames. The entrance on the riverside is very small and inconvenient; it is a covered alley and rather dark. Thence one enters a low hall, and then by a staircase of fifteen or twenty steps to the rooms above. It is very low and has no great appearance for a royal house. There is no great hall, and the place is passing melancholy. There is another entrance on the land side, somewhat finer.[114]

Tudor wine cellar beneath the Ministry of Defence Building, London. (*Courtesy of Amanda Reynolds; www.wikimedia.org*)

Elizabeth's bedroom and library overlooked the River Thames. German visitor Paul Hentzner was granted access to the queen's chambers in Whitehall during 1598. He described her bed chamber, 'The queen's bed, ingeniously composed of woods of different colours, with quilts of silk, velvet, gold, silver and embroidery'.[115]

Elizabeth stayed frequently at Whitehall Palace because its vast size accommodated her court and was close to the Palace of Westminster and Parliament. She spent many Christmases there and favoured this palace above any other. All that remains of the Tudor palace of Whitehall is the wine cellar beneath the Ministry of Defence building and the river wall, from which steps led down to the River Thames.

# 64

# Surviving Wall of Oatlands Palace

## A Forgotten Tudor Palace

**The southern entrance and wall of Oatlands Palace is all that remains of Elizabeth's home. It is located within a quiet residential area of Weybridge in Surrey, along the aptly named Tudor Walk. The construction of Oatlands Palace began in 1537 together with a road that linked Hampton Court Palace during the reign of Henry VIII. Stones from the abbeys at Chertsey, Bisham and Merton, which was dissolved during the dissolution of the monasteries, was used to construct Oatlands Palace.**

Situated 17 miles south-west of London, Oatlands Palace is one of the forgotten Tudor palaces. The palace was demolished during the seventeenth century; however, the surviving southern entrance and wall are now encompassed by residential homes in Weybridge. After passing through the southern entrance there was a yard where there were kitchens, stables and sheds on the right before entering the outer gatehouse. The house was built around three courtyards in the traditional Tudor style. The northern facade contained two towers that separated the queen's gallery, the northern entrance and the king's gallery from which there were commanding views of the River Thames.

It was at Oatlands Palace that Henry VIII married his fifth wife, Katherine Howard, cousin of Anne Boleyn and niece of the Duke of Norfolk, Cromwell's enemy. The marriage ceremony took place while Thomas Cromwell was being executed on 28 July 1540. It was conducted by Bishop Edmund Bonner, but there are no recorded details of any celebrations, so it can be assumed that the king wanted the wedding to be a quiet, low-profile affair. Henry VIII and Katherine Howard would have walked through this entrance to enter the palace for the wedding ceremony. Queen Mary withdrew from Hampton Court Palace to Oatlands Palace after it was discovered that she was not pregnant.

*Above*: The entrance to Oatlands Palace at Tudor Walk, Weybridge. (*Author's Collection*)

*Right*: A plaque marking the site of Oatlands Palace. (*Author's Collection*)

OATLANDS PALACE 1537-1650

THIS TUDOR GATEWAY WAS RE-OPENED BY COUNCILLOR HARRY COHEN OBE DEPUTY MAYOR OF THE BOROUGH OF ELMBRIDGE ON 9TH NOVEMBER 1985

PALACE GARDENS 1985

A seventeenth-century painting of Oatlands Palace. Note that the front wall and entrance gate is all that stands today. The palace was within close proximity of Hampton Court Palace and Nonsuch Palace and could be approached by the River Thames. Construction began in 1537 and building material was sourced from the dissolved monasteries at Chertsey, Bisham and Merton. The palace's name derived from a previous owner of the land in the thirteenth century, Robert de Ottelond. The palace was demolished in 1650.

Elizabeth frequently stayed at Oatlands Palace, especially when she wanted to rest during her annual royal progresses and enjoyed hunting in the nearby woods. On 19 August 1583, Bernardino de Mendoza referred to Elizabeth staying at Oatlands, 'The Queen had gone from Greenwich to Oatlands, where they say she will stay all this month hunting, instead of continuing her progress further.'[116]

# 65

# Beccles Town Sign

## The Granting of a Town Charter to Beccles, Suffolk

**Close to the junction of the A145 London Road with Richard Crampton Road, the Beccles town sign depicts Queen Elizabeth I presenting the town's charter to John Bass on 2 July 1584.**

The charter is a legal document and it established the Beccles Corporation as a municipality and as a town. The bestowing of a charter allowed the inhabitants the right to town privileges under the feudal system. It also granted the surrounding fen land to the people of Beccles. The charter also established the position of portreeve, a local government official charged with keeping the peace and carrying out administrative duties in a port or market town. In presenting the charter, Elizabeth appointed Bass as the first portreeve of Beccles. Elizabeth's successor, James I, confirmed the charter in 1605.

The idea of commemorating this event was conceived by Dr Henry Wood-Hill, Mayor of Beccles, in 1936 and the sign was sculptured by Judy Quinton Barber. Bass is portrayed with a posture that was normal practice and protocol when in the presence of the queen, bending on one knee in a subservient position. Paul Hentzner was in the company of Elizabeth at Greenwich Palace and was able to describe how she interacted with her subjects and how they adopted this position of addressing her while on bended knee:

As she went along with all this state and magnificence, she spoke very graciously, first to one, then to another, or those who attended for different reasons, in English, French and Italian; for besides being well skilled in Greek, Latin and the languages I have mentioned … whoever speaks to her, it is kneeling. Now and then she raises some with her hand. While we were there, W. Slawata, a Bohemian Baron, had letters to present to her; and she, after pulling off her glove, gave him her right hand to kiss, sparkling with

Beccles town sign showing Queen Elizabeth I handing the Charter of the Corporation of Beccles to John Bass, Portreeve, in 1584. (*Courtesy of Adrian Cable/www.geograph.org*)

rings and jewels, a mark of particular favour. Wherever she turned her face, as she was going along, everybody fell down on their knees.[117]

The town sign originally stood at Ballygate until it was vandalised in 1980. It was removed and replaced with a replica. Four additional replicas were produced and positioned at the other main entrances into Beccles.

# 66

# Statue of Sir Walter Raleigh

## Adventurer and Favourite of the Queen

**This statue of Raleigh was unveiled in 1958 at Raleigh Green, Whitehall, close to where he was executed at Old Palace Yard, Whitehall, to commemorate the 350th anniversary of the foundation of the Commonwealth of Virginia. The statue was relocated in 2001 to its current position in the grounds of the Old Royal Naval College, Greenwich.**

Walter Raleigh originated from Devon and was a seafarer, explorer, soldier, politician, writer and poet who became a favourite of Elizabeth. He fought on the Protestant side in the religious wars in France during 1569. Raleigh took part in an expedition to North America with his step-brother, Sir Humphrey Gilbert. He returned to soldiering during the suppression of the Desmond Rebellion in Ireland between 1579 and 1583. His deeds in Ireland brought Raleigh to the attention of the queen in 1580.

During April 1584, Elizabeth allowed Raleigh to explore the Americas, the New World, and granted him permission to colonise territory not governed by Christians in return for giving the queen 20 per cent of the bullion found there. Raleigh did not participate in the actual expedition, but he equipped two vessels and sent them on a voyage to the New World. These vessels returned in August 1584 with produce from the American continent and two native men. Raleigh's expeditions to the New World brought him wealth and the queen's favour. Elizabeth rewarded him with a knighthood in 1585. Raleigh was handsome, witty and intelligent. Although he was twenty-one years her junior, he wrote poems and words of admiration to Elizabeth. Charmed by his attention, Raleigh became a favourite of the queen. Lupold von Wedel, a German nobleman, observed how Elizabeth interacted with Raleigh at a banquet at Greenwich Palace during December 1584.

A statue of Sir Walter Raleigh in the grounds of the Old Royal Naval College, Greenwich. (*Author's Collection*)

… as long as the dancing lasted, she summoned young and old and spoke continuously. All of them, knelt before her. She chatted and jested most amiably with them, and pointing with her finger at the face of one Master or Captain Rall [Raleigh] told him there was smut on it. She also offered to wipe it off with her handkerchief, but he anticipating her removed it himself. They say that she now loved him beyond all others, and this one may easily credit, for but a year ago he could scarcely keep one servant, whereas now owing to her bounty he can afford to keep five hundred.[118]

Raleigh financed expeditions to North America in 1584, 1585 and 1587 which led to the colonisation of Roanake Island, which he named Virginia, after the Virgin Queen. He is widely thought to have introduced tobacco to England, but it is most probable that Sir John Hawkins brought it to England in 1566. Raleigh was knighted by Elizabeth on 6 January 1585.

Although Raleigh gave the impression he was devoted to Elizabeth, his role as Captain of the Gentleman Pensioners gave him regular access to the queen's chambers where he flirted and seduced several members of the queen's maids of honour. He kept his dalliances concealed from Elizabeth until Raleigh and Elizabeth 'Bess' Throckmorton conceived a child during July 1591 and Bess pleaded with Raleigh to marry her. They married in secret and kept the pregnancy hidden. Bess continued to serve the queen and when she was eight months pregnant in February 1592, she left court for a month for the birth of her son which took place on 29 March. Elizabeth was furious when she discovered during that summer that Raleigh had married Bess. She dispatched both to the Tower of London in disgrace. Raleigh wrote letters in an attempt to regain favour with the queen. Bess was unrepentant and revelled in the fact that her marriage to the most eligible man in court was public knowledge and she brazenly signed her letters as Elizabeth Raleigh, much to the annoyance of the queen. Elizabeth forgave Raleigh and ordered his release from the Tower of London, but she felt so bitter towards Bess, that one of her closest confidantes had betrayed her, that she kept her imprisoned. Elizabeth showed no compassion towards Bess when her son died prematurely during October 1592 and it was only two months after this loss that the queen finally ordered that Bess should be released. Raleigh returned to the queen's favour after playing a prominent role in the attack upon Cádiz in July 1596.

# 67

# Second Great Seal of Elizabeth I

## The Sovereign's Symbol of Power

**The Great Seal was used by Elizabeth to authorise official documents such as Acts of Parliament and announcements. Commissioned to be made in 1586, it is known as the Second Great Seal and was used by the Chancery, the equivalent of the Civil Service during the Tudor period, to stamp official documents during the second half of Elizabeth's reign between 1586 and 1603. The stamp from a seal of an official document was used to provide proof that the document was either written or approved by the owner of the seal, in this case the sovereign.**

The first seal used during Elizabeth's reign had become worn and needed replacing after twenty-eight years of use. The artist Nicholas Hilliard and Derick Anthony, a mint engraver, were commissioned to design a new Great Seal on 8 July 1584 when they received a letter from the queen. She wrote:

> As our Great Seal by much use waxes unserviceable, we have resolved that a new one shall be made. We therefore desire you to emboss in lead, wax or other fit stuff, patterns for a new one, according to the last pattern made upon parchment by you, Hidyard [*sic* Hilliard], and allowed by us; and by the same pattern engrave and bring to perfection with speed a new Great Seal in silver, of convenient massiveness, to form as near as may be to the former; and when finished, deliver it to our Chancellor, to be by him brought to us.[119]

Seals depicted the image of the owner of the seal and a motto. Hilliard engraved a series of images of the queen which she reviewed. Hilliard and Anthony were then instructed to 'emboss in lead, wax or other fit stuff patterns ... according to the last pattern made upon parchment by you Hildyard, and allowed by us, and by the same pattern to engrave and bring to perfection a new great seal in silver'.[120]

The Second Great Seal of Elizabeth I. (*The National Archives*)

The second Great Seal is important because it shows how Elizabeth wanted to be perceived and was used to assert her power as sovereign. On the front of the seal, she is portrayed holding the orb and sceptre with the sun's rays shining above her head. The reverse side shows Elizabeth on horseback flanked by the Tudor rose and the royal arms. In Latin, the words *Elizabetha dei gracia Anglie Francie et Hibernie Regina Fidei Defensor* are inscribed around the edge of the seal, which translates as, 'Elizabeth, by grace of God, Queen of England, France and Ireland, Defender of the Faith'.

# 68

# Coded Letter Relating to the Babington Plot

## An Attempt to Usurp Queen Elizabeth I During 1586

**Sir Francis Walsingham had established a network of spies which would form the beginnings of England's security service and eventually evolve into MI5 four centuries later. This coded postscript and cipher was used by Walsingham as evidence against Mary, Queen of Scots and the Babington Plot co-conspirators to implicate them in their involvement to overthrow Queen Elizabeth.**

Bernardino de Mendoza, former Spanish ambassador to London who was implicated and exiled for his involvement in the Throckmorton Plot to oust Elizabeth, and John Gifford, a Catholic priest who had rallied supporters in England, spurred on Anthony Babington, an affluent, young Catholic. Babington coordinated an attempt to depose Queen Elizabeth before a Spanish invasion and restore Catholicism to England by placing Mary, Queen of Scots on the English throne. Babington sent Mary, Queen of Scots a coded letter on 6 July 1586, secreted in a beer barrel sent to her room at Tutbury Castle in Staffordshire, which contained details of the enterprise that was known as the Babington Plot and asked for her to sanction the attempt. Mary responded and agreed to the plot, however, her servants were acting as double agents working for Sir Francis Walsingham, who intercepted these communications, including Mary's response which was written on the 17 July. Thomas Phelippes was a Cambridge-educated language expert and a leading code-breaker who was recruited by Walsingham. He was able to decipher these coded letters which revealed that Mary, Queen of Scots authorised the usurpation of Elizabeth and an invasion of England.

Walsingham ordered Phelippes to forge an additional postscript to Mary's response to Babington, requesting him to use the broken cipher to reveal the names of his co-conspirators. It read:

I would be glad to know the names and qualities of the six gentlemen which are to accomplish the assignment, for that it may be, I shall be able upon knowledge of the parties to give you some further advise necessary to be followed therein … as also from time to time particularly how you proceed and as soon as you may for the same purpose who bee already and how far every one privy hereunto.[121]

Mary, Queen of Scots' communications with Babington implicated her in the plot to usurp Elizabeth and would seal her fate. Babington and his conspirators were arrested and imprisoned in the Tower of London. They were taken to St Giles-in-the-Field and executed on 20 September 1586.

The discovery of the Babington Plot to assassinate Elizabeth during July 1586 compelled Elizabeth to act. It hastened the trial and condemnation of Mary, Queen of Scots, who was implicated in the attempt. Elizabeth was placed under enormous pressure from her Privy Council to put Mary on trial for plotting her assassination and eventually agreed to their request.

The coded postscript and cypher used by Walsingham as evidence of Mary, Queen of Scots' involvement in the Babington Plot. (*The National Archives*)

# 69

# Remains of Fotheringhay Castle

## The Imprisonment and Execution of Mary, Queen of Scots

**Fotheringhay Castle in Northamptonshire was built in about 1100. It became an administrative centre for the House of York during the Wars of the Roses and was the birthplace of Richard III in 1452. Mary, Queen of Scots was imprisoned at Fotheringhay Castle during late 1586, tried in the Great Hall and executed there on 8 February 1587. The castle fell into disrepair and was dismantled in 1628. All that remains is the motte where the keep once stood while some of castle masonry serves as a monument to its royal connections.**

Mary was imprisoned at Fotheringhay Castle after the discovery of her involvement in the Babington Plot. On 12 October 1586, lords from Elizabeth's Privy Council, including Lord Burghley and Sir Francis Walsingham, arrived at the castle to prepare for her trial. Two days later on 14 October in the Great Hall the examination of Mary, Queen of Scots commenced. She complained that she was unable to see the evidence against her and that she did not recognise the legitimacy of the English judiciary, given that she was Scottish, but she attended to proclaim her innocence. Mary had previously written to Elizabeth protesting that being Scottish she was not under the jurisdiction of an English court.

The commissioners brought the evidence submitted at the trial at Fotheringhay Castle to the Star Chamber at Westminster Palace in London on 25 October 1586, where in her absence Mary, Queen of Scots was found guilty of plotting to assassinate Elizabeth and sentenced to death. Elizabeth was reluctant to give her assent for the sentence to be carried out despite being petitioned by Parliament on 12 and 14 November 1586. The guilty verdict was publicly announced on 4 December 1586 and Burghley drafted the death warrant two days later.

Elizabeth was indecisive and did not sign the death warrant until 1 February 1587. She feared that executing a sovereign would galvanise an uprising and was worried that Mary's son, King James VI, might want to avenge his mother's death. Elizabeth was also concerned about the reaction of Catholic Spain and France if Mary, Queen of Scots was executed. Despite these ramifications, Elizabeth eventually signed the death warrant on 1 February 1587, although there was still doubt in her mind because she gave it to her secretary, William Davison, but instructed him to hold it and leave it unsealed. Davison did not follow her instructions and gave it to Burghley who, on 3 February 1587, agreed with the Privy Council to seal and send it to Fotheringhay Castle. Elizabeth felt deceived by these actions. She sent William Davison to the Tower of London for disobeying her orders with regard to not withholding the death warrant unsealed and for passing it to Burghley. He was released in 1588. Burghley was banished from court for four months.

Mary continued to protest her innocence in letters to Elizabeth, but there was no response. On 4 February 1587, the executioner arrived at Fotheringhay Castle with his axe concealed in a trunk. The commissioners, including the Earls of Kent and Shrewsbury, arrived three days later on 7 February and during that evening informed Mary that she would be executed the next morning. Appearing unperturbed, she told them that she did not believe that Elizabeth would have consented to her execution. She asked her clergy to come to her, but the commissioners refused that request. Instead, they proposed sending the Bishop of Peterborough, but Mary declined their offer. Her servants were disturbed by the news that she was to die the next morning and Mary spent time comforting them. After supper, she reviewed her will. She spent her final hours devoted to prayer holding a crucifix. At 8 am on 8 February she was led into the Great Hall, which was decorated with black curtains,

Masonry from the keep of Fotheringhay Castle preserved as a monument. (*Author's Collection*)

*The Execution of Mary, Queen of Scots, 1542–1587*, depicting the queen's execution in the great hall at Fotheringhay Castle, 8 February 1587. The Dean of Peterborough is seen pointing to Mary as she clutches a crucifix as the executioner wields his axe to deliver the fatal blow. Among those observing this horrific tragedy are her attendants, Elizabeth Curle and Jane Kennedy, sat to the left of the scaffold, while the Earls of Kent and Shrewsbury are seated on the right. (*National Portrait Gallery of Scotland/Public Domain*)

where in the centre scaffold had been erected and upon which a black cushion lay. Three noblemen were present to witness the execution, which was horrific for the executioner missed her neck and struck Mary on her back, the second blow severing her neck except for some sinews which were sliced with an axe. The executioner then held up her decapitated head and declared 'God save the queen' but to his dismay, he dropped her head, leaving just her auburn wig in his hand. Her head fell to the floor revealing that she had grey hair. Her body was initially buried in Peterborough Cathedral, but it is believed that her heart was buried at Fotheringhay.

Although the date cannot be ascertained, Elizabeth did visit Fotheringhay Castle during one of her progresses to Stamford. She lamented over the graves of the Dukes of York, including the father of Richard III, which was neglected amongst the ruins of the choir and ordered that his remains be moved into Fotheringhay church and interred either side of the Communion table.

# 70

# Statue of James VI of Scotland

## Elizabeth's Heir

**The birth of James Stuart at Edinburgh Castle on 19 June 1566 provided Mary, Queen of Scots with an heir to the Scottish throne and strengthened her claim to the throne of England. Mary also named Elizabeth as his godmother. The execution of Mary, Queen of Scots would affect Anglo-Scottish relations.**

When Mary was sentenced to death in 1586, James VI made attempts to secure a pardon. He sent his personal servant William Keith with a letter for Elizabeth about the issue on 28 November 1586. In that letter he argued that Henry VIII had blemished his reputation by executing her mother, Anne Boleyn, and used that reasoning to enforce the point that if the execution of his mother was carried out, her reputation was at stake, which infuriated Elizabeth. In December 1586, James sent diplomats Sir Robert Melville and Lord Patrick Gray to initiate friendly dialogue with Elizabeth and formally ask for Mary's release, but the initiative failed.

On 26 January 1587, in a final letter to prevent the execution and save his mother's life, he urged Elizabeth to intervene and pardon Mary. His approach was conciliatory, addressing Elizabeth as his 'dearest sister'. He emphasised that he was compelled as a son and for the Scottish nation to champion her release. He acknowledged that Elizabeth was offended by his letter that he had sent in November 1586 in which he had written 'you have already taken so evil with my plainness'.[122] James then asked, 'What thing in honour, that both is a king and a son, then that my nearest neighbour being in straightest friendship with me, shall rigorously put to death a free sovereign prince, and my natural mother.'[123] He continued by emphasising that the execution of Mary, Queen of Scots would tarnish her reputation. The letter was measured and respectful, pleading for the life of his mother and to maintain peace between England and Scotland. He presented this 'earnest request' to pardon his mother as a personal favour to him.[124]

A statue of James VI and I of Scotland and England, holding orb and sceptre, at Glamis Castle. (*Reimar/Shutterstock*)

After the execution of Mary, Queen of Scots, James was disturbed, distraught and incensed that Elizabeth had ignored his petition. Elizabeth too became anxious about how James VI would react to the news. Elizabeth sent her cousin, Sir Robert Carey, to Edinburgh to deliver a letter that she wrote to James VI on 17 February 1587 absolving herself of any responsibility in ordering his mother's death. James was concerned for Carey's safety because the Scottish were furious that Mary, Queen of Scots had been executed, so he sent courtiers to meet Carey at Berwick on the border to receive the letter, which read:

Mr Dear Brother, I would you knew (though not felt) the extreme dolour that overwhelms my mind for that miserable accident, which (far contrary to my meaning) hath befallen. I have now sent Sir Robert Carewe, this kinsman of mine, whom here now, yet hath pleased you to favour, to instruct you truly of that which is too irksome for my pen to tell you. I beseech you, that has God, and many more know how innocent I am in this case, so you believe me, that if I had bid ought, I would have bid by it. I am not so base-minded, that fear of any living creature or prince should make me afraid to do that were just: or done to deny the same: I am not of so base a lineage, not carry so vile a mind. But as not to disguise fits most a king, so will I never dissemble my actions, but cause them to show even as I meant them. Thus, assuring yourself of me, that as I know this was deserved: yet, if I meant it, I would never lay it upon the shoulders of, no more will I not damnifie myself that thought it not. The circumstances yet may please you to learn from this bearer; and, for my part, think you have not in the world a more loving kinswoman, not a more dear friend, than myself, nor any that will watch more carefully to preserve you and your estate. And who shall otherwise persuade you, judge them more partial to others than you. And thus haste, I leave to trouble you, beseeching God to send you a long reign. Your most assured loving sister and cousin. Elizabeth R.[125]

Relations with Scotland became strained, but despite calls amongst the Scottish populace for vengeance against England for the death of Mary, Queen of Scots and his own personal bereavement, James VI, who was a Protestant, resisted cooperating with Spain in its plans to invade England. Elizabeth remained tormented by the tragic episode. Sir Robert Carey later recalled that 'for all in my life-time before I never knew her fetch a sigh, but when the Queen of Scots was beheaded. Then, upon my knowledge, she shed many tears and sighs, manifesting her innocence that she never gave consent to the death of that queen.'[126] Prior to her death, Elizabeth named James VI of Scotland as her successor. This was an important lasting legacy because he would unify England and Scotland, Protestants and Catholics during his reign as James I of England.

# 71

# Queen Elizabeth's Dockyard at Chatham

## More than a Dockyard

**Chatham was an ideal location to build a Royal Dockyard and accommodate Elizabeth's navy. It was established in 1567, comprising a wharf, slipway and storehouses. The first recorded ship built here was a pinnace named *Merlin*, which was launched in 1579. The ship displaced 50 tons, carried ten guns and was crewed by thirty-five men and took part in the battle against the Spanish Armada. The dockyard positioned along the River Medway was strategically placed to deploy ships into the Thames Estuary to defend the approaches to London from the sea. Chatham Dockyard was an important legacy left by Elizabeth because it was used by the Royal Navy for four centuries until 1984.**

The dockyard was expanded throughout the reign of Elizabeth. A mast pond was established in 1570 and a forge operated and was able to make anchors for the queen's ships from 1571. Matthew Baker, Master Shipwright, was transferred from Deptford Royal Dockyard to Chatham in 1572 and he made further additions to the dockyard which included workshops, sawpits for cutting timber and a wharf which featured a treadmill crane. In 1581 the first dry dock was operational at Chatham and was able to repair ships. André Hurault de Maisse, French ambassador, passed through Rochester on 1 December 1597 and commented that 'this place is the port of the Queen of England's ships, and some are very fine. Great ships can come there and remain at high tide.'[127]

During the summer progress of 1573, Elizabeth spent four days in Rochester at the Crown Inn from 18 September. During her stay she attended a service at Rochester Cathedral and visited Chatham Dockyard for the first time, where she surveyed the site and gave instructions on expanding the dockyard to ensure the security of her vessels in the harbour. *Holinshed's Chronicles* recorded that Elizabeth returned to Chatham Dockyard on 1 February 1582 with Francis, Duke of Anjou and Alençon when she showed him English ships that were berthed in the dockyard.

Chatham Dockyard was used to build ships for the English navy that would eventually be employed in the fight against the Spanish Armada. When John Hawkins was appointed Treasurer of the English Navy in 1578 he became responsible for building new ships and upgrading existing vessels. Being a shipwright, he championed the construction of faster vessels capable of operating from long distances. Among the innovative features he introduced were longer vessels with lowered forecastle and aftcastle to increase speed and detachable topmasts, which could be raised during favourable weather, but stowed away during rough seas. In 1583 he reviewed the expenses of operating Chatham Dockyard. Despite resistance from officers, Hawkins was able to implement cost-reducing measures. Elizabeth recognised his strengthening of her navy by appointing him rear admiral. By 1587, Hawkins had expanded the English navy to twenty-five renovated ships and eighteen smaller warships. Hawkins was also an advocate of mitigating the risks of abuses and corruption within the royal dockyards.

Chatham Historic Dockyard. The Tudor dockyard was positioned where the river bends on the left bank in the photograph. It expanded in 1618 to the dry docks holding the submarine HMS *Ocelot* and the Second World War destroyer HMS *Cavalier*, which can be seen bottom left of the photograph. (*Rob Oldland/Shutterstock*)

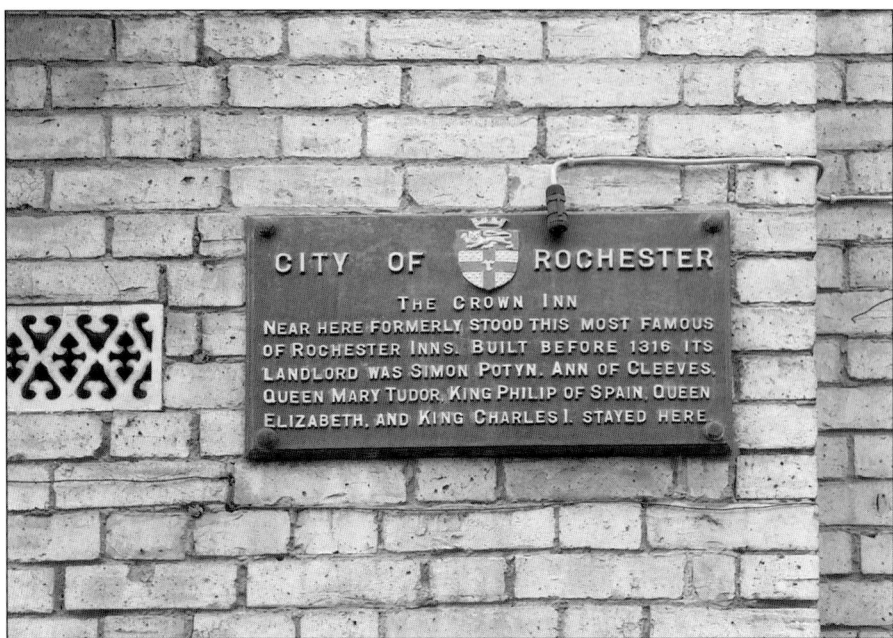

A plaque commemorating Queen Elizabeth's stay at the Crown Inn, Rochester. (*Author's Collection*)

Elizabeth ordered the preparation of the English fleet for conflict with Spain during 1587. Work began on 1 November and the fleet was ready to sail by 28 December 1587. In January 1588 intelligence reports were received from Spain that Philip II was ready to launch a large armada destined to attack and invade England. A council was established led by Lord Charles Howard, John Hawkins, Sir Francis Drake and Martin Frobisher to ensure that the English navy was ready to confront the Spanish threat. In March 1588, the majority of the English Fleet left Chatham Dockyard to assemble in Plymouth to wait for the Spanish invasion.

When English warships that had defeated the Spanish Armada returned to Chatham in August 1588, Elizabeth had not apportioned funds to take care of maimed sailors that had been wounded during the campaign and those that had succumbed to typhoid. Hawkins supported Drake to establish a relief fund at Chatham Dockyard known as 'the chest at Chatham' to provide finances that would enable medicines and food to be bought for the ailing crews. Elizabeth and the State had abandoned those who had so valiantly defended the nation, but 'the chest at Chatham' would become the precursor of the Greenwich Hospital which was established to aid retired sailors in need.

# 72

# Replica of the Spanish Galleon
## *El Galeon*

---

## The Threat of the Spanish Armada

**This replica of a Spanish galleon is typical of the vessels used in the Spanish Armada. In May 1588, Philip II sent the Spanish Armada to England to avenge the death of Mary, Queen of the Scots, usurp Elizabeth as queen and restore Catholicism to the country. The Armada was the greatest threat to English shores since the Norman conquest in 1066.**

There were other reasons why Philip II felt aggrieved by Elizabeth. Although she wanted to avoid a direct war with Spain, primarily because England could not afford a conflict, Elizabeth had conducted policies which were averse to Spanish interests. For several years, Elizabeth had encouraged those such as Sir Francis Drake to raid Spanish ports and molest Spanish vessels, stealing their wealthy cargoes. Elizabeth also permitted financial support of Dutch Protestants in the Netherlands who resisted Spanish rule and allowed Dutch rebels to use English ports to replenish supplies, which further infuriated Philip II.

The Spanish Armada was an invasion force of 138 vessels.[128] It comprised galleons and requisitioned merchant vessels armed with cannon. Philip II of Spain instructed the Duke of Medina Sidonia to sail through the English Channel to the French coast near Gravelines, between Dunkirk and Calais. From here he would escort and protect barges transporting the Duke of Parma's forces to land on the Isle of Thanet, close to Margate, where the Spanish Army could launch a direct assault along the River Thames and capture Chatham Dockyard and attack London. Philip II ordered:

> Taking one of the enemy's ports where the Armada may refit … and impress upon you how important it would be for you to enter and make yourself safe in the Thames itself … it will have the effect of compelling the enemy to

A replica of the Spanish galleon *El Galeon*. (*Courtesy of ElGaleon@elgaleonandalucia*)

maintain two armies, one on each side of the river, as they will be uncertain where the attack upon them will be made. If they do not do this the road to London will be open to us on the unprotected side, whilst otherwise they will divide their forces, and may be attacked where they are weakest.[129]

On 30 May 1588 the Spanish Armada, crewed by 7,050 sailors and commanded by the inexperienced Duke of Medina Sidonia, departed Lisbon with 17,097 soldiers and began its journey to invade England.[130] A severe storm off Cape Finisterre scattered the fleet along the Galician coastline causing much damage on 19 June. It was a major setback forcing the Spanish Armada to enter La Coruña, a Spanish port on the north-western coast of Spain, to repair the ships. Reports were received in England that the Spanish Armada had been destroyed, which influenced Elizabeth to order Admiral Lord Howard to stand down four of her largest warships, for economic reasons, because she could not afford overhead expenses incurred in their operation. Howard at his own personal expense maintained these

*The Spanish Armada off the English Coast in 1588*, by Cornelis Claesz van Wieringen.
(*Rijksmuseum*)

four vessels within the English Fleet. If he had followed Elizabeth's instructions, the English would have been seriously disadvantaged.

On 21 July 1588 the Spanish Armada set sail from La Coruña. The Spanish galleons sailed in a defensive crescent formation that stretched for 3 miles. William Camden described the invasion fleet, 'the Spanish ships, with lofty turrets, like castles, in front like a half-moon, the wings thereof spreading out about the length of seven miles, sailing very slowly, though with full sails, the winds being, as it were, tired with carrying them, and the ocean groaning at the weight of them.'[131]

The Spanish Armada reached the English coastline during the afternoon of 29 July 1588. At dawn during the following day, it drew closer to the shoreline and could see the warning beacons being lit along the coast signalling its approach.

# 73

# Drake Statue, Plymouth Hoe

## Sir France Drake, Second-in-Command of the English Fleet

After several years of piracy and plundering Spanish shipping Drake had earned notoriety. He had instilled fear in the Spanish, who called him '*El Draque*', 'The dragon'. In 1587, Drake led a pre-emptive strike upon Cádiz to disrupt Spanish preparations to invade England. During the following year, Drake waited in Plymouth for the arrival of the Spanish Armada.

Walsingham had received intelligence that Philip II was expanding his fleet and renovating his existing warships in Spanish ports, with the intention of invading England. Elizabeth sanctioned Drake to sail to Spain and interrupt that work. On 2 April 1587, Drake led a flotilla and raided Cádiz, plundering the town and destroying twenty-four Spanish vessels. He then ventured to the Azores where he intercepted the carrack named *San Felipe*, which belonged to Philip II, and its cargo of jewels, silks and china valued at £114,000 (the equivalent of £19.6 million in 2017). Drake returned to England in June and reported to Elizabeth, describing the Cádiz raid as 'the singeing of the King of Spain's beard'.[132] The attack disrupted Spanish efforts to build up its fleet, but only caused a temporary delay in the invasion of England. It also bought Elizabeth some time to prepare for war and strengthen England's defences.

On 21 December 1587, Elizabeth mobilised her fleet and appointed Lord Admiral Charles Howard as its commander and Drake as second-in-command. By 3 June 1588, Howard and Drake had assembled 34 warships owned by the queen and requisitioned 178 merchant vessels which were armed.[133] Their objective was to prevent the Spanish Armada from joining with the Duke of Parma's forces and deny them the opportunity of setting foot on English soil.

Once the Spanish Armada was sighted off Lizard Point, the call to set sail was signalled. The legend that Sir Francis Drake was playing bowls on Plymouth Hoe, where his statue stands, and that he wanted to finish his game before confronting the Spanish Armada has been propounded over the centuries, but there is no evidence to suggest that this was true. The actual situation was that strong currents and high winds impeded the departure of the English galleons, which meant that they had to be hauled by ropes from the land out to the open sea. As these vessels proceeded into the English Channel, they encountered the Spanish Armada which they engaged in small skirmishes, the first of which took place near Plymouth on 31 July 1588. The English Fleet followed the Spanish Armada past Start Point on 1 August and on this day Drake captured the *Nuestra Señora del Rosario* (this Spanish vessel was later taken to Chatham Dockyard where it was sunk to form a wharf). Drake realised that the tip of the crescent formation of the Spanish Armada

was the weakest point and it was here that he focused his attack. During the evening the *Rosario*, which carried the pay chest of the armada, amounting to 50,000 escudos, surrendered to Drake. A further battle raged off Portland Bill on 2 August. Nicholas Oseley reported to Sir Francis Walsingham, 'Has been with Sir Fr. Drake in the *Revenge*. Engagement with the Spanish. Capture of two galleons and taking prisoner Don Pedro de Valdes, the third in command of the fleet, and Joan Martinez de Ricaldo, vice-admiral. Great disorder on board the Spanish ships.'[134]

Drake was involved in another engagement off the Isle of Wight during 3 and 4 August 1588 and the Spanish Armada proceeded through the English Channel unmolested and were able to anchor in Calais Roads off the French coast on 6 August where they waited for the arrival of the Spanish forces led by the Duke of Parma.

The statue of Sir Francis Drake on Plymouth Hoe. (*Author's Collection*)

# 74

# Cigarette Card Featuring the Image of the *Ark Royal*

### Flagship of the English Fleet

*Ark Royal* was the flagship of the English fleet in 1588. The name *Ark Royal* was another significant legacy from the reign of Elizabeth I because it was used to name four other Royal Navy warships, aircraft carriers, in the twentieth century. Elizabeth's influence in strengthening the navy was recognised in the twenty-first century by naming one of the Royal Navy's next generation of aircraft carriers HMS *Queen Elizabeth* after the Tudor sovereign.

Sir Walter Raleigh commissioned the construction of a 540-ton galleon as a private enterprise in 1586. Built at Deptford by Robert Chapman, he designed the vessel under the guidance of Sir John Hawkins, with the keel built specifically for speed and manoeuvrability. It was originally called *Ark Raleigh*, following the tradition of naming the ship after its owner. Crewed by 300 sailors and 100 soldiers, *Ark Raleigh* comprised 2 gun decks, a forecastle and a quarterdeck. She was capable of carrying 55 guns, equivalent to larger warships that were in service in Elizabeth's navy. *Ark Raleigh* was launched on 12 June 1587 and was purchased by the Crown to serve in the navy for £5,000 (the equivalent of £850,000 in 2017), the sum being deducted from Raleigh's debt to Elizabeth. The *Ark Raleigh* became the flagship of the English Fleet and was commanded by the Lord Admiral Charles Howard of Effingham. In a letter to Lord Burghley, dated 28 February 1588, he wrote, 'I pray you tell her Majesty from me that her money was well given for the *Ark Raleigh* for I think her the odd ship in the world for all conditions; and truly I think there can be no great ship make me change and go out of her.'[135]

The name of the ship was changed to *Ark Royal* and it was from her masts that the Spanish Armada was first sighted. While off the coast near Plymouth, Admiral Lord Howard wrote the following report to Walsingham on 31 July:

Intelligence of the Spanish fleet off the Lizard. With great difficulty they worked out of harbour, and on Saturday got sight of them, consisting of above 100 sail, many of them of great burden. At 9 o'clock gave them fight, but did not venture amongst them, their fleet being so strong. The captains of Her Majesty's ships behaved themselves most bravely and like men. The southerly wind that brought us back from the coast of Spain brought them out. God blessed us with turning us back. Begs for the love of God to have some powder and shot sent to them.[136]

On 31 July, *Ark Royal* attacked the Spanish galleon named *Rata*, but had to hold back when other Spanish ships came to her aid. Howard decided to disengage for the remainder of that day, until his fleet was joined by forty ships from Plymouth as reinforcements and pursued the Spanish Armada from a safe distance.

FAMOUS BRITISH SHIPS

FIRST ARK ROYAL

A cigarette card featuring the image of the *Ark Royal*. (*Author's Collection*)

The *Ark Royal* was attacked by the *Regazona* at dawn on 2 August off Portland Bill. As she was about to be boarded by Spanish soldiers, Howard gave the order to steer to leeward in the direction of the sea. Joined by the *Victory,* commanded by Hawkins, *Elizabeth Jonas* and *Nonpareil,* the *Ark Royal* launched a counter-attack upon the *Regazona.* The *Ark Royal* also joined in an attack upon Spanish galleons in the lee of Portland Bill. On 7 August 1588, Howard convened a council of war aboard *Ark Royal* when it was agreed to launch a fireship assault upon the Spanish Armada, anchored off the French coast at Gravelines. *Ark Royal* took part in this attack and pursued the fleeing Spanish galleons into the North Sea up to the Firth of Forth.

Howard used *Ark Royal* as flagship during the raid on Cádiz on 15 July 1596 when the Spanish Fleet was almost annihilated. When James I ascended the throne, *Ark Royal* was renamed the *Anne of Denmark* after his wife. She was rebuilt in 1608 at Woolwich but her service ended when she was wrecked off Tilbury in the River Thames in 1636.

The *Ark Royal*, 1587, by Claes Janszoon Visscher. (*Public Domain*)

# 75

# Signalling Beacons

## A Warning System Against Invasion

**The beacon system was established along the south coast of England and prominent high points inland to warn the country against the threat of invasion. Two beacons were erected during 1988 on Folkestone Leas and Sandgate Beach to commemorate the 400th anniversary of the Spanish Armada, which passed along this stretch of the Kent coast on 6 August 1588. The Spanish Armada anchored off the French coast at Gravelines, between Dunkirk and Calais, approximately 25 miles south-east of Folkestone and it was there that the English Fleet launched its fire attack upon them at midnight on 7 August 1588.**

On 28 June 1585, the Privy Council ordered the lords lieutenants of each county to prepare for war, including the muster and training of forces and 'watching the beacons'.[137] On 20 October 1587, the Deputy Lieutenant of Somerset ordered the 'appointment of captains. Watch set in very town, and the beacons to be watched and warded.'[138]

Beacons were established upon high points where once lit the flames would be within the line of sight of one or several other beacons. They formed an important component in the defence of England, being able to signal the approach of enemy forces off the coastline and expedite the mobilization of approximately 76,000 soldiers serving in the English militia. The beacons were not always manned throughout the year, but efforts were made to ensure that each beacon was operational between spring and autumn, when sea conditions were usually calmer, and an invasion was therefore more likely to occur.

The dearth of corn motivated famished citizens to plot to use the beacons to give false alarms of invasion and use the ensuing commotion as a diversion to rob from the houses of wealthy noblemen and acquire provisions for those in need in their district. On 11 July 1586, Thomas Egerton, Solicitor General, reported to Sir Francis Walsingham, 'Examinations of Richard Noyse, Charles Roberts, Zachary Mansell, Robert Elkins, Will Stephens and several others, upon a charge of conspiracy to fire the beacons in the county of Southampton, upon a report of the appearance of the Spanish fleet, and in the tumult to rob provisions for the populace.'[139] The conspirators were sent to gaol in London.

When the Spanish Armada approached the Lizard, the Duke of Medina Sidonia could see the flickering of flames all along the Cornish coastline, for he reported that 'we were seen by the people on land, who made signal fires'.[140]

As the Spanish Armada sailed through the English Channel, the local militia would follow them on land, thus reinforcing other militia forces further along the coastline so that there would be a sufficient force to resist an attempt by the Spanish to land.

This beacon was positioned at Sandgate to commemorate the 400th anniversary of the Spanish Armada's bid to invade England. This image was taken looking south-east towards the English Channel and the French coast where the English Fleet pursued the Spanish Armada. (*Author's Collection*)

After the defeat of the Spanish Armada, some units of the militia manning the beacons were not stood down. John Scudamore wrote to Walsingham on 8 September 1588, 'requests that the county of Hereford may be relieved of the duty of watching the beacons, as other shires had ceased to do so'.[141] A threat of the appearance of a second Spanish Armada in 1590 meant beacons were placed on standby across the nation.

During 1988, to commemorate the 400th anniversary of the defeat of the Spanish Armada, the Folkestone Lions Club installed beacons on Folkestone Leas and at Sandgate as part of the chain of beacons that were lit around the English coastline.

Another beacon was installed on Folkestone Leas in 1988 to commemorate the 400th anniversary of the Spanish Armada's arrival of the English coast. The photograph was taken looking south-east towards the English Channel. The Spanish Armada, pursued by the English Fleet, passed along this stretch of the English Channel on 6 August 1588 from the south-west in an easterly direction towards Calais. On clear days, the white chalk cliffs of Cap Griz-Nez are visible. The Spanish Armada anchored off the French coastline, 15km east of Cap Griz-Nez, and that is where the English Fleet launched its assault using fireships upon the Spanish Armada on 7 August 1588. (*Author's Collection*)

# 76

# Painting, *Elizabeth I and the Spanish Armada*

## The English Fleet's Fireship Assault On the Spanish Armada

**This unsigned painting depicts the engagement between the English Fleet and the Spanish Armada at the Battle of Gravelines at midnight on 7 August 1588. The signalling beacons and Elizabeth addressing her soldiers at Tilbury are also incorporated in this painting.**

The Spanish Armada succeeded in reaching the French coast near Calais on 6 August 1588, where 124 Spanish galleons anchored off Gravelines. They waited to escort barges carrying soldiers led by the Duke of Parma across the English Channel to launch an invasion at Margate, Kent. Once a beachhead was established, the Spanish Army would march upon London. In comparison with the English Fleet, the vessels of the Spanish Armada were superior in size and were fortified with castles on the stern and the bow. However, they were vulnerable to the smaller English ships which could move faster, especially with half a dozen fireships heading in their direction. During the morning of 7 August 1588, Admiral Lord Howard convened a meeting amongst his commanders aboard *Ark Royal* and decided to attack the Spanish Armada using fireships at midnight. Robert Carey was aboard an English galleon and recalled:

> Our Council of war had provided six old hulks, and stuffed them full of all combustible matter fit for burning, and on Monday at two of the clock in the morning they were let loose, with each of them a man in her to direct them. The tide serving, they brought them very near the Spanish fleet, so that they could not miss to come amongst the midst of them, then they set fire on them, and came off themselves, having each of them a little boat to bring him off. The ships set on fire, came so directly to the Spanish fleet, as they

had no way to avoid them, but to cut all their hawsers, and so escape; and their haste was such that they left one of their four great galliasses on ground before Calais, which our men took and had the spoil of, where many of the Spaniards were slain with the Governor thereof, but most of them were saved with wading ashore to Calais. They being in this disorder, we made ready to follow them, where began a cruel fight, and we had such an advantage both of wind and tide, as we had a glorious day of them; continuing fight from four o'clock in the morning, till almost five or six at night, where they lost a dozen or about fourteen of their best ships, some sunk, and the rest ran ashore in divers parts to keep themselves from sinking.[142]

Although the English vessels were smaller than the Spanish galleons, they were manoeuvrable and possessed abundant supplies of gunpowder and cannon to overwhelm them. The Spaniards preferred to board enemy vessels, but they were not given the opportunity of getting close enough to deploy their grappling irons, for the English broadsides fired from cannon broke their ranks and holed their ships. The battle at Gravelines on 8 August 1588 lasted for fourteen hours and the Spanish Armada was dispersed.

Of 124 Spanish vessels that were anchored at Calais, only 86 could be found after the battle. Carried by strong winds, the remnants of the armada were pushed northwards into the North Sea and skirted the eastern English coastline, pursued by the English Fleet.[143]

*Elizabeth I and the Spanish Armada*, 1588, by unknown artist. (*Worshipful Society of Apothecaries of London*)

# 77

# St James's Palace

## Elizabeth's Refuge from the Threat of the Spanish Armada

Henry VIII acquired St James's leper hospital during November 1531. It was situated north-west of Westminster and surrounded by countryside. In 1532 Henry ordered its demolition and a palace was built on the site. Construction was completed in 1540. The palace was named St James's Palace and contained many of the common features incorporated within other palaces, such as courtyards, a tiltyard, tennis court, accommodation for guests, but there was no great hall. It was at St James's Palace that Queen Mary signed the treaty surrendering Calais and she died here on 17 November 1558. Queen Elizabeth would frequently reside here during her reign.

St James's Palace was not favoured by Elizabeth and she would stay here when Whitehall was being cleaned. Her coat of arms was displayed over the main entrance to the Chapel Royal. When Sir Martin Frobisher returned to London from his expedition to locate the North-West Passage on 9 October 1576, he brought with him an Eskimo, who would live at St James's Palace at Elizabeth's expense.[144]

Elizabeth learnt of the approaching Spanish Armada at Richmond Palace during the evening of 1 August 1588, and for the next two days the Privy Council considered and agreed the measures to resist the imminent threat of invasion. Three days after receiving news of the Spanish Armada approaching English shores, it was decided that it would be easier to protect the queen if she was closer to London and its garrison, so on 4 August 1588 Elizabeth left Richmond Palace to reside in the sanctuary of St James's Palace. Lord Hunsdon was responsible for the personal security of the sovereign while she was in the capital and ordered a cordon be placed around St James's Palace comprising 2,000 armed soldiers to protect the queen. These soldiers were known as the Army Royal. Elizabeth stayed at St James's

St James's Palace, where Elizabeth resided as the Spanish Armada was proceeding along the English Channel. (*Author's Collection*)

Palace for four days before leaving to spend two days at Tilbury Fort from 8 August 1588 to rally her troops, and from here she delivered her famous speech. After the threat of the Spanish Armada receded Elizabeth returned to St James's Palace on 10 August.

# 78

# Tilbury Fort

## Rallying Point For Elizabeth's Troops, 1588

**This fort was built on the northern bank of the River Thames by Henry VIII to protect London from a seaborne assault. The defences were strengthened during the reign of Elizabeth in 1588 and Parliamentary forces used it during the English Civil War between 1642 and 1651. Sir Bernard de Gomme expanded the fort during the Third Anglo-Dutch War, 1572–4, into the star-shaped defensive bastion with moat that remains today. None of the Tudor works have survived above ground, but the foundations were used to support the current fort.**

As the Spanish Armada was sailing through the English Channel, Elizabeth assembled an army comprising 23,000 men at Tilbury Fort, London. From here they deployed to meet the Spanish forces that were meant to have landed at Margate and prevent them from advancing along the banks of the River Thames towards London.

Robert Dudley, Earl of Leicester was commander of the Tilbury Garrison with the title Lieutenant General. Of the 10,000 men raised in London 10 per cent were deployed to Tilbury Fort on the condition that they brought their own provisions, especially bread and beer. The London militia wore white caps and a white uniform with the City of London arms embroidered on it in scarlet thread. Armed with halberds and pikes, they marched in companies according to which arms they carried. Leicester was confident in the capabilities of these soldiers. In a letter to Sir Francis Walsingham he wrote, 'I see that their service will be little, except they have their own captains, and having them I look for none at all by them when we shall meet the enemy.'[145]

On 23 July 1588, Leicester reported on the state of the fortifications at Tilbury and Gravesend to Walsingham: 'Those at Tilbury are more out of order than at Gravesend. Requests that they may be supplied with powder, ordnance and implements. Tilbury might be made impregnable; each fort must be well furnished with provisions.'[146]

A bridge formed of barges was positioned across the River Thames between Tilbury and Gravesend, to prevent Spanish ships from sailing into London and to allow English troops to cross between Kent and Essex according to which side of the river the Spanish landed.

Robert Devereux, 2nd Earl of Essex, the step-son of Robert Dudley, Earl of Leicester, had been appointed captain general of the cavalry. He was aged 22 and inexperienced but was received by Elizabeth when she visited the camp at Tilbury. Essex would later become a favourite courtier of the queen.

Although the threat of the Spanish invasion had been thwarted in 1588, work continued to bolster the defences of Tilbury Fort during the following year, when an out ditch was excavated and a counterscarp bank was raised. The castle was used as an artillery bastion, which ensured that no enemy fleet could sail up the River Thames and attack London. A physical barrier was also installed at Tilbury in the form of a boom positioned across the River Thames, built from ship's masts, cables and chains which were fixed by anchors.

An aerial view of Tilbury Fort on the north bank of the River Thames. (*Courtesy of Mervyn Rands*)

# 79

# Engraving of Elizabeth Arriving at Tilbury Fort

## Inspecting the Troops

**On 8 August 1588, Elizabeth insisted on leaving the safe sanctuary of St James's Palace to visit her troops. During that day she was transported by royal barge along the River Thames to Tilbury Fort where she was received by Robert Dudley, Earl of Leicester.**

After her arrival at Tilbury Fort, Elizabeth inspected her troops. Stow reported that she 'passed through every rank of them, to their great comfort and rejoicing'.[147] The queen spent the night at nearby Arden Hall and she returned to the fort the following day, 9 August 1588, wearing a steel breastplate and delivered the following speech as a battle cry for her troops, even though at that time it was not known that the Spanish Armada had been defeated at the Battle of Gravelines and the threat had receded:

My loving people, we have been persuaded by some, that are careful of our safety, to take heed how we commit ourselves to armed multitudes, for fear of treachery; but I assure you, I do not desire to live to distrust my faithful and loving people. Let tyrants fear; I have always behaved myself, that, under God, I have placed my chiefest strength and safeguard in the loyal hearts and good will of my subjects; and therefore, I am come amongst you, as you see, at this time, not for my recreation and disport, but being resolved, in the midst and heat of the battle, to live or die amongst you all; to lay down, for my God, and for my kingdom, and for my people, my honour and my blood, even in the dust. I know I have the body but of a weak and feeble woman; but I have the heart and stomach of a king, and of a king of England too; and think foul scorn that Parma or Spain; or any Prince of Europe, should dare to invade the borders of my realm; to which, rather than any dishonour shall grow by me,

I myself will take up arms; I myself will be your general, judge and rewarder of every one of your virtues in the field. I know already, by your forwardness, you have deserved rewards and crowns: and we do assure you, on the word of a prince, they shall be duly paid you. In the mean my Lieutenant-General shall be in my stead, than whom never prince commanded a more noble or worthy subject; not doubting by your obedience to my General, by your concord in the camp, and your valour in the field, we shall shortly have a famous victory over the enemies of my God, of my kingdom and my people.[148]

The speech was written by Elizabeth and shows her ability to reassure her subjects that although she was a woman, she was just as brave as a king. It shows her

An engraving showing the arrival of Queen Elizabeth at Tilbury, displayed at St Faith's Church, Gaywood, Norfolk. (*Courtesy of Evelyn Simak/www.geograph.org*)

determination to stand by her troops and her willingness to bear arms and fight for her kingdom like a king. The soldiers who heard her speech cheered and their spirits were roused, many shouting 'Gloriana'. Leicester wrote of the effect the queen's presence at Tilbury had upon the men to the Earl of Shrewsbury:

> Our royal mistress hath been here with me, to see her camp and people, which so inflamed the hearts of her good subjects, as I think the weakest person among them is able to match the proudest Spaniard that dares land in England. But God hath also fought mightily for her majesty, and I trust they be too much daunted to follow their pretended enterprise.[149]

After addressing her troops, Elizabeth dined with Leicester, and as they ate, they received news that the Duke of Parma would leave France on the spring tide. With the imminent prospect of enemy forces landing on English soil, Elizabeth vowed to stay at Tilbury, refusing to return to the safety of St James's Palace, London, and favouring standing alongside her troops. News had not reached Tilbury that the Spanish Armada was scattered and fleeing the English Fleet, but later that day George Clifford, 3rd Earl of Cumberland brought news from Gravelines that the Spanish had been defeated. Once the Spanish Armada had been dispersed, the camp at Tilbury was stood down on 17 August 1588.

# 80

# Tomb of Robert Dudley, Earl of Leicester

## Death of Elizabeth's Closest Confidant

**Leicester was devoted to Elizabeth up to the last days of his life. While he was in command of the Tilbury Garrison, Leicester was concerned for the queen's safety and urged her to seek sanctuary at St James's Palace, protected by her army instead of venturing to Tilbury. He ended a letter addressed to her, 'for himself, for her gracious favour to him he can only yield the like sacrifice he owes to God, which is a thankful heart, and to offer his body, life and all to do her service'.[150]**

As soon as the threat of the Spanish Armada receded and the militia under his command had been disbanded, Dudley left Tilbury for Kenilworth. During the journey he was taken ill and developed a fever. On 29 August he reached Rycot, the same house that Elizabeth stayed in when she was released from the Tower of London and transferred to Woodstock House in 1554. Both Elizabeth and Dudley visited Henry Norris and his wife at Rycot during September 1566. During that night Dudley wrote the following letter to Elizabeth:

I most humbly beseech your majesty to pardon your poor old servant to be this bold in sending to know how my gracious lady doth and what ease of her late pain she finds, being the chefest thing in the world I do pray for and for her to have good health and long life / for my none poor case, I continue still your medicine and find it amended much better than with any other thing that hath been given me. Thus, hoping to find perfect cure at the bath, with the continuance of my wanted prayer for your majesty's most happy preservation. I humbly kiss your foot. From your old lodging at Rycot this Thursday morning ready to take on my journey. By your most faithful and obedient servant. R Leicester.[151]

This would be the last letter that Dudley wrote to Elizabeth because on 4 September 1588, Dudley died at a hunting lodge that he owned at Cornbury Park in Oxfordshire. She kept this letter in a casket by her bedside until her death and marked it as 'Dudley's last letter'. Elizabeth was distraught when she heard the news of his death. She had known him for many years and while the nation rejoiced at the defeat of the Spanish Armada, Elizabeth grieved in private. Spanish diplomats received the following report from England, 'The Queen is sorry for his death, but no other person in the country. She was so grieved that for some days she shut herself in her chamber alone, and refused to speak to anyone until the Treasurer and other Councillors had the doors broken open and entered to see her'.[152]

Dudley left Elizabeth a diamond and emerald pendant and 600 pearls, but he was also bankrupt and left his debts to his second wife, Lettice Knollys. Much of the debt was owed to Elizabeth and she reclaimed everything that she had given to Dudley including Kenilworth Castle. She showed no sympathy to his widow and insisted that Lettice auction his belongings to raise funds.

Dudley's remains were transferred to Warwick where he was interred in the Beauchamp Chapel within the Church of St Mary the Virgin. Lettice Knollys died in 1634 and was buried next to him. His tomb is surmounted by an effigy depicting Leicester wearing full armour and a coronet.

The tomb of Robert Dudley, Earl of Leicester at the Church of St Mary the Virgin, Warwick. (© Copyright Julian P Guffogg and licensed for reuse under this Creative Commons Licence: www.geograph.org.uk)

# 81

# Spanish Bronze Siege Gun

## Symbol of the Destruction of the Spanish Armada

**The Spanish Armada galleon *La Trinidad Valencera* was badly damaged by heavy seas and struck a reef in Kinnagoe Bay, County Donegal, on 16 September 1588. This bronze siege gun was recovered from the wreck in 1971 and is displayed in the Ulster Museum.**

The surviving galleons of the Spanish Armada were unable to return home through the English Channel and due to high winds, currents and being pursued by the English Fleet they were forced to take the long route home. On 12 August 1588 the Duke of Medina Sidonia issued orders for the remnants of the Spanish Armada to sail north towards the Shetland Isles and then proceed west and then south through the Atlantic Ocean towards La Coruña. Howard's pursuit had to be stopped along the eastern English coastline due to depleted supplies of ammunition and was forced to return to Chatham Dockyard.

The crews on the Spanish ships were suffering with the low temperatures and from starvation as they sailed around Scotland. Five sailors a day were dying from hunger. In order to conserve supplies of drinking water, horses were thrown overboard. As they entered the Atlantic Ocean the remnants of the Spanish Armada encountered heavy storms and many galleons ran aground along the Irish coastline, with numerous bodies washed ashore. Secretary Fenton reported to Lord Burghley on 28 October 1588 that while walking for 5 miles along the Sligo coast he counted 'above 1,100 dead corpses men, which the sea had driven upon the shore'.[153]

The English government was concerned that if the Spanish landed in Ireland, they could use it as a base to attack England and ordered the execution of Spanish personnel that landed along with any Irish individuals who assisted them. Ministers in England were unaware of the effect the bad weather was having on the Spanish and that they were in no position to fight. Those Spaniards that survived received

*Above and below:* The bronze siege gun recovered from the wreck of the Spanish Armada vessel *La Trinidad Valencera* at Kinnagoe Bay, County Donegal. (*Courtesy of Bozonka*)

the most violent reception when they reached the Irish shore and were massacred. It was reported that:

> … the loss of life by shipwreck was enormous and thousands who had a chance of their lives by swimming were mercilessly slain on reaching the shore. A large ship was cast away in Tyrawly; so miserably distressed were they on coming on land, that one man named Melaghin McCabb, boasted that he had killed 80 of them with his galloglass axe.[154]

The bronze siege gun was transported on the Spanish Armada vessel *La Trinidad Valencera*, a large requisitioned Venetian merchant vessel of 1,100 tons that belonged to the Levantine Squadron. Her complement comprised 75 sailors and 338 soldiers. *La Trinidad Valencera* was transporting arms and equipment for the purpose of carrying out a siege, possibly upon London. On 12 September 1588 *La Trinidad Valencera* sailed into a heavy storm and was forced to head for land after sustaining damage. She ran aground on a reef at Kinnagoe Bay and on 16 September the stricken vessel broke up. If the Spanish Armada had successfully landed its army along the Kent coastline, it would have been used to besiege London. Instead, it sank to the bottom of the sea.

# 82

# Spanish Armada Memorial at Streedagh, Sligo, Ireland

## Spanish Armada Shipwrecks

**The memorial was erected in 1988 to commemorate the 400th anniversary of the shipwrecking of the *Lavia*, *Santa Maria de Vison* and *Julianna* at Streedagh Strand on 21 September 1588. Approximately 1,200 Spanish sailors and soldiers perished and 300 were rescued between Streedagh Point and Black Rock. Directly to the north of Black Rock is the Carraig na Spáinneach, the Spaniard's Rock.**

The *Lavia*, *Santa Maria de Vison* and *Julianna* belonged to the Levantine Squadron of the Spanish Armada. The *Lavia* was the vice flagship. The *Santa Maria de Vison* was a merchant vessel operating in the Adriatic Sea. Having been requisitioned, she was armed with 18 guns, crewed by 70 sailors and transported 236 soldiers, but went on to serve as a hospital ship for the Spanish Armada. The *Julianna* was a merchant vessel from Barcelona and was commandeered in Palermo in 1586.

Captain Francisco de Cuéllar was the commander of the Spanish galleon *San Pedro*, but when he failed to respond to a signal from the Spanish flagship to stand to and prepare to resist the English Fleet during the Battle of Gravelines, he was relieved of his command and transferred to the *Lavia* where he was placed under the jurisdiction of Judge Advocate General of the Fleet, Martín de Aranda. Cuéllar was stripped of his rank and sentenced to death, but this was later commuted as the Spanish Armada sailed north. The *Lavia* was formerly a 728-ton Venetian merchant vessel and was requisitioned during February 1588 while discharging its cargo of sugar at Lisbon. She was armed with 25 guns and her crew comprised 71 sailors and 231 soldiers. Don Diego Enrique, referred to by Cuéllar as the 'hunchback', was the commander of the *Lavia*.

As the surviving galleons of the Spanish Armada were passing the western Irish coastline, they were forced to anchor close to Streedagh. On 21 September a severe storm forced the *Lavia*, *Santa Maria de Vison* and *Julianna* onto the rocks at Streedagh and the vessels sank. Cuéllar wrote:

> On the fifth day there sprang up so great a storm on our beam, with a sea up to the heavens, so that the cables could not hold the sails serve us, and we were driven ashore with all three ships upon a beach, covered with very fine sound, shut in on one side and the other by great rocks. Such a thing was never seen: for within the space of an hour all three ships were broken in pieces, so that there did not escape three hundred men, and more than one thousand drowned.[155]

Don Diego Enrique and the son of the Count of Villa Franca and two Portuguese noblemen left the wreck of the *Lavia* with jewels worth 16,000 ducats. As they headed for the shore, seventy sailors jumped from the wreck and swam for their boat. A huge wave capsized the boat washing them all into the sea. Don Diego Enrique and the occupants of the boat drowned. A day later, their bodies washed up and were stripped, the jewels being taken by locals from nearby villages. Cuéllar wrote of his escape from the wreck of the *Lavia*:

> I placed myself on the top of the poop of my ship, after having commended myself to God and to Our Lady, and from thence I gazed at the terrible spectacle. Many were drowning within the ships; others casting themselves into the water, sank to the bottom without returning to the surface; others on rafts and barrels, and gentlemen on pieces of timber; others cried allowed in the ships calling for God; captains threw their chains and crown-pieces into the sea; the waves swept others away, washing them out of the ships. While I was regarding this solemn scene, I did not know what to do, nor what means to adopt, as I did not know how to swim, and the waves and the storm were very great; and; on the other hand, the land and the shore were full of enemies, who went about jumping and dancing with delight at our misfortunes; and when any one of our people reached the beach, two hundred savages and other enemies fell upon him and stripped him of what he had on until he was left in his naked skin. Such they maltreated and wounded without pity, all of which was plainly visible from the battered ships, and it did not seem to me that there was anything good happening on any side … I managed to find another resource, which was to take the cover of a hatchway, about as large

*Above*: The memorial commemorating the 400th anniversary of the loss of the Spanish Armada galleons *Lavia*, *Santa Maria de Vison* and *Julianna* at Streedagh Strand on 21 September 1588. (*Courtesy of Kenneth Allen; www.geograph.org.uk*)

*Below*: A viewing platform looking towards Streedagh where the Spanish galleons *Lavia*, *Santa Maria de Vison* and *Julianna* sank. (*Courtesy of Kenneth Allen; www.geograph.org.uk*)

as a good-sized table … When I tried to place myself upon it, it sank with me to a depth of six times my height below the surface, and I swallowed so much water, I nearly drowned. When I came up again, I called to the Judge Advocate and I managed to get him upon the hatchway with myself. In the act of casting off from the ship, there came a huge wave, breaking, over us in such a manner that the Judge Advocate was unable to resist it, and the wave bore him away and drowned him, crying out and calling to God while drowning.[156]

A piece of timber crushed Cuéllar's legs and when he reached the shoreline he could not stand. The bloodstained Cuéllar was not touched by the Irish people on the shore but found a place to seek refuge for the night. During the following morning he saw that many of his drowned countrymen were denied the dignity of a decent burial and were eaten by crows and wolves. Cuéllar eventually found a way home to Spain, via Scotland and Flanders, however, before he reached the European continent, he was shipwrecked a second time.

Irish chieftains such as O'Rourke of Briefne and McClancy of Dartry offered refuge to some of the survivors of these Spanish vessels who reached the Irish shore. Don de Aranada, commander of the *Julianna*, was among those who drowned, but Pedro Blanco was one of the crew who survived and he became the bodyguard and servant to Hugh O'Neill, Earl of Tyrone.

# 83

# The 'Armada Portrait'

## Elizabeth at the Pinnacle of her Power

**The defeat of the Spanish Armada was celebrated through this portrait of Elizabeth. It was used to galvanise the perception of a youthful, triumphant monarch who had beaten an army of superior numbers.**

Adorned with lavish jewellery, Queen Elizabeth projects an image of wealth and affluence. The abundance of pearls, the Tudor symbol of chastity, alludes to the queen's virginity. A mermaid, regarded by English seaman as a bad omen and a prophesier of disasters, is visible bottom right of the portrait; and this mermaid foresees the destruction of the Spanish Armada off the western coast of Ireland, which is depicted above right. It acknowledges that the English were lucky that huge storms were a factor in defeating the Spanish Armada. The English fireships were also another major element in the successful suppression of the Spanish invasion, which are seen in the top left of the image. Her right hand is placed on a globe over the North American continent, asserting her ambitions for expanding beyond the colonialisation of Virginia, which was already under English control. The English Crown is firmly placed between the English Fleet and above the globe. The 'Armada Portrait' presents Elizabeth as 'the great Empress of the World' and signifies England's emergence as a major international power.

However, behind the splendour and grandeur of this image of the victorious queen there were negative undertones, as mentioned earlier. Firstly, Elizabeth was also mourning the loss of her close friend Robert Dudley, while the country was celebrating the defeat. Secondly, the sailors who formed the crew of the English warships that fought the Spanish Armada were suffering. Despite being portrayed as wealthy and opulent in the 'Armada Portrait', Elizabeth was unable to keep to her word when she told her soldiers at Tilbury that 'I myself will be your general, judge and rewarder of every one of your virtues in the field. I know already, by your forwardness, you have deserved rewards and crowns.' Elizabeth did not have sufficient

The 'Armada Portrait' of Elizabeth I, previously owned by Sir Francis Drake and his descendants. (*Woburn Abbey/ Public Domain*)

funds to pay their wages and many were either wounded or infected with typhoid and scurvy, and overall, they were neglected and abandoned. Although hundreds had died in battle fighting the Spanish, many thousands more succumbed to disease. Admiral Lord Howard split his fleet into two positions on the Downs near Sandwich and Margate. Four days after the English fleet had dispersed the Spanish Armada at Gravelines, Lord Howard wrote to Lord Burghley from Margate on 10 August 1588:

> Sickness and mortality begins to grow wonderfully among them: it is a most pitiful sight to see the men die in the streets of Margate. The *Elizabeth Jonas* had lost half her crew. Of all the men brought out by Sir Ric. Townsend he has but one left alive. Proposes that 1,000l. worth of new clothing should be sent to the fleet, as the men were in great want.[157]

The condition of the sailors and the English vessels was so dire that if there had been another attack upon England, the country would not have been able to defend itself. On 22 August 1588, Admiral Lord Howard reported to the queen that, 'the fleet is suffering much from infection which has broken out. Those that come in fresh are soonest affected; they sicken one day and die the next.'[158] He also reported to the Privy Council that day that 'the infection in the fleet is so great that many of the ships have hardly enough men to weigh their anchors'.[159] On 26 August 1588, Admiral Lord Howard attributed inferior beer from Sandwich to exacerbating the situation regarding illness onboard those vessels. 'The beer brewed at Sandwich was sour; belike there are some great fault in the brewer. The mariners think it was one great cause of the infection. Nothing displeaseth them more than to have sour beer.'[160] Elizabeth blamed captains of vessels for not controlling budgets and for allowing these men to get into this situation, but it was undoubtedly her failure. Admiral Lord Howard, Drake and Hawkins showed compassion and at their own expense paid for medicines to improve the sailors' general welfare.

# 84

# Old Medieval St Paul's Cathedral

## Thanksgiving for the Defeat of the Spanish Armada

**This depiction of London was engraved by C.J. Visscher and published in 1616, thirteen years after the death of Elizabeth. It shows the London that would have been familiar to Elizabeth, particularly on 24 November 1588, when a thanksgiving service was held at St Paul's Cathedral to celebrate the victory against the Spanish Armada. Protestant England believed that the victory over Catholic Spain was a validation from God and that its cause was righteous and championed the Protestant faith.**

St Paul's Cathedral is seen without its steeple which was struck by lightning during the afternoon of 4 June 1561, Corpus Christi Eve, and set ablaze. The steeple was destroyed and Catholics in London believed that it was God's judgement and anger at the Protestant reforms made in England during the first years of Elizabeth's reign. This was particularly so because lightning had also caused the steeple of St Margaret's Church, Ludgate, to collapse hours earlier on the same day. Nicholas Jones witnessed the destruction of the steeple of St Paul's Cathedral and he gave a detailed account of what happened in a letter to Sir Nicholas Throckmorton the following day. Jones recalled that it rained all day:

> … when suddenly a thunder-bolt, with a great thunder following, hit within a yard of the very top of the steeple, which forthwith showed his effect, and appeared a little fire, like unto the light of a torch, which, increasing towards the weather-cock, caused the same within a quarter of an hour to fall down. Whereby the wind, which was great, and the more vehement by reason of the opening of the steeple and the height thereof, caused the flame so to augment, and burn the steeple, which no man could succour, as with an hour the steeple of St Paul's, which was so long in building, and so renowned, was utterly consumed to the very battlements; which being of some breadth and

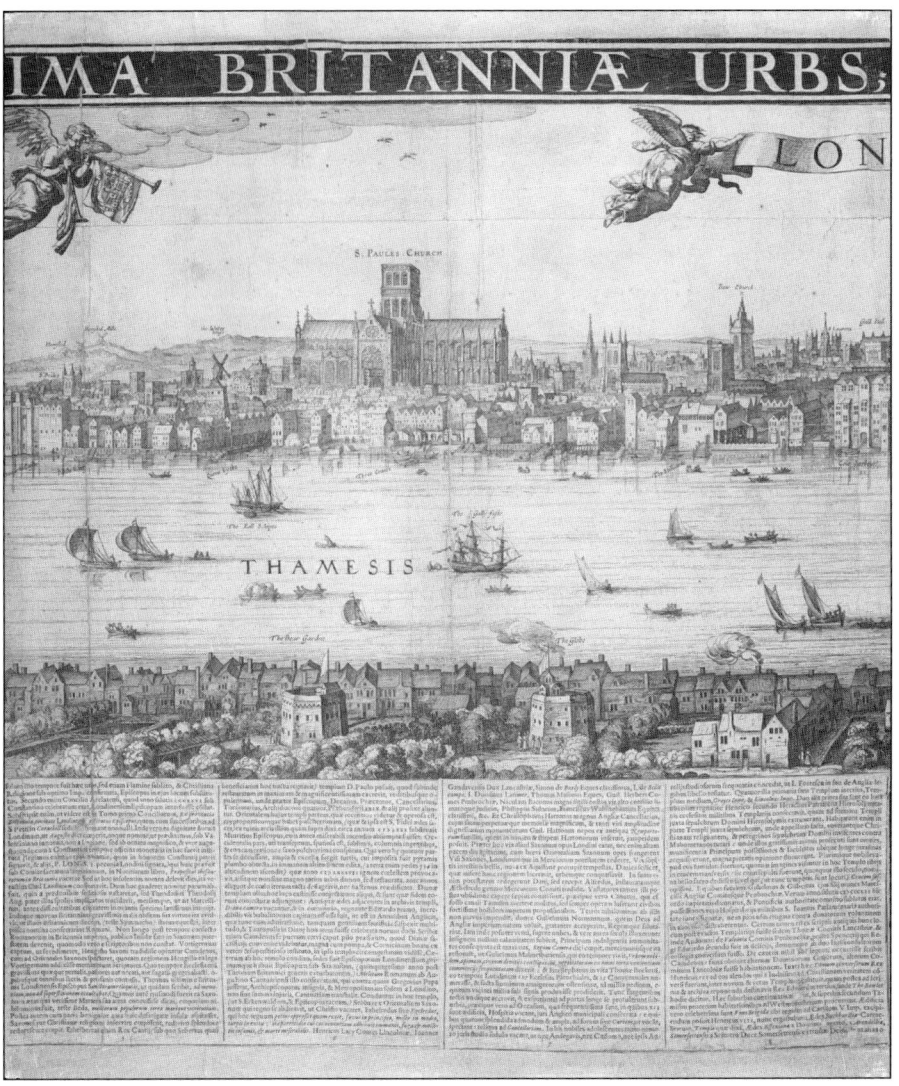

A depiction of St Paul's Cathedral engraved by C.J. Visscher and published in 1616, which also shows the Bear Garden where bear baiting took place and Shakespeare's Globe Theatre in the foreground on the south bank of the River Thames. (*British Library/Public Domain*)

strength, as was needful to uphold such a weight, received most part of the timber which fell from the spire, and began to burn with such vehemence, as all the timber was burnt, the iron and bells melted and fallen down upon the stairs within a short space ... All good and honest men are sorry for it, and impute it to a terrible remembrance of God's anger towards us for our offences.[161]

A plan of the layout of the medieval St Paul's Cathedral is marked out on the ground outside the south-western corner of the building today. (*Author's Collection*)

Twenty-six years later St Paul's Cathedral was central to celebrating the defeat of the Spanish Armada. On 8 September 1588, eleven ensigns captured from Spanish ships were displayed in the cathedral. A service of thanksgiving for the victory over Spain was held at St Paul's Cathedral on 24 November 1588 which was attended by Elizabeth, members of the Privy Council, bishops, representatives from the judiciary and the French ambassador. Elizabeth had to put her grief for Dudley to one side as she attended the service and celebratory feast. She arrived 'in a chariot throne made with four pillars behind to have a canopy on the top whereof was made a crown imperial and two lower pillars before whereon stood a lion and a dragon holding the arms of England'.[162] Robert Devereux, 2nd Earl of Essex had succeeded his step-father, the Earl of Leicester, as Master of the Horse and rode by her side. Elizabeth was received by the Bishop of London and the Dean of St Paul's at the west door.

# 85

# Model of Greenwich Tiltyard

## Jousting and Displays of Power

**Elizabeth shared her father's interest in jousting and tournaments were held on two occasions annually on the tiltyards at her palaces at Greenwich, Whitehall and Hampton Court to celebrate her birthday on 7 September and her accession day on 17 November.**

Jousting tournaments were popular during the reigns of the Tudor monarchs, the sport being a demonstration of courage, physical strength and horsemanship. Armour that was worn for jousting was used to display style and wealth. These jousts were held to celebrate prestigious events such as royal occasions and state visits and provided Elizabeth with opportunities to posture and parade in front of her subjects, foreign sovereigns and diplomats. With the queen observing such tournaments, this was the only chance the masses had to come into contact with royalty.

In 1516, Henry VIII ordered the construction of a permanent tiltyard at Greenwich Palace and this is depicted in this model. It was built to the south-east of the palace and ran northwards from where Queen's House stands, across the lawn and the Romney Road to the Old Royal Naval College. The foundations of these towers were excavated beneath the lawns of the Queen's House. This tiltyard continued to be used for jousting tournaments during the reign of Elizabeth.

The tiltyard at Whitehall Palace was located west of the palace on the site of Horse Guards Parade. During a tournament that was held here during 1570 a scaffold collapsed killing and injuring the spectators that were standing upon it. Lupold von Wedel attended a tournament at Whitehall Palace to celebrate accession day in 1584, which was attended by Elizabeth. He wrote the following account of the event:

The 17th November, the date on which the tournament is annually held having arrived, the Queen at twelve o'clock seated herself with her ladies at

A model of the tiltyard at Greenwich Palace on display at the Old Royal Naval College Visitor Centre. (*Author's Collection*)

the windows of a long room facing Whitehall, near Westminster. A broad staircase before the tiltyard leads up to this room. Round the yard are erected stands. Everyone who wishes to look on and have a seat on the stands must pay 18 pence ... On the stand were very many thousands of men, women and girls, to say nothing of those who were in the tiltyard and had nothing to pay. The tournament began with two knights who were desirous of contending with one another, riding simultaneously into the lists to the loud blare of trumpets and other music. And this mode of procedure was observed throughout the tournament. Every knight taking part in the tournament had dressed himself and his attendants in particular colours although none of the underlings rode into the lists with the knights had bedizened themselves and their train like savages; some like the natives of Ireland with their hair streaming like a woman's down to their girdles. Some had crescent moons upon their heads; some came into the lists with their horses caparisoned like elephants; some came driving, their carriages drawn by people most oddly attired ... all the knights had their horses with them and being ready accoutred for the fight mounted their steeds, some of them however were dressed like horsemen and bravely decked out. If any failed to take part in the tournament it cost him some thousands of crowns.

Now when a knight entered the lists with his following, he rode up to the staircase that led up to the room into which the Queen was. Then one of his followers ascended the staircase into the Queen's presence. This servant wore a very fine livery in the colours of his master. He then addressed the Queen at length in rhymes that he had learnt by rote and at the same time quaintly and decorously cut merry capers. This evoked laughter from the Queen and those around her. When the man had finished his speech, he in the name of his master handed the Queen a beautiful present which she accepted and then gave the donor permission to take part in the tournament. Now the knight jousted and broke lances in the lists two at a time. On this day there were to be seen many fine horses and beautiful women, not only amongst the ladies of the Queen, but also amongst those of the gentry, nobility and burghers. This tournament lasted until five o'clock. Then my Lord Leicester, the Queen's Master of the Horse, bade the knights cease from combat. The Queen then presented the prizes to the Earl of Oxford and to the Earl of Arundel, the eldest son of the Duke of Norfolk, whom the Queen had beheaded ... Lastly each knight who had acquitted himself well and nobly received a gift, and so this tournament closed.[163]

# 86

# Armour Garniture of George Clifford, 3rd Earl of Cumberland

## Suit of Armour of Queen Elizabeth's Champion

**George Clifford, 3rd Earl of Cumberland was born in 1558, the year of Elizabeth's accession. He was a naval commander, navigator, mathematician and courtier who was renowned for his jousting abilities on the tiltyard. During the action against the Spanish Armada, he commanded the *Elizabeth Bonaventure* and after the Battle of Gravelines he brought news of its defeat to the camp at Tilbury. This suit of armour was worn by Cumberland on the tiltyard during jousting tournaments in the presence of Queen Elizabeth.**

Manufactured in 1586, this is the best-preserved armour garniture from the royal workshops at Greenwich. It was made by master armourer Jacob Halder when the workshop was at its technical and decorative peak. Cumberland chose the Tudor rose, the French fleur-de-lys (which was part of the English arms) and the cipher of Elizabeth, which comprised two Es back-to-back, to form the decoration.

Elizabeth observed Cumberland's prowess on the tiltyard. He took part in a jousting tournament on 19 August 1588, shortly after the defeat of the Spanish Armada, which was held by Robert Devereux, 2nd Earl of Essex. The Genoese merchant and spy Marco Antonio Messia was present and reported:

The review was held in a field in front of the house, and her Majesty witnessed it from a window. A joust was then held in an open field (without lists), and the earl of Essex ran two tilts against the earl of Cumberland. As they are two of the best horsemen in the country, the spectators were much pleased at this. Several other gentlemen then joined, and they tilted first two against two, and then four against four; the earl of Essex always running against the earl of Cumberland. When they had finished with the lance, they drew their swords, but when her Majesty saw this, she made a sign with her hand that they were to cease, but they set to and she shut the window, in order not to see them.[164]

In 1590 Cumberland was appointed the Queen's Champion and she would refer to him as 'my knight'. To mark the occasion, Nicholas Hilliard was commissioned to paint a miniature portrait of him dressed in jousting attire. Two years later, Cumberland was elevated to a Knight of the Garter. Cumberland is best remembered for his capture of the Spanish fort in San Juan, Puerto Rico, in 1598.

*Right*: The armour garniture of George Clifford, 3rd Earl of Cumberland. (*Courtesy of Metropolitan Museum of Art, New York*)

*Below*: A detail of the armour garniture of George Clifford, 3rd Earl of Cumberland, showing the Tudor rose, the French fleur-de-lys (which was part of the English arms) and the cipher of Elizabeth, which comprised two Es back-to-back. (*Courtesy of Metropolitan Museum of Art, New York*)

# 87

# Monument to Blanche Parry, St Faith's Church, Bacton

## A Faithful Nurse

**Blanche Parry served Elizabeth as a nurse when she was an infant and taught her the Welsh language. Throughout her life she served her queen as her faithful attendant. When Parry died in 1590 a monument featuring her alongside Elizabeth was erected in St Faith's Church, Bacton, Herefordshire, the village of her birth.**

During the final ten years of her life, many of Elizabeth's courtiers and attendants who served her passed away and each death represented another link to her past that was lost and she became isolated. Blanche Parry was a close companion who had attended upon Elizabeth as a nurse since she was 3 months old. Given that she had no mother, Blanche became a maternal figure for Elizabeth, remaining a source of comfort and a close confidante throughout her life. When she ascended the throne, Elizabeth appointed Blanche as Keeper of the Royal Books. Blanche was a cousin of William Cecil and was responsible for introducing him to the queen. Blanche remained unmarried and would devote her life to serving the queen. She was extremely loyal and Elizabeth later appointed her as Chief Gentlewoman of the Privy Chamber and Keeper of the Queen's Jewels. She was trusted to read official papers before the queen's scrutiny and drafted her private correspondence.

In later life, Blanche became infirm and eventually lost her sight. Elizabeth requested that her own apothecary attend upon her during her final years. On 12 February 1590 Blanche died aged 82. Elizabeth was sad because Blanche could remember her mother, Anne Boleyn, and represented a link to her own childhood.

It was originally intended that Blanche should be buried within St Faith's Church, Bacton, but since she had served the queen for fifty-seven years and was her longest serving attendant, Elizabeth held Blanche in high esteem and commanded that she be buried with the dignity and status of a baroness. She was therefore buried in St Margaret's Church, Westminster. St Faith's Church contains an empty tomb upon which Blanche is shown kneeling adjacent to Elizabeth. This is an early example of Elizabeth depicted as Gloriana.

*Right*: Blanche Parry's empty tomb at St Faith's Church, Bacton, with sculptures of Elizabeth as Gloriana and Parry kneeling. (*Courtesy of Philip Pankhurst; www. geograph.org.uk*)

*Below*: A detail of the sculptures of Elizabeth and Blanche Parry above the latter's empty tomb at St Faith's Church, Bacton. (*Courtesy of Fabian Musto; www. geograph.org.uk*)

# 88

# Chislehurst Town Sign

## The Walsinghams

**Sir Francis Walsingham, Elizabeth's Secretary of State and spymaster, was born *c.* 1532 in the family home at Scadbury Hall, near Chislehurst. A village sign at Royal Parade, Chislehurst, depicts Queen Elizabeth I knighting his relative, Thomas Walsingham, in 1597 for raising and funding soldiers from Kent in preparation for another Spanish invasion attempt. Bricks from Scadbury Hall, which was demolished in 1738, are positioned at the foot of the Chislehurst town sign.**

Francis Walsingham began his career as a diplomat at the French court in Paris, where he sheltered Huguenots, French Protestants, escaping from the Massacre of St Bartholomew on 23 August 1572. Walsingham returned to England during the following year and on 20 December 1573 Elizabeth appointed him Secretary of State and a privy councillor. Walsingham was responsible for the queen's security and became England's first spymaster and is reputed to be the founder of the British intelligence service. He established a network of spies across Europe which enabled him to source valuable information about plots to depose Elizabeth I.

Towards the end of 1596 the Privy Council was concerned that Philip II would send a second Spanish Armada to invade England. The Privy Council appealed for militias to be raised across the southern counties to prepare to defend England. Thomas Walsingham, who lived in the manor house at Scadbury, near Chislehurst, and had served as a Justice of the Peace for the north-west Kent district of Rokesley since 1592, recruited soldiers from the Kent village for that militia and provided financial support to fund them. Walsingham and five other captains were ordered to take these soldiers to Upnor Castle to man boom defence ships that were placed across the River Medway to defend Chatham Dockyard.

*Right*: The sign at Royal Parade, Chislehurst, Kent, showing Elizabeth I knighting Sir Thomas Walsingham. (*Courtesy of Ian Capper/www.geograph.org*)

*Below*: The ruins of Scadbury Hall. This was the home of the Walsingham family and it was where Sir Francis Walsingham, Elizabeth's spymaster, was born. Bricks from these ruins were used for the base of the memorial in Chislehurst. (*Courtesy of Ian Yarham*)

Thomas Walsingham was a distant relative of Sir Francis Walsingham who employed him on diplomatic missions to the French court. He was also an enthusiastic patron of literature and sponsored the playwright Christopher Marlowe. Walsingham was also the employer of Ingram Frizer, Marlowe's murderer. When Marlowe's poem *Hero and Leander* was published posthumously in 1598, his publisher dedicated the work to Walsingham, 'knowing that in his lifetime you bestowed on him many favours'.

During her royal progress in Kent in 1597, Elizabeth visited Scadbury and acknowledged Walsingham's leadership in raising and funding the local militia with a knighthood. A town sign depicting Elizabeth I knighting Walsingham was inaugurated in nearby Chislehurst in 1953 to commemorate the coronation of her forebear, Elizabeth II. The current sign is a replica dating from 1981, which was restored in 2003.

# 89

# Elizabeth's Lost Dress

## Fabric Possibly from the Wardrobe of Elizabeth I

In her later years Elizabeth's wardrobe was reputed to have comprised 1,900 dresses, and that each of these had only been worn twice. Her clothes were so expensive that when they became unfashionable, they were unpicked and reused for other purposes such as a seat cover or a cushion and given as gifts to members of her household. In St Faith's Church at Bacton there is an embroidered altar cloth exhibited in a glass case on a wall and it is believed to have originated from the wardrobe of Elizabeth. It has been on display for the last 400 years.

The altar cloth from St Faith's Church, Bacton, believed to have been made from a dress worn by Elizabeth I, who then gave the garment to Blanche Parry. Recent research and conservation have confirmed that this is the case. (*Philip Pankhurst/www.geograph.org*)

The altar cloth was made from silver chamblet silk fabric. It dates from the 1590s and features a collage of plants and flowers and a menagerie of various animals, including stags, bears, butterflies and caterpillars. There is also an image of a sea monster and an empty boat. These images were embroidered onto the cloth. A small dart in the material indicates that it was once a dress and the design is similar to the pattern of the dress worn by Elizabeth in the 'Rainbow Portrait', which is displayed at Hatfield House, Hertfordshire.

Blanche Parry was highly favoured by her mistress and Elizabeth passed down some of her disregarded gowns to her in recognition of her service and loyalty. The 'Rainbow Portrait' was produced a decade after Blanche died, but this fabric might have been given to the Parry family to honour her memory after the death of Elizabeth in 1603. Perhaps Blanche had a hand in creating the dress. As previously mentioned, Blanche Parry was meant to have been buried at St Faith's Church, Bacton, and there are sculptures of Blanche and Elizabeth on her empty tomb in the church.

# 90

# The 'Rainbow Portrait' of Elizabeth I

## A True Representation?

There is confusion regarding who painted this portrait with both **Isaac Oliver** and **Marcus Gheeraerts the Younger** being attributed as the artist. The portrait was painted in 1600 when Elizabeth was in her late 60s. This image is known as the 'Rainbow Portrait' because it appears that Elizabeth is holding an object which is curved like a rainbow and on it are inscribed the latin words '*Non sine sole iris*', which translate as 'No rainbow without sun'. Elizabeth represents the sun for without the sun there is no rainbow.

The portrait was either commissioned by Elizabeth or someone within her inner circle. In later life, Elizabeth had lost her hair and relied upon wigs to conceal her baldness. Her skin was pockmarked having suffered with smallpox and her teeth were rotten. Nature had not treated Elizabeth kindly in old age, but Isaac Oliver produced this iconic image which portrays the queen as ageless, beautiful and graceful, with her hair adorned with jewels and a crown. It is a visual representation of Edmund Spenser's interpretation of Gloriana written in his poem *The Faerie Queen*. Elizabeth is depicted wearing an elaborate costume with eyes and ears interwoven into the design which enforces the notion that the queen saw and heard everything at court. The dress worn by Elizabeth in the 'Rainbow Portrait' resembles the design of the altar cloth at Bacton.

Paul Hentzner accompanied German aristocrats on tours around Europe and watched the queen's procession at Greenwich Palace as she and her entourage entered the chapel in 1598. He recalled the image of Elizabeth and made observations that were not consistent with Isaac Oliver's portrayal of her in the 'Rainbow Portrait':

And next came the queen, in the sixty-fifth year of her age, as we were told, very majestic; her face oblong, fair, but wrinkled; her eyes small, yet black and

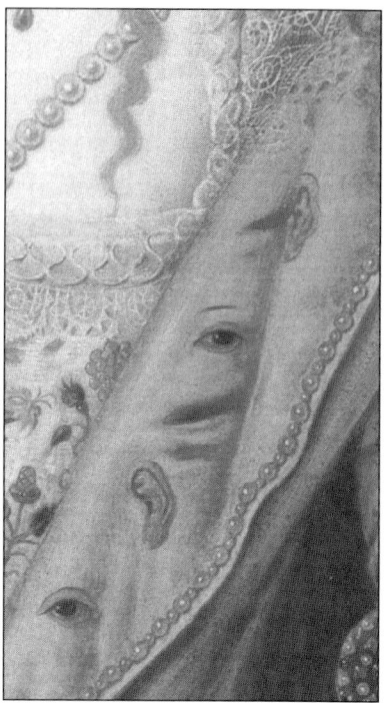

*Above left*: The 'Rainbow Portrait' of Elizabeth I attributed to both Isaac Oliver and Marcus Gheeraerts the Younger, *c.* 1600. (*Hatfield House/Marquess of Salisbury/Public Domain*)

*Above right*: A detail from the 'Rainbow Portrait' showing images of eyes and ears in the pattern of her dress which enforces the point that Elizabeth saw and heard everything in her court and kingdom. (*Hatfield House/Marquess of Salisbury/Public Domain*)

pleasant; her nose a little hooked; her lips narrow, and her teeth black; a defect, the English seem subject to, from their great use of sugar. She had in her ears two pearls, with very rich drops; she wore false hair, and that red; upon her head she had a small crown. Her bosom was uncovered, as all the English ladies have it, till they marry; and she had on her a neckless of exceedingly fine jewels; her hands were small, her fingers long, and her stature neither tall nor low; her air was stately, her manner of speaking mild and obliging.[165]

Isaac Oliver's depiction of Elizabeth was probably close to her actual appearance when she was made up and wearing elaborate clothing. Her ladies-in-waiting ensured that she was immaculately attired and that the make-up applied to her face made her look younger to conceal her age, facial blemishes and rotting teeth. Thomas Platter described Elizabeth's appearance when he saw her at Nonsuch Palace during September 1599:

She was most lavishly attired in a gown of pure white satin, gold-embroidered, with a whole bird of paradise for panache, set forward on her head studded with costly jewels, wore a string of huge round pearls about her neck and elegant gloves over which were drawn costly rings. In short, she was most gorgeously apparelled, and although she was already seventy-four [Platter was wrong about her age, for in September 1599 she celebrated her 66th birthday], was very youthful still in appearance, seeming no more than twenty years of age. She had a dignified bearing, and, as noted above, rules her kingdom with great wisdom in peace and prosperity and the fear of God, has up till now successfully confronted her opponents with God's help and support … and although her life has been threatened by poison and many ill designs, God has preserved her wonderfully at all times.[166]

The 'Rainbow Portrait' is displayed within the Marble Hall at Hatfield House, Hertfordshire.

# 91

# Nonsuch Palace Marker in Nonsuch Park, Surrey

## Nonpareil

**Elizabeth's father, Henry VIII, built Nonsuch Palace but it was incomplete on his death in 1547. His daughter, Mary I, sold the palace to the Earl of Arundel in 1556. For most of Queen Elizabeth's reign, Nonsuch Palace remained in the possession of the earl and his family, but in the early 1590s she bought the palace from the now dead earl's son-in-law, John, Baron Lumley. The palace soon became her favourite residence.**

In 1538 Henry VIII purchased the village named Cuddington, near Ewell in Surrey. The entire village, including the church, was completely demolished so that work could begin on building a new palace for the king called Nonsuch. Its name derived from the fact that no other building in England could rival its grandeur with its southern face featuring ornate octagonal towers and turrets. Henry wanted to use this new palace, containing two courts, as a place for sport and entertainment. It was close to one of his principal hunting grounds within this area.

Elizabeth used Nonsuch Palace during her royal progresses and liked hunting in the forests close to the palace. She also used the palace for receiving ambassadors. On 19 August 1585 she signed the Treaty of Nonsuch with Dutch rebels showing her support for their opposition to Spanish rule. This was the first international treaty signed with the Dutch republic.

Thomas Platter was a Swiss tourist who was given access to the royal palaces and visited Nonsuch Palace on 26 September 1599. He described the appearance and features of the palace during Elizabeth's reign:

> Nonsuch (or Nuntzich) is a fine royal residence; it takes its name from its magnificence, for Nonesuch is equivalent to (non pareille) without equal, for there is not its equal in England. ...The palace exterior is built entirely of

great blocks of white stone on which are represented numerous Roman and other ancient stories. Above the doors of the inner court, stone statues of three Roman emperors are erected. Then, in the inner court, I noticed a very handsome and elaborate snow-white stone fountain, showing a griffin angrily spewing water with great violence. ... We were led very soon into the presence chamber where we were placed well to the fore, so as better to behold the queen. This apartment like the others leading into this one was hung with fine tapestries, and the floor was strewn with straw or hay; only where the queen was to come out and up to her seat were carpets laid down worked in Turkish knot. After we had waited awhile there, somewhere between twelve and one, some men with white staffs entered from an inner chamber, and after them a number of lords of high standing followed by the queen, alone without escort, very straight and erect still, who sat down in the presence chamber upon a seat covered with red damask and cushions embroidered in gold thread, and so low was the chair that the cushions almost lay on the ground, and there was a canopy above, fixed very ornately to the ceiling.[167]

A concrete marker denoting the position of the outer gatehouse, which was the northern entrance into Nonsuch Palace. (*Author's Collection*)

It was at Nonsuch Palace, on 28 September 1599, that Robert Devereux, 2nd Earl of Essex burst into the queen's room without permission after returning from Ireland and saw her without a wig or make-up. She was angered that he had set eyes upon her without her mask of youth. This was the last time he saw Elizabeth and the following day he was interrogated by the Privy Council who questioned him on his conduct in Ireland. It concurred that his truce with the Irish was undefendable and placed him under house arrest.

Nonsuch Palace. (*Author's Collection*)

# 92

# Shakespeare Memorial, Stratford-upon-Avon

## Elizabethan Theatre

Shakespeare's plays were performed for Elizabeth in her palaces during the latter part of her reign. Elizabeth and her court enjoyed the theatre. Theatre companies would tour the country performing in towns, but it was during her reign that permanent theatres opened in London. Here the people could enjoy performances of plays written by prominent playwrights of the time, such as Ben Jonson, Christopher Marlowe and William Shakespeare. A statue in Bancroft Gardens, Stratford-upon-Avon, celebrates William Shakespeare and features well-known characters from his plays, Hamlet, Lady Macbeth, Falstaff and Henry V.

The first theatre was opened by James Burbage in 1576 in Shoreditch, and was called 'The Theatre'. The theatre's company was patronised by Robert Dudley, Earl of Leicester and was known as the 'Leicester Men'. Shakespeare's *The First Part of King Henry VI* was recorded as being performed at the Rose Theatre on 3 March 1592. The Rose Theatre was the first of several theatres built on the south bank of the River Thames in 1587. During 1594 Shakespeare and the actor Richard Burbage founded a theatre company called 'Lord Hunsdon's Men', after its patron Henry Carey, 1st Baron Hunsdon, Elizabeth's cousin. When he became Lord Chamberlain in 1597, it became known as the 'Lord Chamberlain's Men'.

The Globe Theatre was constructed on the South Bank in 1599 and during that year, Shakespeare and the Lord Chamberlain's Men began to perform on this stage. No evidence exists to suggest that Elizabeth visited the public theatres, but theatre companies were invited to perform for the queen in the royal palaces. The earliest recording of Shakespeare and his fellow players from the Lord Chamberlain's Men performing before Elizabeth was during Christmas 1594 when two plays, including Shakespeare's *The Comedy of Errors*, were performed at Greenwich Palace. Elizabeth was so enthralled by the experience that Shakespeare was invited to perform at court on several occasions. During Christmas 1597, Shakespeare returned to court for a performance of his play *Love's Labour's Lost* at Whitehall Palace.

It has been speculated that after seeing a performance of *The Second Part of King Henry IV* during 1597, Elizabeth was so delighted by the escapades of the charismatic rogue Sir John Falstaff that she requested that Shakespeare write a play where Falstaff fell in love, and wanted this to be ready to perform for a celebration on 23 April 1597. By royal command, Shakespeare wrote *The Merry Wives of Windsor* in which the penniless Falstaff arrives in Windsor and attempts to seduce Mistress Page and Mistress Ford. They were both married, but that did not prevent him from writing identical love letters to each in the forlorn hope that at least one of them would share their husband's wealth with him. The two women were close friends and showed each the letters they had received from him. Outraged by his intent, they set about planning his downfall and eventually he ends up being dumped from a laundry basket into the River Thames while disguised as the old woman of Brentford. A 1602 publication of Shakespeare's comedy that featured Falstaff confirmed that Elizabeth also saw this play. It declared that, 'As it hath been divers times Acted by the right Honorable my Lord Chamberlaines servants. Both before her Majestie and else-where.'

It is also believed that Elizabeth saw a production of Shakespeare's *Twelfth Night* performed on Twelfth Night in 1601 in the Great Hall of Whitehall Palace in honour of her guest, the young Italian nobleman Virginio Orsino, Duke of Bracciano. Shakespeare named one of the main characters Orsino after him, and it is he who opens the play with the words 'If music be the food of love, play on.'

Shakespeare wrote *The Tragedy of King Richard III* in *c.* 1592 and used the works of Tudor historians such as Holinshed and Sir Thomas More as sources, which were biased against the last Plantagenet monarch. Shakespeare's depiction of Richard III as a deformed, despotic murderer would be used by the Tudor propaganda machine to enforce the notion that the Tudors were the rightful rulers of England.

Falstaff and Shakespeare. (*Shutterstock*)

# 93

# Queen Elizabeth's Kitchen

## Protocol for Feeding the Queen

**The only example of kitchens that served food for Henry VIII and Elizabeth I can be seen at Hampton Court Palace. Elizabeth did not like the odours that emanated from this kitchen and another one had to be built in 1567, which is now the Privy Kitchen Café.**

The largest surviving sixteenth-century kitchens are at Hampton Court Palace. The kitchens were expanded when Henry VIII took possession of the palace from 1529–30 to accommodate his large entourage of 800 courtiers. These kitchens would also serve Elizabeth during her reign. The kitchens comprised fifty rooms and three cellars. One kitchen specifically cooked for the household, another was devoted primarily to preparing meals for officers of the household and the king and queen's privy kitchen cooked solely for them. Sheep, deer, oxen, pigs and wild boar were cooked in these kitchens for Elizabeth. The cooks also catered for the queen's sweet tooth, for she adored sugar to the extent that she was served with cakes, confectionery and the majority of food that she ate featured sugar. Her penchant for sugar resulted in tooth decay at an early age.

Once food had been cooked in the kitchens, there followed an elaborate process to serve the queen, which included her soldiers tasting a portion of the food before she ate it. Elizabeth was perpetually at risk from the threat of assassination so it was imperative that any food served to the queen was tested for poison. Thomas Platter observed luncheon being served to Elizabeth during a visit to Nonsuch Palace in September 1599:

When the queen had returned to her chamber, her guardsmen wearing tabards, red, if I remember, with the royal arms on their backs embroidered in gold, carried two tables into the room with trestles, and set them down where the queen had been sitting. Then another two entered each bearing a mace and bowed three times; first at their entrance, and by the door, then in the centre of the room and lastly in front of the table, and after they had laid it, they withdrew again. Soon two more guards in tabards appeared bowing with plates and other things which they laid on the table. Following them came another two bowing, and placed the carving-knives, bread and salt upon the table. Then a gentleman bearing a mace entered, together with a charming gentlewoman or lady-in-waiting, who bowed very gracefully, as described above, thrice to the empty table, at the same time a gentleman with a mace arrived with another gentleman and all four stood before the table.

Then straightaway came the queen's guardsmen with red tabards folded back, one behind the other, and if I am not mistaken, a weapon at their sides, each one bearing a single covered dish of food. They are all very tall, fine, strong men, and all similarly attired, so that I never in my life saw their like. I believe there must have been forty of them.

The kitchen at Hampton Court Palace that was used to prepare food until 1567. (*Shutterstock*)

When they had handed over the foods gentlemen removed the cover, while the lady-in-waiting served and carved a large piece off, which she gave to the guard, who had carried it in, and who was supposed to eat the portion, though they generally took it out or merely tasted a morsel.

Two of them brought wine and beer which was also poured out and tasted. And after this long table had been fully laid and served and the same obeisance and honours performed as if the queen herself had sat there, whatever dishes there were, were offered to the queen in her apartment for her to make her choice. These were sent into her and she ate of what she fancied, privily however, for she very seldom partakes before strangers, and the remainder was carried out again to the Lord's table; and the guards brought out other fresh dishes, which were served like the former, and I observed amongst them some very large joints of beef, and all kinds of game, pasties and tarts. After the third course had been thus brought in, served and removed again, and the dessert prepared and cleared off.[168]

Elizabeth usually dined in private and only ate in public on feast days.[169]

# 94

# The Essex Ring

## Robert Devereux, 2nd Earl of Essex Falls from the Queen's Favour

**The ring, known as the 'Essex Ring', was reputed to have been given by Queen Elizabeth to her ill-fated favourite, Robert Devereux, the 2nd Earl of Essex, with a promise of clemency, should he return it to her when in need.**

Born in 10 November 1565, Robert Devereux was the son of Walter Devereux and Lettice Knollys. His great-grandmother on his mother's side of the family was Mary Boleyn, the sister of Anne Boleyn, which meant that he was a cousin of Queen Elizabeth. Devereux succeeded his father as 2nd Earl of Essex when his father died in 1576. Lord Burghley became his legal guardian. Robert was educated at Trinity College, Cambridge, and graduated in 1581. His mother remarried in 1578 to Robert Dudley, Earl of Leicester, Queen Elizabeth's favourite.

Essex was a soldier who served during the Dutch Revolt, the invasion threat by the Spanish Armada and the raid on Cádiz in 1596. Devereux married the widow of Sir Philip Sidney, Frances Walsingham, who was the daughter of Sir Francis Walsingham, Elizabeth's spymaster. Devereux was also involved with espionage and discovered that the queen's physician, Dr Lopez, was plotting to poison Elizabeth in 1594.

When Robert Dudley died in 1588, Essex succeeded him as Master of the Horse. He became a favourite of Elizabeth and an influential figure at court and within the Privy Council. He cemented his position at court when he led a successful assault upon the Spanish port at Cádiz during 30 June–15 July 1596. When he returned home, it is believed that Elizabeth gave Essex this ring and told him to return it to her if he found himself in difficulties and she would come to his aid.

The relationship deteriorated in late June/early July 1598 when Essex argued with Elizabeth and she rebuked him for turning his back on her and struck him on the ear. He reacted by turning and drawing his sabre, when the Earl of Nottingham intervened and dissolved the situation.

In 1599, in his role as Governor General of Ireland, he was sent to Ireland to supress the rebels, but he realised that he did not have sufficient resources to defeat them and instead negotiated a truce. Despite being banished by Elizabeth from returning to England for his dereliction of duty in Ireland, he arrived unannounced at Nonsuch Palace and saw her with no wig, gown or make-up on 28 September 1599. Following this Essex was interrogated by the Privy Council and placed under house arrest. He was tried and acquitted, but Essex lost the queen's favour, together with his wealth and influence. Essex began to plot against Elizabeth and gathered support. On 6 February 1601, representatives of Essex called at The Globe Theatre and asked the Lord Chamberlain's Men, with whom Shakespeare was associated, to perform his play *The Tragedy of King Richard II*. They declined on the grounds that it would not be popular, but after being offered 40 shillings more than their usual wage the company agreed to perform the play. Essex also requested that they reinsert the scene where Richard II was deposed to demonstrate how easy it was to remove a king. The actors were unaware that this was part of a plot to depose

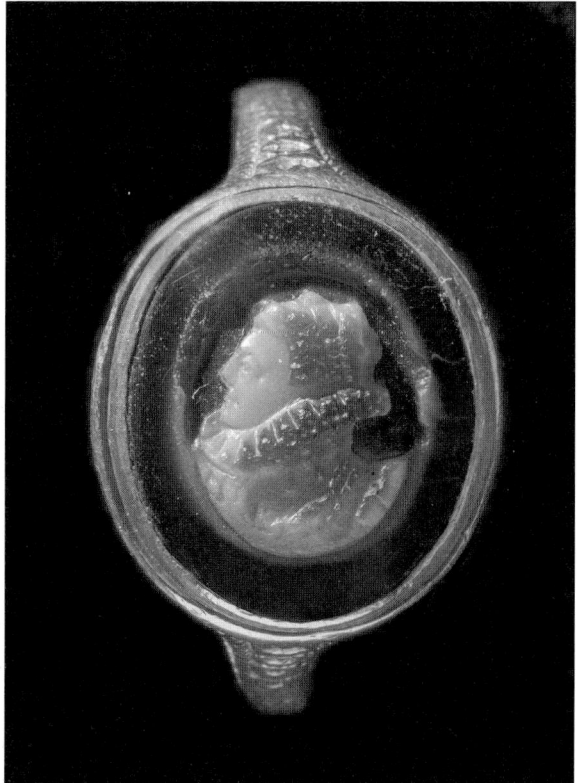

The Essex Ring. (*Copyright Dean and Chapter of Westminster*)

Elizabeth. On 7 February, they performed the play that depicted the usurpation of Richard II, but it did not stir the crowd to revolt. On 8 February 1601, Essex and 200 fellow conspirators tried to enter the City of London to seek an audience with the queen. They were repelled by a blockade at Ludgate and he returned to his home, Essex House in the Strand, where four privy councillors were held hostage. When Robert Cecil proclaimed Essex a traitor, some of the conspirators became unnerved and released the hostages without Essex's consent. They were besieged by men led by Lord Cobham and Sir Walter Raleigh. Essex was compelled to surrender. On 19 February 1601, Essex was tried for treason, for attempting to usurp and assassinate the queen, and was found guilty seven days later and condemned to death by decapitation. The actors belonging to the Lord Chamberlain's Men were questioned, but their innocence was accepted and they were exonerated.

While under the sentence of death, Essex attempted to send this ring to the queen, in a last-ditch attempt to receive mercy, but the ring fell into the hands of his adversaries and never reached Elizabeth.

After Essex's execution the ring was given to his widow and passed through the family until it was sold by the Thynne family in 1911. The gold ring features the image of Queen Elizabeth wearing an auburn wig. The ring was originally fixed on a mount on the side of Elizabeth's tomb but was later displayed in Westminster Abbey.

# 95

# Block and Axe

---

## The Execution of Robert Devereux, 2nd Earl of Essex

**Prisoners of noble birth who were condemned as traitors were executed using an axe. Although this block was used for the last public beheading at Tower Hill on 9 April 1747, to execute Simon Fraser, Lord Lovat, it is typical of those used for executions during the Tudor period and in particular the one used to execute Devereux during Elizabeth's reign.**

The axe is believed to have originated in the sixteenth century and may have been used during high-profile executions. It weighs 3.2kg (7lb) and as it was wielded to strike a victim's neck, the force of the swing was absorbed by the block, which weighed 56.7kg (125lb). Beheading was believed to be a swift and humane punishment, which was reserved for the nobility and distinguished persons of stature. It was considered to be an honourable and merciful way to die.

The execution would take place on a wooden scaffold covered with straw, which soaked up the blood. The top of the block was carved with a curve on both sides, to accommodate the victim's head and chest and to ensure that the head was placed comfortably on the block with the neck exposed. A minister was present on the scaffold to provide spiritual comfort to the condemned prisoner if required. The prisoner was expected to pay the executioner and offer forgiveness for what he was about to do. The prisoner was allowed to address those who observed the execution before placing their neck upon the block. A skilled executioner with a sharpened axe would conduct the beheading swiftly within seconds. If the executioner was not experienced, had a blunt axe or the prisoner moved, then it would take several strikes and some minutes to detach the head from the body, as was the case with the execution of Thomas Cromwell.

Once the decapitation was complete, the executioner displayed the severed head to the watching crowd, shouting 'behold the head of a traitor!'. The purpose was not to show the spectators the head, but to allow the head to see the crowd and its own decapitated body. Despite the head being severed, the brain still functions for a further 8 seconds until the oxygen supply is exhausted, when the head loses consciousness and dies. On some occasions, the features on the decapitated head moved.

At 1 am on 25 February 1601, the Lieutenant of the Tower of London informed Essex that he was to be executed that day. He had previously written to the queen requesting that he die privately within the confines of the Tower of London, and she granted her former favourite that wish. He spent the remainder of the early morning at prayer with Chaplain Ashton. Essex was taken from his cell between 7 and 8 am and led to Tower Green within the Tower of London, where a scaffold had been erected and the executioner, Thomas Derrick, was waiting for the condemned prisoner. There were approximately a hundred spectators present including alderman from the City of London and several knights amongst whom

Block and axe. (*Author's Collection*)

were Sir Walter Raleigh, Lord Thomas Howard and the Earl of Cumberland. Essex addressed the crowd and acknowledged the sins of his past life, especially towards the queen. An eyewitness reported that Essex:

> … putting off his gown, he kneeled down on the straw before the block, with hands clasped and eyes raised towards heaven and prayed unpremeditatedly … he asked the executioner how to fit himself to the block, and gave him his forgiveness saying 'Thou art the minister of justice; spare not, nor be not afraid.' Then he undressed, commended his spirit to God, and begged those present to do the same, when his arms were stretched out, saying 'Lord, into thy hands I commit my spirit, Lord Jesus receive my soul.' The executioner had to strike three times, but neither arms, body, nor head stirred; then he lifted up the head, saying 'God save the queen.' His eyes were still fixed to heaven.[170]

Essex was the last person to be beheaded within the Tower of London.

# 96

# Gatehouse, Richmond Palace

## Elizabeth's Final Days

All that remains of Richmond Palace, which was built along the southern bank of the River Thames, is the outer gateway and a small part of the house known as the Old Palace which is on the western perimeter of Richmond Green. This gatehouse formed the principal access to Richmond Palace on the landward side. It comprised a large opening which once held a pair of sizeable doors (the surviving hinge pins still exist) and a now-blocked entrance to the right of the gatehouse. The arms of Elizabeth's grandfather, Henry VII, restored in 1976, are carved above the entrance. Confirming the significance of this palace for the Tudor dynasty, a plaque on the wall states 'Richmond Palace. Residence of King Henry VII, King Henry VIII, Queen Elizabeth I'.

Richmond had been used as a royal residence since Henry I when there was a manor house on this site. Edward III transformed this building into the Palace of Shene, and he died here in 1377. When Anne, the wife of his successor, Richard II, died here in 1394, the king, being so distraught in his bereavement, ordered the destruction of the palace. Henry V started construction of a new palace, which was completed by Henry VI. This palace became a favourite residence of Henry VII but was destroyed in a fire during Christmas 1497. The king immediately ordered the construction of another palace on the same site and it took four years to build. The new palace was built of red brick, with pinnacles and turrets topped with domes with gold and silver weathervanes mounted on them. The palace featured courtyards and galleries that were inspired by the Burgundian court. A plumbing system was installed that piped spring water into the palace. When construction was completed, Henry VII named it the Palace of Richmond, which was the earldom held by him before his accession to the throne.

Henry VII died at Richmond Palace in 1509 and Henry VIII made use of this residence during his early reign and spent his first Christmas as king at the palace.

The Christmas feast was followed by jousting which took place outside these gates on the site of Richmond Green on 12 January 1510. Henry VIII had always been fascinated by jousting, but he was forbidden to participate by his father. After the passing of his father, Henry could pursue that interest and it was during this tournament that he took part in his first joust. Later during his reign Henry became disinterested with Richmond Palace and it became a residence for Princess Mary. The palace was later given by Henry VIII to Anne of Cleves on 24 June 1540, as part of their divorce settlement, but she later returned it to Edward VI.

Richmond Palace became a favourite residence for Elizabeth because the compactness of the building made it warm inside, and she would spend the winter months there. She also enjoyed hunting in the vicinity. In 1596, Sir John Harington, Elizabeth's godson, invented a toilet water closet and installed one in Richmond Palace for the queen to use. It contained most of the basic features of conveniences that we use today and Elizabeth appreciated it because it was hygienic and the waste flowed away instead of stagnating in a pit. However, Harington's invention was not recognised by Tudor society and not widely taken up until the 1730s.

Elizabeth was suffering with a cold infection during January 1603. On the advice of John Dee, her long-serving astrologer, Elizabeth left Whitehall on 14 January

The outer gateway, Richmond Palace. (*Author's Collection*)

Richmond Palace drawn by Wenceslaus Hollar in 1638.

Richmond Palace drawn by Wenceslaus Hollar in 1638. (*Author's Collection*)

to rest at Richmond Palace. Elizabeth recovered; however, she fell ill with similar symptoms on 28 February. She was aged 69, her health was failing and two weeks later her Privy Council was summoned. Courtiers noted that during her final days Elizabeth devoted more time to prayer and no doubt she was thinking about the future, her successor and her own mortality. Elizabeth declared on her deathbed, 'My throne was a Throne of Kings, that I would not have any mean person succeed me. I will that a king succeed me: and who that should be but my nearest kinsman, the king of the Scots? That I do, neither doth my mind at all wander from him.'[171]

On 24 March 1603 Elizabeth died at Richmond Palace.

# 97

# Painting, *The Death of Elizabeth I*

## The Days Following the Queen's Death

**This depiction of the final hours of Elizabeth I was painted by the French artist Paul Delaroche in 1828.**

Elizabeth began to suffer from swollen glands in her throat and lost her appetite for food during February 1603. Noblemen within the court were writing to King James VI of Scotland in an effort to curry favour with the heir to Elizabeth's throne. Amongst these was her cousin, Sir Robert Carey, who kept James updated on Elizabeth's condition and arranged to travel to Edinburgh to inform him once the queen had died. Courtiers noticed that:

> ... she gave herself over wholly to melancholy, and seemed to be much troubled with a peculiar grief for some reason ... Hereupon she looked upon herself as a miserable, forlorn woman, and her grief, and indignation extorted from her such speeches as these: *They have yoaked my neck, I have none whom I can trust; My condition is strangely turned upside down.*[172]

The Irish Rebellion, the betrayal and execution of Robert Devereux, Earl of Essex and the loss of close confidantes such as her cousin, Catherine Howard, Countess of Nottingham, who had died on 24 February 1603, would have caused the queen anxiety. She may also have reflected upon her life and may have had regrets at not finding a husband and not producing an heir that would continue the Tudor dynasty and might have felt remorse for her hand in the death of her cousin, Mary, Queen of Scots.

Sir Robert Carey recalled that, 'I found the queen ill-disposed, and she kept her inner lodging ... I found her in one of her withdrawing chambers, sitting low upon her cushions.'[173] A dozen physicians were in attendance but they could not persuade her to go to bed and she remained on those cushions.

This painting depicts the death of Elizabeth I by the French artist Paul Delaroche in 1828. (*Louvre Museum, Public Domain*)

Elizabeth advised the Privy Council that it was her wish that King James VI of Scotland succeed her after her demise. Carey recalled that, 'the queen grew worse and worse ... on Wednesday the twenty-third of March she grew speechless. That afternoon, by signs, she called for her Council, and by putting her hand to her head, when the King of Scots was named to succeed her, they all knew he was the man she desired should reign after her.'[174] Naming her successor before her death ensured that there was a peaceful transition from England's last Tudor sovereign to the first Stuart king.

At about 6 pm on 23 March, Elizabeth summoned her chaplains and John Whitgift, Archbishop of Canterbury and they provided spiritual solace and comfort through prayer. During her final hours she was attended by her ladies. On 24 March 1603 between 1 and 2 o'clock in the morning, Elizabeth died and her reign which had lasted forty-four years and four months came to a conclusion. She had set a record at that time for being the longest serving English sovereign, as William Camden remarked 'to which no king of England had ever attained before'.[175]

The corpse of Elizabeth was embalmed against her wishes, placed in a coffin and remained at Richmond Palace for several days. Sir Robert Cecil gave instructions to her surgeon to conduct an autopsy, which was carried out despite attempts by her ladies-in-waiting to prevent this. It was thought that they resisted a post-mortem to maintain the queen's reputation as a virgin. Blood poisoning, cancer, pneumonia and streptococcus (an infection of the tonsils) were cited as reasons for death, although the cause was never ascertained. Elizabeth's remains were transferred to a barge, draped in black and transported along the River Thames to Whitehall Palace where her body lay in state in one of the chambers for three weeks. Her Maid of Honour, Lady Elizabeth Southwell, wrote that:

> … now the queen's body being cered up, was brought by water to Whitehall, where being watched every night by six several ladies, myself that night watching as one of them, and being all in our places about the corpse, which was fast nailed up in a board coffin, with leaves of lead covered with velvet, her body burst with such a crack that it splitted the wood, lead and cere-cloth, wherefore upon, the next day, she was fain to be new trimmed up.[176]

Southwell was describing the natural explosion of gas that had accumulated within the corpse of the queen.

# 98

# Queen Elizabeth's Locket Ring

## In Memory of Anne Boleyn?

**Elizabeth carried her mother's memory throughout her life with this ring which was removed from her finger after her death.**

William Camden served Elizabeth in the role of Clarenceux King of Arms and would write the first biography of Elizabeth after her death. He heard from courtiers that she:

> … commanded that Ring where with she had been as it were joined in marriage to her kingdom at her inauguration, and had, never since been taken off, to be filed off from her finger, because it was so grown into the flesh, that it could not be drawn off. Which was taken as a sad omen, as if it portended that her marriage with kingdom, contracted by that Ring, would now be dissolved.[177]

Elizabeth was referring to the coronation ring and it was removed from her finger within a week of her death. Another ring was also removed from her hand and this ring is known as 'the Chequers Ring'. Made from mother-of-pearl, it has rubies set in the band and six diamonds form the letter 'E' over a blue enamel letter 'R', signifying Elizabeth Regina. The ring opens to reveal an image of Elizabeth and an image of a woman dressed in clothes dating from the reign of Henry VIII. Some historians believe that the other woman is Anne Boleyn and that this is evidence that Elizabeth acknowledged her mother, despite her fall from her father's favour and execution in 1536. Other theories suggest that the unknown woman could be Katherine Parr, her step-mother, with whom she shared a close, warm relationship. However, although Elizabeth was aged 2 years and 8 months when Anne Boleyn was executed and her memories of her relationship with her mother were vague, it might have served as remembrance of her mother out of respect and as a warning that making the wrong political decisions could have fatally detrimental consequences. Elizabeth never made her feelings about the execution of her mother publicly known, but this ring could be seen as evidence that she never forgot her. Elizabeth indirectly expressed her belief that her mother was innocent of the charges brought against her by elevating the son of Sir Henry Norris to a peerage and looking after his family. Norris was one of the courtiers accused of committing adultery with Anne and was executed as a consequence. Elizabeth visited Norris's son several times at his home at Rycot.

The rear of the oval bezel features an enamelled phoenix with coronet and Elizabeth may have received it as a gift from Edward Seymour, Earl of Hertford, because they both shared the phoenix as an emblem. It is thought that the ring was produced *c.* 1575 because the image of Elizabeth resembles her image in the Phoenix Badge produced at about the same time.

The ring was presented to Elizabeth's successor, James VI of Scotland, when he was informed of her death and that he was proclaimed James I of England. The ring is housed at Chequers, the country residence of the British Prime Minister in Buckinghamshire.

Queen Elizabeth's locket ring.
(*Heritage Image Partnership Ltd/ Alamy*)

# 99

# Engraving of Funeral Procession of Elizabeth I

## The Queen's Final Journey

**This is a detail of an engraving with etching by J. Basire, 1791, after a drawing by William Camden. It shows the funeral procession of Elizabeth I with the Gentlemen Pensioners, the queen's personal bodyguard, carrying flags and banners above the cortège.**

King James I refrained from entering London until the funeral of Queen Elizabeth. The funeral took place on 28 April 1603 and the procession started its journey to Westminster Abbey at Whitehall Palace.

Elizabeth's coffin was covered with purple velvet, on which lay a life-sized wooden effigy of the deceased queen in the image of Gloriana, wearing her crown and crimson parliamentary robes and holding her sceptre. The coffin and effigy were placed on a chariot which was pulled by four horses draped in black. Four knights walked beside the chariot carrying a canopy. The canopy was richly decorated with heraldic symbols of England, Wales and Ireland, the Tudor Rose and the arms of Elizabeth with her motto '*Semper Eadem*', meaning 'always the same'. The coffin was followed by noblemen, the members of the Privy Council and representatives of all ranks of society. William Camden was appointed Clarenceux King of Arms and would be among the mourners that followed Elizabeth's cortège to Westminster Abbey and would write the first biography of the queen after her death. The queen's household also formed part of the procession, including ladies of the court, kitchen staff and stable workers. Tens of thousands of Londoners lined the route of the funeral procession and many were genuinely upset at the death of Elizabeth. The effigy of the deceased queen looked lifelike and affected all those who saw it. John Stow wrote that:

> ... the city of Westminster was surcharged with multitudes of all sorts of people in their streets, houses, windows, leads and gutters that came to see

the obsequie; and when they held the statue or picture lying upon the coffin set forth in royal robes, having a crown upon her head thereof, and a ball and sceptre in either hand; there was a general sighing, groaning and weeping, as the like hath not been seen or known in the memory of man, neither doth any history mention any people, any time, or state to make like lamentation for the death of their sovereign.[178]

The funeral procession of Queen Elizabeth I showing the Gentlemen Pensioners carrying flags and banners. Detail of an engraving with etching by J. Basire, 1791, after a drawing by William Camden. (*Wellcome Collection*)

# 100

# Tomb of Elizabeth I

## Elizabeth is Buried with her Sister Mary

**The remains of Elizabeth I lie in north aisle of the Lady Chapel within Westminster Abbey alongside the tombs of other members of the Tudor dynasty, including her great-grandmother, Lady Margaret Beaufort, her grandparents, Henry VII and Elizabeth of York, her brother, Edward VI, and her sister, Mary I.**

Elizabeth was initially interred beneath the main altar of the Lady Chapel at Westminster Abbey, in the vault alongside her grandparents, Henry VII and Elizabeth of York. Despite her ordering the execution of his mother, Mary, Queen of Scots, James I commissioned the design and building of a tomb for Elizabeth.

Elizabeth's large white marble tomb cost £1,485 (approximately equivalent to £205,000 in 2017) and reposes beneath a regal canopy which is supported by four lions. The head of the queen rests upon two tasselled and embroidered cushions. It was sculptured by the Flemish sculptor Maximilian Colt and painted by Flemish artist Jan de Critz. Colt sculptured the effigy of Elizabeth based on images of her in her elder years. The tomb was completed in 1606 and Elizabeth's remains were transferred to the north aisle in Westminster Abbey below the effigy and on top of the coffin of her step-sister, Mary I. Elizabeth was the last sovereign to have an effigy surmounted above her tomb until the death of Queen Victoria in 1901 when a marble effigy was placed upon her tomb in the Royal Mausoleum at Frogmore. Jan de Critz's paint has disappeared from the effigy and it is now just white marble, however, a drawing was found in Germany dated 1618–20 which shows the colour used upon the effigy, the ermine-lined crimson robe, the orb painted blue and the face upon the effigy flesh-coloured which made it lifelike. The crown, cross on the orb and the sceptre held by the queen were stolen and had to be replaced, together with the railings around the tomb.

The base of the memorial remembers both Elizabeth and Mary with the words, 'Partners in throne and grave, here we sleep Elizabeth and Mary, sisters in [the] hope of the Resurrection'. Just to the west of the tomb there is a plaque dedicated to the martyrs of the reformation, which was unveiled in 1977:

NEAR THE TOMB OF MARY AND ELIZABETH REMEMBER BEFORE GOD ALL THOSE WHO DIVIDED AT THE REFORMATION BY DIFFERENT CONVICTIONS LAID DOWN THEIR LIVES FOR CHRIST AND CONSCIENCE' SAKE.

Mary, Queen of Scots was initially buried on 1 August 1587 in Peterborough Cathedral. On 28 September 1612, James I ordered that the remains of Mary, Queen of Scots be transferred from Peterborough Cathedral to Westminster Abbey and decreed that his mother's tomb should be more elaborate than the tomb of Elizabeth. His mother's remains were interred in a tomb in the south aisle of the Lady Chapel and this is slightly taller in stature than Elizabeth's tomb. In life Elizabeth I, Mary I and Mary, Queen of Scots were divided by their religious beliefs, but in death they were joined in their internments within the Lady Chapel at Westminster Abbey. The tomb of Elizabeth I serves as a monument to the last Tudor monarch and a symbol of her legacy.

The tomb of Elizabeth I in the Lady Chapel within Westminster Abbey. (*Copyright Dean and Chapter of Westminster*)

# Notes

1. James Gairdner, *Letters and Papers, Foreign and Domestic, Henry VIII, Volume 11* (London: 1888), p. 90.
2. It was during this voyage that after passing Resolution Island, he turned north-west and discovered what is now known as the Frobisher Strait. Anonymous, *Colburn's United Services Magazine, Naval & Military Journal, Part II* (London: 1875), p. 437.
3. Clare Williams, *Thomas Platter's Travels 1599* (London: Jonathan Cape, 1937), p. 225.
4. Mandell Creighton, *Queen Elizabeth* (London: Longmans Green & Co., 1901), p. 39.
5. Gairdner, *Letters and Papers, Foreign and Domestic, Henry VIII, Volume 11*, p. 204.
6. Robert Lemon, *Calendar of State Papers, Elizabeth, 1581–1590* (London: Longmans, 1865), p. 304.
7. Gairdner, *Letters and Papers, Foreign and Domestic, Henry VIII, Volume 11*, p. 90.
8. Victor von Klarwill, *Queen Elizabeth and Some Foreigners* (London: Bodley Head, 1928), pp. 322–3.
9. MS Cherry 36, fol. 2r, Bodleian Library, University of Oxford.
10. R.H. Brodie and James Gairdner (eds), *Letters and Papers, Foreign and Domestic, Henry VIII, Volume 19 Part 2, August–December 1544* (London: 1905), p. 466.
11. Creighton, *Queen Elizabeth*, pp. 38–9.
12. Leah S. Marcus, Janel Mueller and Mary Beth Rose (eds), *Elizabeth I, Collected Works* (Chicago: University of Chicago Press, 2000), p. 9 and British Library: MS Royal 7 D.X.
13. Marcus, Mueller and Rose (eds), *Elizabeth I, Collected Works*, p. 9.
14. ibid., p. 10.
15. Creighton, *Queen Elizabeth*, p. 38.
16. John Nichols, *The Progresses and Public Processions of Queen Elizabeth, Volume 1* (London: 1823), p. 28.

17. *Letters and Papers, Foreign and Domestic, Henry VIII, Volume 21, Part 2, 1546–7* (London: His Majesty's Stationery Office, 1910), p. 320.

18. ibid.

19. Charles Wriothesley, *The Chronicle of England During the Reign of the Tudors, Volume 1* (Camden Society, 1875), p. 36.

20. *Letters and Papers, Foreign and Domestic, Henry VIII, Volume 21, Part 2, 1546–7*, p. 230.

21. Tracy Borman, *The Private Lives of the Tudors* (London: Hodder & Stoughton, 2016), p. 227.

22. Samuel Haynes, *A Collection of State Papers relating to Affairs in the Reigns of King Henry VIII, King Edward VI, Queen Mary and Queen Elizabeth from the year 1542 to 1570* (London: Bowyer, 1740), p. 99.

23. Marcus, Mueller and Rose (eds), *Elizabeth I, Collected Works*, p. 10 and British Library: MS Royal 7 D.X.). p. 20.

24. Fredrick Chamberlin, *The Private Character of Queen Elizabeth* (New York: Dodd, Mead & Company, 1922), p. 9 and British Library, MS Cotton Otho C.X., fol. 236v, p. 20.

25. Haynes, *A Collection of State Papers*, p. 103.

26. Gladys E. Locke, *Queen Elizabeth: Various Scenes and Events in the Life of Her Majesty* (Boston: Sherman French & Company, 1913), p. 18.

27. Marcus, Mueller and Rose (eds), *Elizabeth I, Collected Works*, p. 10.

28. Letter written by Elizabeth, the future Queen Elizabeth I, to her brother, King Edward VI of England, 21 April 1552. Houghton Library, Harvard University, MS Typ 686.

29. Royall Tyler (ed.), *Calendar of State Papers, Spain, Volume 12, 1554* (London: 1949), pp. 164–80.

30. Williams, *Thomas Platter's Travels*, p. 155.

31. Paul Hentzner, *A Journey into England in the Year MDXCVIII* (London: 1757), p. 5.

32. Williams, *Thomas Platter's Travels*, p. 155.

33. John Stow, *Annals of England* (London: 1603), p. 1259.

34. Creighton, *Queen Elizabeth*, pp. 29–30.

35. John Bailey, *History and Antiquities of the Tower of London* (London: Jennings & Chapman, 1830), p. 448.

36. ibid., pp. 448–9.

37. Tyler (ed.), *Calendar of State Papers, Spain, Volume 12, 1554*, pp. 206–15.

38. Agnes Strickland, *Memoirs of Elizabeth* (Philadelphia: Blanchard & Lea, 1853), p. 76.

39. Bailey, *History and Antiquities of the Tower of London*, p. 428.

40. John Foxe, *Foxe's Book of Martyrs* (London: 1856), p. 926.

41. Creighton, *Queen Elizabeth*, pp. 34–5.

42. ibid., pp. 35–6.

43. Williams, *Thomas Platter's Travels*, p. 203.

44. Creighton, *Queen Elizabeth*, p. 41.

45. Strickland, *Memoirs of Elizabeth*, p. 103.

46. Nichols, *The Progresses and Public Processions of Queen Elizabeth, Volume 1*, p. 16.

47. The National Archives: Elizabeth's first speech, Hatfield, 20 November 1558 (SP12/1 f. 12).

48. Henry Machyn, *The diary of Henry Machyn, citizen and merchant-tailor of London, from A. D. 1550 to A. D. 1563* (London: Camden Society, 1848), p. 178.

49. Sir John Hayward, *Annals of the First Four Years of the Reign of Queen Elizabeth* (London: John Bowyer Nichols and Son, 1840), p. 10.

50. ibid.

51. G. Cavendish Bentinck and Rawden Brown, *Calendar of State Papers, Venice. Volume 7, 1558–80* (London: 1890), pp. 10–24.

52. Bentinck and Brown, *Calendar of State Papers, Venice*, pp. 10–24.

53. Hayward, *Annals*, pp. 17–18.

54. Bentinck and Brown, *Calendar of State Papers, Venice*, pp. 10–24.

55. ibid.

56. ibid.

57. Creighton, *Queen Elizabeth*, p. 52.

58. Martin A.S. Hume (ed.), *Calendar of State Papers, Spain (Simancas), Volume 1, 1558–1567* (London: Eyre & Spottiswoode for HMSO, London, 1892), pp. 21–6.

59. Creighton, *Queen Elizabeth*, p. 53.

60. William Camden, *The history of the most renowned and victorious Princess Elizabeth, the late queen of England* (London: 1675), p. 29.

61. Creighton, *Queen Elizabeth*, p. 57.

62. Klarwill, *Queen Elizabeth and Some Foreigners*, p. 314.

63. Mary Anne Everett Green, *Calendar of State Papers, Domestic Series, Elizabeth, 1595–97* (London: HMSO, 1869), p. 310.

64. ibid., p. 305.

65. Robert Lemon, *Calendar of State Papers, Edward VI, Mary, Elizabeth 1547–80* (London: Longmans, 1856), p. 120.

66. Joseph Stevenson (ed.), *Calendar of State Papers Foreign: Elizabeth, Volume 3, 1560–1561* (London: 1865), p. 327.

67. Joseph Stevenson (ed.), *Calendar of State Papers Foreign: Elizabeth, Volume 2, 1559–1560* (London: 1865), pp. 543–71.

68. ibid.

69. Stevenson (ed.), *Calendar of State Papers Foreign: Elizabeth, Volume 3, 1560–1561*, pp. 24–42.

70. ibid.

71. Klarwill, *Queen Elizabeth and Some Foreigners*, p. 113.

72. Lemon, *Calendar of State Papers, Edward VI, Mary, Elizabeth 1547–80*, p. 159.

73. ibid., p. 160.

74. ibid., p. 161.

75. ibid., p. 160.

76. Hume (ed.), *Calendar of State Papers, Spain (Simancas), Volume 1*, pp. 261–5.

77. Christopher Hibbert, *The Virgin Queen: Elizabeth I, Genius of the Golden Age* (London: Addison-Wesley Publishing Company, 1991), p. 86.

78. Hume (ed.), *Calendar of State Papers, Spain (Simancas), Volume 1*, pp. 261–5.

79. ibid.

80. ibid.

81. ibid.

82. Neville Williams, *Royal Homes of Great Britain from Medieval to Modern Times* (London: Lutterworth Press, 1971), p. 25.

83. Strickland, *Memoirs of Elizabeth*, p. 147.

84. Nichols, *The Progresses and Public Processions of Queen Elizabeth, Volume 1*, p. 162.

85. ibid.

86. Martin A.S. Hume (ed.), *Calendar of State Papers, Spain (Simancas), Volume 2, 1568–1579* (London: Eyre & Spottiswoode for HMSO, 1894), p. 211.

87. ibid., p. 233.

88. Camden, *The history of the most renowned and victorious Princess Elizabeth*, p. 146.

89. ibid., p. 147.

90. Hume (ed.), *Calendar of State Papers, Spain (Simancas), Volume 2, 1568–1579*, p. 267.

91. Williams, *Thomas Platter's Travels*, p. 156.

92. G.B. Harrison and R.A. Jones (eds), *De Maisse: a journal of all that was accomplished by Monsieur de Maisse ambassador in England from King Henri IV to Queen Elizabeth, anno domini 1597* (London: Bloomsbury, 1931), p. 2.

93. British Library: MS Cotton Caligula C.III, fol. 2421.

94. William Cecil, *Cecil Papers in Hatfield House: 1306–1571* (London: HMSO, 1883).

95. ibid.

96. Camden, *The history of the most renowned and victorious Princess Elizabeth*, pp. 177–8.

97. ibid., p. 178.

98. ibid.

99. John Nichols, *The Progresses and Public Processions of Queen Elizabeth, Volume 2* (London: 1823), p. 55.

100. Thomas Birch, *Memoirs of the Reign of Queen Elizabeth Volume 1* (London: A. Miller, 1754), p. 22.

101. Nichols, *The Progresses and Public Processions of Queen Elizabeth, Volume 1*, p. 345.

102. ibid., pp. 345–6.

103. Sir Walter Besant, *London in the times of the Tudors* (London: Adam & Charles Black, 1904), p. 176.

104. ibid., p. 81.

105. Sir James Mackintosh, MP, *History of England, Volume III* (London: Longman, 1832), p. 170.

106. Harrison and Jones (eds), *De Maisse*, p. 14.

107. Besant, *London in the times of the Tudors*, p. 106.

108. Williams, *Thomas Platter's Travels 1599*, pp. 225–6.

109. James Halliwell (ed.), *Private Diary of Dr John Dee* (London: Camden Society, 1842), pp. 8–9.

110. Lemon, *Calendar of State Papers, Edward VI, Mary, Elizabeth 1547–80*, p. 682.

111. Martin A.S. Hume (ed.), *Calendar of Letters & State Papers relating to English Affairs, Elizabeth 1580–1586, Archives of Simancas, Volume III* (London: Eyre & Spottiswoode for HMSO, 1896), p. 75.

112. ibid., p. 95.

113. Camden, *The history of the most renowned and victorious Princess Elizabeth*, p. 658.

114. Harrison and Jones (eds), *De Maisse*, p. 27.

115. Hentzner, *A Journey into England*, p. 31.

116. Hume (ed.), *Calendar of Letters & State Papers relating to English Affairs*, p. 501.

117. Hentzner, *A Journey into England*, pp. 49–50.

118. Klarwill, *Queen Elizabeth and Some Foreigners*, pp. 338–9.

119. Mary Ann Everett Green, *Calendar of State Papers, Elizabeth I and James I, Addenda 1580–1625* (London: Longmans, 1872), p. 125.

120. David Starkey, *Elizabeth* (London: Chatto & Windus, 2003), p. 49.

121. The National Archives, SP 12/193/54: The Babington Cipher, 1586.

122. Nichols, *The Progresses and Public Processions of Queen Elizabeth, Volume 2*, p. 501.
123. ibid.
124. ibid.
125. ibid., pp. 507–8.
126. John Nichols, *The Progresses and Public Processions of Queen Elizabeth, Volume 3* (London: 1823), p. 603.
127. Harrison and Jones (eds), *De Maisse*, p. 2.
128. National Maritime Museum, *Armada* (London: published by Penguin Books, 1988), p. 31.
129. Martin A.S. Hume (ed.), *Calendar of State Papers, Spain (Simancas), Volume 4, 1587–1603* (London: Eyre & Spottiswoode for HMSO, 1899), p. 363.
130. National Maritime Museum, *Armada*, p. 31.
131. Strickland, *Memoirs of Elizabeth*, p. 429.
132. John Barrow, *The Life, Voyages and Expeditions of Sir Francis Drake* (London: John Murray, 1844), p. 113.
133. National Maritime Museum, *Armada*, pp. 156–8.
134. Robert Lemon, *Calendar of State Papers, Domestic Series, Elizabeth, 1581–1590* (London: Longman, 1865), p. 510.
135. Hume (ed.), *Calendar of State Papers, Spain (Simancas), Volume 2*, p. 205.
136. Lemon, *Calendar of State Papers, Domestic Series, Elizabeth, 1581–1590*, p. 507.
137. ibid., p. 248.
138. ibid., p. 363.
139. ibid., p. 339.
140. Hume (ed.), *Calendar of State Papers, Spain (Simancas), Volume 4*, p. 395.
141. Lemon, *Calendar of State Papers, Domestic Series, Elizabeth, 1581–1590*, p. 615.
142. G.H. Powell, *The Memoirs of Robert Carey, Earl of Monmouth* (London: Alexander Morin Ltd, 1905), p. 9.
143. Lemon, *Calendar of State Papers, Domestic Series, Elizabeth, 1581–1590*, p. 517.
144. Anonymous, *Colburn's United Services Magazine, Naval & Military Journal, Part II*, p. 437.
145. Besant, *London in the times of the Tudors*, p. 77.
146. Lemon, *Calendar of State Papers, Domestic Series, Elizabeth, 1581–1590*, p. 509.
147. Stow, *Annals of England*, p. 1259.
148. Nichols, *The Progresses and Public Processions of Queen Elizabeth, Volume 2*, p. 536.
149. Strickland, *Memoirs of Elizabeth*, p. 440.
150. Lemon, *Calendar of State Papers, Domestic Series, Elizabeth, 1581–1590*, p. 514.

151. The National Archives: Robert Dudley, Earl of Leicester to Elizabeth, 29 August 1588 (SP 12/215 f.114).

152. Hume (ed.), *Calendar of State Papers, Spain (Simancas), Volume 4*, p. 431.

153. Lemon, *Calendar of State Papers, Domestic Series, Elizabeth, 1581–1590*, p. 543.

154. ibid.

155. Hugh Allingham and Robert Crawford, *Captain Cuéllar's Adventures in Connaught & Ulster A.D. 1588* (London: Elliott Stock, 1897), p. 48.

156. Allingham and Crawford, *Captain Cuéllar's Adventures in Connaught & Ulster A.D. 1588*, pp. 49–50.

157. Lemon, *Calendar of State Papers, Domestic Series, Elizabeth, 1581–1590*, p. 529.

158. ibid., p. 534.

159. ibid.

160. ibid., p. 536.

161. Besant, *London in the times of the Tudors*, p. 158.

162. Stow, *Annals of England*, p. 1260.

163. Klarwill, *Queen Elizabeth and Some Foreigners*, pp. 330–2.

164. Hume (ed.), *Calendar of State Papers, Spain (Simancas), Volume 4*, p. 419.

165. Hentzner, *A Journey into England*, p. 48.

166. Williams, *Thomas Platter's Travels*, pp. 190–2.

167. ibid., pp. 190–2.

168. ibid., pp. 194–5.

169. Klarwill, *Queen Elizabeth and Some Foreigners*, p. 334.

170. Mary Anne Everett Green, *Calendar of State Papers, Domestic Series, Elizabeth, 1598–1601* (London: 1869), pp. 595–6.

171. Camden, *The history of the most renowned and victorious Princess Elizabeth*, pp. 660–1.

172. ibid., p. 658.

173. Nichols, *The Progresses and Public Processions of Queen Elizabeth, Volume 3*, p. 603.

174. ibid., p. 605.

175. Camden, *The history of the most renowned and victorious Princess Elizabeth*, p. 661.

176. Strickland, *Memoirs of Elizabeth*, p. 577.

177. Camden, *The history of the most renowned and victorious Princess Elizabeth*, p. 659.

178. Nichols, *The Progresses and Public Processions of Queen Elizabeth, Volume 3*, p. 616.

# Bibliography

Ackroyd, Peter, *Tudors: The History of England from Henry VIII to Elizabeth I*, New York: Thomas Dunne Books, 2012

Allingham, Hugh and Crawford, Robert, *Captain Cuéllar's Adventures in Connaught & Ulster A.D. 1588*, London: Elliott Stock, 1897

Anonymous, *Cabala; mysteries of state, in letters of the great ministers of K. James and K. Charles*, London: M.G. Bedell & T. Collins, 1654

Anonymous, *Colburn's United Services Magazine, Naval & Military Journal, Part II*, London: 1875, p. 437

Bailey, John, *History and Antiquities of the Tower of London*, London: Jennings & Chapman, 1830

Barrow, John, *The Life, Voyages and Expeditions of Sir Francis Drake*, London: John Murray, 1844

Beesly, Edward Spencer, *Queen Elizabeth*, London: Macmillan & Co., 1892

Bentinck, G. Cavendish and Brown, Rawden, *Calendar of State Papers, Venice. Volume 7, 1558–80*, London: 1890

Besant, Sir Walter, *London in the times of the Tudors*, London: Adam & Charles Black, 1904

Birch, Thomas, *Memoirs of the Reign of Queen Elizabeth Volume 1*, London: A. Miller, 1754

Borman, Tracy, *The Private Lives of the Tudors*, London: Hodder & Stoughton, 2016

Boys, William, *Collections for a history of Sandwich in Kent*, Canterbury: printed, Simmons, Kirkby and Jones, 1792

Brown, Rawdon (ed.), *Calendar of State Papers Relating to English Affairs in the Archives of Venice, Volume 6, 1555–1558*, London: 1877

Brodie, R.H. and Gairdner, James (eds), *Letters and Papers, Foreign and Domestic, Henry VIII, Volume 19 Part 2, August–December 1544*, London: 1905

Camden, William, *The history of the most renowned and victorious Princess Elizabeth, the late queen of England*, London: 1675

Cecil, William, *Cecil Papers in Hatfield House: 1306–1571*, London: HMSO, 1883

Chamberlin, Fredrick, *The Private Character of Queen Elizabeth* New York: Dodd, Mead & Company, 1922

Creighton, Mandell, *Queen Elizabeth*, London: Longmans Green & Co., 1901

Foxe, John, *Foxe's Book of Martyrs*, London: 1856

Gairdner, James, *Letters and Papers, Foreign and Domestic, Henry VIII, Volume 11*, London: 1888

Green, Mary Anne Everett, *Calendar of State Papers, Elizabeth, Addenda 1566–79*, London: Longmans, 1871

Green, Mary Anne Everett, *Calendar of State Papers, Elizabeth I and James I, Addenda 1580–1625*, London: Longmans, 1872

Green, Mary Anne Everett, *Calendar of State Papers, Domestic Series, Elizabeth, 1591–1594*, London: HMSO, 1867

Green, Mary Anne Everett, *Calendar of State Papers, Domestic Series, Elizabeth, 1595–1597*, London: HMSO, 1869

Green, Mary Anne Everett, *Calendar of State Papers, Domestic Series, Elizabeth, 1598–1601*, London: 1869

Haynes, Samuel, *A Collection of State Papers relating to Affairs in the Reigns of King Henry VIII, King Edward VI, Queen Mary and Queen Elizabeth from the year 1542 to 1570*, London: Bowyer, 1740

Halliwell, James (ed.), *Private Diary of Dr John Dee*, London: Camden Society, 1842

Harrison, G.B. and Jones, R.A. (eds), *De Maisse: a journal of all that was accomplished by Monsieur de Maisse ambassador in England from King Henri IV to Queen Elizabeth, anno domini 1597*, London: Bloomsbury, 1931

Hayward, Sir John, *Annals of the First Four Years of the Reign of Queen Elizabeth*, London: John Bowyer Nichols and Son, 1840

Hentzner, Paul, *A Journey into England in the Year MDXCVIII*, London: 1757

Hibbert, Christopher, *The Virgin Queen: Elizabeth I, Genius of the Golden Age*, London: Addison-Wesley Publishing Company, 1991

Hume, Martin A.S. (ed.), *Calendar of State Papers, Spain (Simancas), Volume 1, 1558–1567*, London: Eyre & Spottiswoode for HMSO, 1892

Hume, Martin A.S., *Calendar of State Papers, Spain (Simancas), Volume 2, 1568–1579*, London: Eyre & Spottiswoode for HMSO, 1894

Hume, Martin A.S., *Calendar of State Papers, Spain (Simancas), Volume 4, 1587–1603*, London: Eyre & Spottiswoode for HMSO, 1899

Hume, Martin A.S., *Calendar of Letters & State Papers relating to English Affairs, Elizabeth 1580–1586, Archives of Simancas, Volume III*, London: Eyre & Spottiswoode for HMSO, 1896

Kingsford, Charles Lethbridge, *Two London Chronicles from the Collections of John Stow*, London: Royal Historical Society, 1910

Klarwill, Victor von, *Queen Elizabeth and Some Foreigners*, London: Bodley Head, 1928

Knight, Charles, *Popular History of England, Volume III*, London: Bradbury, Evans, 1856

Lemon, Robert, *Calendar of State Papers, Edward VI, Mary, Elizabeth 1547–80*, London: Longmans, 1856

Lemon, Robert, *Calendar of State Papers, Elizabeth, 1581–1590*, London: Longmans, 1865

Lemon, Robert, *Calendar of State Papers, Domestic Series, Elizabeth, 1581–1590*, London: Longman, 1865

Locke, Gladys E., *Queen Elizabeth: Various Scenes and Events in the Life of Her Majesty*, Boston: Sherman French & Company, 1913

Machyn, Henry, *The diary of Henry Machyn, citizen and merchant-tailor of London, from A. D. 1550 to A. D. 1563*, London: Camden Society, 1848

Mackintosh, MP, Sir James, *History of England, Volume III*, London: Longman, 1832, p. 170

Marcus, Leah S., Mueller, Janel and Rose, Mary Beth (eds), *Elizabeth I, Collected Works*, Chicago: University of Chicago Press, 2000

Markham, Clement R., *Hawkins' Voyages During the Reign of Henry VIII, Queen Elizabeth & James I*, London: The Hakluyt Society, 1878

National Maritime Museum, *Armada*, London: published by Penguin Books, 1988

Nichols, John, *The Progresses and Public Processions of Queen Elizabeth, Volume 1*, London: 1823

Nichols, John, *The Progresses and Public Processions of Queen Elizabeth, Volume 2*, London: 1823

Nichols, John, *The Progresses and Public Processions of Queen Elizabeth, Volume 3*, London: 1823

O'Donoghue, Freeman M., *A Descriptive and Classified Catalogue of Portraits of Queen Elizabeth*, London: Bernard Quaritch, 1894

Powell, G.H., *The Memoirs of Robert Carey, Earl of Monmouth*, London: Alexander Morin Ltd, 1905

Roche, John (ed.), *Acts of the Privy Council of England Volume 7, 1558–1570*, London: 1893

Starkey, David, *Elizabeth*, London: Chatto & Windus, 2003

Stevenson, Joseph (ed.), *Calendar of State Papers Foreign: Elizabeth, Volume 1, 1558–1559*, London: 1863

Stevenson, Joseph (ed.), *Calendar of State Papers Foreign: Elizabeth, Volume 2, 1559–1560*, London: 1865

Stevenson, Joseph (ed.), *Calendar of State Papers Foreign: Elizabeth, Volume 3, 1560–1561*, London: 1865

Stow, John, *Annals of England*, London: 1603

Stow, John, *A Survey of London, written in the year 1598*, London: Whittaker & Co., 1842

Strickland, Agnes, *Memoirs of Elizabeth*, Philadelphia: Blanchard & Lea, 1853

Tyler, Royall (ed.), *Calendar of State Papers, Spain, Volume 12, 1554*, London: 1949

Weir, Alison, *Elizabeth the Queen* , London: Vintage Books, 2008

Williams, Clare, *Thomas Platter's Travels 1599*, London: Jonathan Cape, 1937

Williams, Neville, *Royal Homes of Great Britain from Medieval to Modern Times*, London: Lutterworth Press, 1971

Williams, Neville, *The Life and Times of Elizabeth I*, London: Weidenfeld & Nicolson, 1972

Wriothesley, Charles, *The Chronicle of England During the Reign of the Tudors, Volume 1*, Camden Society, 1875